Exits to the Posthuman Future

Exits to the Posthuman Future

Arthur Kroker

polity

First published in 2014 by Polity Press

Polity Press
65 Bridge Street
Cambridge CB2 1UR, UK

Polity Press
350 Main Street
Malden, MA 02148, USA

ISBN-13: 978-0-7456-7162-8
ISBN-13: 978-0-7456-7163-5(pb)

A catalogue record for this book is available from the British Library.

Typeset in 10 on 12 pt Palatino
by Toppan Best-set Premedia Limited

Printed and bound in Great Britain by T.J. International, Padstow, Cornwall

The publisher has used its best endeavours to ensure that the URLs for external websites referred to in this book are correct and active at the time of going to press. However, the publisher has no responsibility for the websites and can make no guarantee that a site will remain live or that the content is or will remain appropriate.

Every effort has been made to trace all copyright holders, but if any have been inadvertently overlooked the publisher will be pleased to include any necessary credits in any subsequent reprint or edition.

For further information on Polity, visit our website: www.politybooks.com

Contents

1

Introduction:
Trajectories of the Posthuman

Trolley to Tijuana and transit of Venus

I'm in downtown San Diego, just about to board the trolley to Tijuana, on a day, unlike most days, that is clearly marked by the spectral signs of cosmology because in far-off galactic space, Venus prepares to transit the sun and, in that transit, for the briefest of periods makes itself visible to the shielded human eye. This astronomical event last occurred in 1882 and will only occur again in 2117. And, so, I'm on a trolley to Tijuana, bracketed by astronomy between the past and the unknown, and certainly unknowable, future of the twenty-second century, with the spectral sign of Venus in transit across the fires of the sun and the earthbound signs of that trolley ride to the borderland following its own low visibility, perhaps even minoritarian, transit across the bright sunshine of the California technological way.

Following the Spanish philosopher José Ortega y Gasset's fateful insight that "I am I in the human circumstance and the human circumstance is I," I ask myself this question enigmatic about my present circumstance on this day of cosmology: What is the connection, if any, between the trolley to Tijuana and the transit of Venus?

Now, the trolley to Tijuana is a down-to-earth story, about migrant workers from Tijuana who begin lining up at 4 am each morning in order to catch the trolley to the houses and stores and construction camps of San Diego. There's a lot of humiliated necessity in those early-morning border crossings. All the immense wealth, restless energy, and sheer disciplined willpower of the California Way pushed to the border, and just stopped with walls of surveillance running into the sea and pitilessness running into the heart. Like everything else on the border, the trolley to Tijuana is a kind of strange fold in the space-time of two cultures, a site of possible cultural intersections that don't really happen, broken mediations, and bodies on the move, some perhaps upward bound, but most disappearing into the routines of daily labor.

And the transit of Venus? That's a different (astronomical) matter altogether. Not just its rarity, although the event dazzles with the fact that it won't happen again for another century. A heavenly messenger linking the twenty-first and twenty-second centuries. Nor even the fact that the transit of Venus cannot be viewed directly, but only with a heavy filter to shield your eyes. But use that filter and the occasion is one of wonderment, that vision of the planet Venus tracking across the face of the sun. In this, the most scientific of times, the event has been stripped of its mystery, reduced to the language of scientific precision or perhaps to celestial celebrity status pumped up by the mass media as another passing interest story for the day – an astronomical punctuation, in this case, supposedly signifying nothing. But still, "I am I in the human circumstance and the human circumstance is I" and there's that irrepressible doubled sense of awe at being witness to the motion of the planets and the stars but also something else, an inexpressible, and certainly prohibited, feeling that what is really being witnessed is something less scientific than cosmological. The transit of Venus is an omen, but an omen of what?

Living at the tip of the posthuman

We are already living at the accelerating tip of the posthuman future. Seemingly everywhere, the highly experimental, definitely utopian language of technology has delivered us to a future that is unmistakably novel, from the hybrid experiments of genetic engineering, the viral growth of increasingly complex databases, the massive diffusion of social networking technologies to enthusiastic pronouncements that the layered world of virtual augmentation represents the next stage of the fully realized technological society. Yet, for all that, contemporary society is also marked by a growing uncertainty concerning both the ultimate ends of technological innovation and the ways of understanding – and negotiating – the uncertain digital future.

Digitally, the onrushing adventure of technology with its coding of seemingly every element of social existence and utopian ambitions towards global connectivity is met by a counterbalancing fascination with images of the abject, the uncanny, the liminal in popular imagination, accompanied by an increasing focus in mass media, with the spectral world of zombies, clones, avatars, and aliens. The real world of digital technology might pursue the aims of greater national security, economic austerity, and highly centralized corporate governance of networked communication, but the popular world of cultural imagination seems to be increasingly preoccupied with fantasy novels, stories of vampire love, and online battles among zombies, robots, and always-besieged defenders of a lost humanity.

Politically, the global sovereignty of virtual capitalism with its emergency programs involving economic austerity and the strengthening of the disciplinary state is met by the resurgence, in country after country, in city after city, of a politics of the street that challenges the economic contents of virtual capitalism, as well as its increasingly undemocratic modes of deployment. While the disciplinary state imposes strict austerity measures on the social economy of governance involving the young, the unemployed, the poor, and the vulnerable, the growing ambition of politics in the streets flows in the opposite direction towards a radical rethinking of the terms of political power and social justice with and against the fully realized technological society.

Economically, it is as if two warring visions are at work across the uncertain spectrum of political economy: one based on a technological intensification of the commodity-form according to the dictates of old-fashioned primitive capitalism with its global outsourcing of labor, destruction of labor organizations, and reliance on the extraction of fossil fuels; and the other an emerging vision of a new economy made possible by creative technological innovations, specifically new communicative forms of media, medicine, education, and labor, all motivated by a cultural preference for a green economy and a social preference for practically realizing the utopian benefits of technological creativity.

Ideologically, the uncertainties of the digital future with its pitched battles between official defenders of labor austerity, political discipline, and the security state and proponents of a new vision of social economy and public democracy has given rise to a global situation of considerable political complexity, namely the development of a growing legitimation crisis, first at the political level and now increasingly at the cultural and social levels. While street protests in Quebec, the Occupy Movement, Idle No More, the Arab Spring, and political resistance in the urban centers of Greece, Spain, Mexico, France, and Russia often focus on specific political demands, what we may be witnessing today is the rise of an alternative trajectory of the posthuman future that is born out of a fundamental crisis of legitimation, specifically the growing belief among the proponents of a progressive vision of civil society that the alliance between governments and large corporations that initially realized the corporate ends of technological innovation may be at odds with popular demands for rethinking the aims and means of the fully realized technological society. In essence, technology itself may, in fact, be experiencing a cascading series of legitimation crises, sometimes overtly at the level of politics in the streets but, at other times, implicitly but with no less intensity, at the level of popular imagination, artistic expression, and social concerns. In this case, while the fundamental drivers of the technological future remain a determined global alliance of virtual capitalism and the disciplinary state in favor of economic austerity and unrestricted access to the life-space of increasingly digital subjects, there has just as quickly emerged a counter-alliance, whether openly or by a particular conjunction of network circumstances, which calls into question the social, political, and economic destiny to which the future of technology delivers us.

Curiously, the global social revolts that mark the early years of the twenty-first century originate in that which was first deemed surplus to the requirements of virtual capitalism and the disciplinary state: revolts by the economic "remainder" that is the unemployed; revolts by a growing artistic counter-culture motivated by aspirations towards a future that is authentically "liminal"; and resistance by social environmentalists determined to reawaken the possibility of the "undecidability" of nature itself as the essence of the technological future. It is as if the dynamic drive to the technological mastery of social and non-social nature has awakened in its path not only the most powerful, consolidated, and recidivist of corporate, media, and political forces but has also called into active social and political being that which was originally designated as prohibited, excluded, and silenced by the awesome power of technology. Indeed, the quintessential definition of technological posthumanism may be as that site where the algorithms of virtual power and the liquid flows of the undecidable, the liminal, the remainder, and the prohibited combine in an increasingly complex world-picture. If it is the case that the sheer force of technological innovation quickly pushes traditional conceptions of humanism aside to make way for all the emerging signs of the posthuman – drift culture, recombinant technology, figural aesthetics, distributive consciousness – then it is true that something indispensably human, whether articulated by conscious political protest, mobilized by social unrest, or motivated by the persistence of human memory itself, remains as the phantasmagorical essence of the future of technological posthumanism.

For example, how are we to account for technological experimentalism and an increasing fascination with dead affect, this strangest of all apparent contradictions, as the essence of the emerging world of technological posthumanism? Not a culture of dead affect as a shadowy side effect of technology, but precisely the tangible hint of the return of the repressed as that which motivates technological society and on behalf of which technology functions to deliver us to a future that is distinctly posthuman in its radical undermining of all the previous markers of the "human" – unitary species-logic, private subjectivity, hierarchical knowledge – with human beings as the universal value-standard of all events. For the contemporary generation, the digital generation, this received framing of the primacy of human subjectivity has suddenly been swept away by the data storm and the genomic rapture of technological innovation. Confidence in unitary species-logic has been challenged not only by progressive perspectives concerning the equivalence of species multiplicity, but also by biotechnologies that literally reveal the vibrancy of the life of the object, the metal, the code. Ontological faith in private subjectivity has been successfully undermined by the objective appearance of technological media of communication based precisely on the exteriorization of the human nervous system, and with it the flipping inside out of the putatively opposed worlds of subject and object. Hierarchical knowledge has been effectively eclipsed by spectacular technological creations, including social networking technologies, mobile devices, and circulating loops of media information, that emphasize the diffuse, the fragmentary, the connected. Finally, the indisputably biblical regime of the supremacy of the human has now been rendered uncertain by genomic technologies that put into question the very markers of being human, effectively providing greater visibility to an emerging world of unexpected species-mediations – technological beings who are part code/part skin.

What renders posthumanism "posthuman" is the truly paradoxical nature of the fully realized digital universe. Indeed, the paradoxical, complex, and often contradictory implications of the posthuman condition have constituted the central focus of the most important intellectual explorations of the emerging episteme. For example, Katherine Hayles's eloquent theorization, *How We Became Posthuman*,[1] situates the emergence of posthuman consciousness in direct relationship to the dynamic appearance of the "regime of computation," investigating, in turn, the reductive and transformative possibilities of an era when "information loses its body" and consciousness itself is increasingly patterned by the language of codes. Equally, Cary Wolfe's landmark text, *What is Posthumanism?*,[2] rethinks the future of the posthumanities under the sign of profound ecological consciousness involving respect for multiplicity (whether for species difference or for new transgenic remixes of animals, plants, objects, and humans). In Wolfe's vision, the posthuman condition contains, in equal measure, clashing tendencies towards a profound ethical breakthrough to a new way of reconciling relationships among diverse species, in the absence of which present tendencies towards anthropomorphism and hierarchical knowledge will only intensify. On the other hand, Francis Fukuyama's *Our Posthuman Future*[3] understands the swiftly developing "biotech century" as an essentially dystopian fable of imminent genetic accidents and transgenic experiments gone wrong. Indeed, when the concept of posthumanism slips beyond the boundaries of theoretical discourse and becomes something else, becomes the dominant technopoeisis – the new material, cultural, political, and semiotic reality – of the technologically enabled twenty-first century, then the deeply paradoxical character of the posthuman finally begins to reveal itself. Neither solely utopian nor fatally dystopian, neither fully historically materialized nor inaugurating a culture of immateriality, the posthuman is that elusive, truly enigmatic gap that appears when the will to technology intersects the endlessly complex social-reality machine. In this case, reflecting upon the question of the posthuman would require, in the first instance, a form of thought that listens intently for the gaps, fissures, and intersections, whether directly in the technological sphere or indirectly in culture, politics, and society, where incipient signs of the posthuman first begin to figure. But it would also require a form of consciousness that is prepared to turn away from the strictly technological in order to make visible what has been lost with the coming-to-be posthuman future, not only in terms of Baudrillard's "terrorism of the code" but also of its flip side, specifically the *boredom of the code*.

Of course, it is customary to consider the human impact of technology in terms of its powers of facilitation as well as its costs, seeking to establish some ethical balance between regimes of technological intelligibility that sustain the digital code as well as the bio-genome and a critical appreciation of that which has been "disappeared" by the coming-to-be of technological society. The underlying argument of this book complicates this interpretation of contemporary developments by proposing a different understanding, namely that the essence of the posthuman axiomatic inheres in the fact that technology now eagerly seeks out that which was previously marginalized as simultaneously ways of mobilizing itself as it effectively recodes every aspect of social and nonsocial existence and ways of drawing attention to a greater technological seduction. In other words, the technological posthuman is that historical moment when the power of technology turns back on itself, effectively undermining traditional concepts such as subjectivity, privacy, and bounded consciousness in order to render all things truly uncertain and unknowable. Not necessarily intentionally, but for the reason that the dynamic drive that is revealed by technological interpellation can only succeed on the basis of making the familiar unknowable, the bounded liminal, the certain uncanny, the subjective a fatal remainder. While Heidegger understood this, he was still sufficiently modernist to claim a doubled vision at the heart of technology, specifically that technology contains a "danger" as well as a "saving power." In this respect, *Exits to the Posthuman Future* is post-Heideggerian to the extent that it claims that the essence of technology today is that every technological innovation, every wrinkle of creativity in social networking technologies, every advance in mobility, every genomic redesign of the species-logic, draws together the danger and the saving power into co-equal and co-attractive magnets of technological seduction. What is liminal about technology is precisely that it is a field of undecidability, with its truly uncanny essence as a major cultural force-attractor. With this in mind, I would like to tell the following two stories concerning technological interpellation and the question of (human) remainders.

Synching your heart to the smartphone

There is a patent application for a new iPhone app that involves synching your heart to the smartphone. The immediate function of this app is to repurpose the iPhone as a mobile heart monitor ("seamlessly embedded heart rate monitor").[4] Dispensing with the need for medical infrastructure housing EKG machines, individuals would simply need to touch the side of their own mobile device, specifically an iPhone, thus transmitting their most vital biological data – heart rate, blood rhythm and velocity – directly to a central digital heart monitoring station. If the data flow suggests that your heart is about to go into frenzied hyperdrive or, at the other extreme, cease functioning, you will be immediately alerted to take your body to the nearest ER. And not only that but the inventors claim that the mobile heart monitor has a second important purpose. Since everyone has a distinctive heart signature, the mobile heart monitor opens up the possibility of a third major form of body recognition software. Not just iris scanners or fingerprint analysis, but in the future the mobile heart monitor will be a way of scanning the body to verify its authenticity. Since all hearts move to their own internal rhythm with their own electronic signature, what could be a better way of securing identity than the beat-beat of an often unruly heart? A world of instant biofeedback: everything is fine. There is a disturbance in the rhythm of your heart.

What does it mean when we literally synch our hearts to the iPhone? On the face of it, this is a useful medical app – social networking technology in the service of better health. In the context of contemporary cultural anxieties about fatal heart attacks and catastrophic strokes, who would not want to secure their good health with 24/7 monitoring of the often errant signature of the individual heart? With data uploaded onto a smart grid for hearts, there is also the added benefit that this stream of heart data will provide an organic basis for digital authentication with your heartbeat proving that you are the person whom your very singular heart rhythm says you actually are. Understood as a medical device facilitating health, the mobile heart monitor augments good health. Considered as an "extension of man," this technological innovation suddenly provides global outreach to what was heretofore the private and unpredictable history of an individual heart. Considered as data, the history of the heart discovers that it has given birth to a digital echo, a duplicate reality in which individuals possess two hearts: one organic, the other virtual. Conceived as a technological device, the mobile heart monitor can be repurposed at will, from medical therapy to security requirements. However, it is when the heart intersects with the language of code that things become very interesting. We know that for more than fifty years, the electronic sensorium of the mass media have increasingly mimicked the logic of biology, first exteriorizing the human senses by way of the amplified senses of the electronic sensorium and then imitating the process of evolution itself. While McLuhan predicted in *Understanding Media* that the effect of accelerated technological change would be the triumphant transformation of mass media into an electronic nervous system, what happens with new media such as the mobile heart monitor is something deeply uncanny: the production of a digital heartbeat by the electronic nervous system. At some indefinable point, the massing together of individual heart signatures provides the electronic nervous system with a heart of its own, the pumping sound of a virtual heart cut to the normativity of a heterogeneous world of individual hearts. Are we witnessing here the first tentative steps in a greater migration from body to code, a data archive housing the biorhythms of the remotely scanned heart, with its own history of blood velocity, arterial blocks, and sudden failures? Or are we witness to something different? By bringing the rhythms of the bodily heart into a greater public visibility, are we suddenly creating the necessary condition for a new order of bio-politics, with its potential drive to bring its data archive of individual heart signatures within the boundaries of normative intelligibility – an alias heart? In other words, the potential resynching of the beat-beat of our own heart to that of society as a whole – the surveillance heartbeat, the repressive heartbeat, the beyond suspicion heartbeat. And all this simply by initializing your heart to the digital recognition software of the smartphone.

Misprinted organs

I believe we can grow organs just as we bake cakes.
Anthony Atala[5]

Recently, there was an intriguing TED presentation by Anthony Atala, the director of Regenerative Medicine at Wake Forest Baptist Medical Center, involving the 3-D printing of bodily organs. In this case, not the printing of an actual organ with its complex internal physiognomy, but the 3-D printing of a kidney mold, like a probe into the future of tissue engineering, stem cells, organ fabrication, and redesigning the genetic code. In an interview with a science reporter, Atala described the technology involved in engineering new human organs for a future of artificial transplants:

> Researchers have already used printers to build quarter-sized two-chamber hearts, Atala told CBC Radio's *Quirks & Quarks*. They spontaneously start beating about four to six hours later.
> "All the cells in your body are already pre-programmed," Atala said. "There's a genetic code within all your cells that drives them to do what they are supposed to do if you place them in the right environment."
> Researchers have already taken advantage of that programming to build and implant simpler organs like urethras and bladders. They layer the appropriate types of cells from the patient's own body on a dissolvable scaffold. After implantation, the cells mature inside the body, connecting to blood vessels and nerves.[6]

And not just kidneys, but there are multiple reports of other 3-D organ printer sightings at university research labs in the United States and around the (biotechnological) world, involving hearts, blood vessels, skin, and other bodily organs including the use of inkjet printers at the University of Washington to create human bone replacements. While images of bionic beings – half flesh/half metal – have been, until now, the focus of science fiction and fantasy novels, the development of 3-D printing definitely opens up the biological gateway to the infinite reproduction of duplicate organs. In this scenario, the mythic divide of life and death, this most privileged subject of religious passion and philosophical ethics, has literally been "inkjetted" away. In the near future, it may not be a question of when we will die, but will we bother to die? After all, when death can be indefinitely deferred by the availability through vital body organs likely purchased from a biometric Kinko's of the future, the markers of life and death will suddenly be subjected to an unanticipated precession of events, that is, to a fatal reversal of the magnetic polarities of life and death. In the future anticipated by 3-D printing of bodily organs, life itself may take on the quality of a fatal remainder – bodies that have become their own prosthetic replacements, indefinitely reproduced, cloned, artificially prolonged. In this case, a society of the living dead, repaired by print, transmitted by code, manufactured one molecular layer at a time, a staged construction of complex bio-scaffolding – the new zombies.

And who can say whether at some point in this future of 3-D organ printing that the machines will not themselves come "alive" with a new bodily possibility, namely the printing of working organs for all the increasingly lifelike robotic beings of the digital world? While the literature of robotics presently likes to refer to the "uncanny valley" as a way of describing that supposedly ominous species crossover point where robots and humans begin to bear an eerie resemblance, robotic literature of the 3-D future will likely have to refigure the concept of the uncanny valley, this time taking into account that the gift of (robotic) life that is the ultimate mythic legacy of 3-D body organ printing. And, of course, if science fiction literature proves to be correct in its long-standing claim of bitter rivalry between the human species and its robotic successors, then who can say with confidence that the robotic 3-D organ printers of the future, now equipped with artificial intelligence and drone-like telemetry, will not, by accident or design, misprint organs, reducing the life of the human species to another necessary accident along the way to the once and certain future of technological posthumanism?

The posthuman axiomatic

Synching Your Heart to the Smartphone, Misprinted Organs: exits such as these to the posthuman future are seemingly everywhere today, proliferating with abandonment, transforming all of the leading signs of contemporary life – the signs of technology, codes, history, archives, media, art, warfare, genomics – into simultaneous moments of departure and arrival. *Signs of departure* because we are caught up in the violent particle stream of the will to technology, here overturning chronological time in favor of light-time, there imploding the lived extensiveness of natural space into the virtual mapping of light-space, capriciously overcoming the fixed boundaries of gender, sexuality, and identity, and always evaporating the hitherto hardened silos of economy, culture, war, and aesthetics into code-matter that is liquid, porous, interchangeable. And *signs of arrival* as well because there is in the cultural air we breathe today the detectable, indeed unmistakable, scent of the fractured, the indeterminate, the paradoxical. While at one time technological futurism could be focused on speculative projections about the likely, and sometimes unanticipated, consequences of scientific innovations, today technological futurism begins by putting the future itself in doubt.

This book explores the future anticipated by accelerated technological innovation. Marked neither by nostalgia for what has been left behind nor by fear over the radical uncertainty of our shared technological destiny, these stories attempt to raise to a greater visibility the complexities involved with a future replete with technological devices, software innovations and genetic engineering that thrive on the undecidable, the liminal, the uncertain. Three key concepts guide this search for a method of understanding the technological posthuman: accelerate, drift, and crash.

Accelerate

Technologies of acceleration

TOKYO – At a university lab in a Tokyo suburb, engineering students are wiring a rubbery robot face to simulate six basic expressions: anger, fear, sadness, happiness, surprise, and disgust. Hooked up to a database of words clustered by association, the robot – dubbed Kansei, or "sensibility" – responds to the word "war" by quivering in what looks like disgust and fear. It hears "love," and its pink lips smile.
Hiroko Tabuchi, "Japanese Robots Enter Daily Life"[7]

All our lives have been spent as crash victims of violent, but deeply seductive, technologies of acceleration – speed technologies that move bodies, our bodies of earth and air and fire and water, to escape velocity.[8] As Tabuchi shows in the excerpt above, we may, as a species, have literally achieved technological liftoff with the fast translation of material history into data streams, networked connectivity, artificial intelligence, and remote sensing. When events move at the speed of light, traditional frameworks of interpretation are themselves destabilized, weakened in detail and definition as useful indicators of what a future of technological acceleration entails.

Whether viewed as an "information bomb" (Virilio), a "Gutenberg Galaxy" (McLuhan), or a "driftworks" (Lyotard), the result is the same. When the human sensorium has been simultaneously dematerialized and hyper-accelerated by digital media and the metaphysical framework of time and space reengineered into the "light-time" and "light-space" of networked society, we suddenly find ourselves in drift culture – a space and time of weightlessness, vertiginous media spin, remix culture. The eclipse of clearly definable boundaries between bodies and machines, the interpellation of human perception and algorithmic codes, the active remixing of borders among humans, animals, plants, and inanimate objects have all resulted in the injection of a fundamental element of drift into the human condition. While, from one perspective, the world today could be considered in terms of "after the accident," drift culture is that strangest of all phenomenon, simultaneously a series of cultural, social, and economic implosions following in the wake of accelerating technologies, but also an equally vital series of creative reinventions, boundary lines between different species, different bodies, different social elements.

You can hear its sounds everywhere – the sounds of slow suicide. Sometimes, it is the slow drip of polar ice caps melting; at other times, the unexpected blasts of radiation from nuclear plants flooded; at other points, the excited murmur of the global techno crowd waiting anxiously through the night for a newly augmented iPhone; and yet, again and again, it has the passionate sound of Occupy, the Indigenous resistance that is Idle No More, the street politics of bodily resistance against state austerity programs in Spain and Greece, collective resistance against the politics of oppression in Syria, Bahrain, Libya, Egypt, and Tunisia – movements for social justice that crowd space global media ecology in their urgent demands for a minimum of political justice and social mercy. And sometimes it is the sound of global ethical silence that is the invisible moral accompaniment of news reports about tortured children in the security prisons of all the Damascuses and Aleppos of the world.

The question of technology is not immune to deeper currents in the history of subjectivity pitting utopian visions of transcendence against the complex reality of immanence as part of the human condition. For example, while Freud expressed this entanglement in terms of the charged relationship between eroticism and the death instinct, Nietzsche argued that the transcendent will-to-power was countered in the games of human passions by the chestnuts of revenge-taking – the hallmark of a culture of *ressentiment*. Later, this would become a contemporary cultural tendency of such pressing significance that Wendy Brown would describe it as politics under the sign of "states of injury." For Heidegger, the dynamic technological drive towards the mastery of human and nonhuman existence by the "will to will" was tempered by the ineluctability of human experience. In this case, Heidegger's concept of the "world-picture" was effectively undone by his insight that nihilism, most of all, contained equal possibilities for political abuse and the poetic imagination. Finally, in Jean-Paul Sartre's active struggle to think history in terms of justice, the transcendence of projecting oneself into social history was always in danger of being undermined by the reality of being dragged down into the inertial mud of the "practico-inert."

Contemporary technological reality is fundamentally different. Expressed in the technical language of algorithms, augmentation, and digital devices, but representing, in essence, a great metaphysical rebellion against the framing of the posthuman condition by the polarities of immanence and transcendence, the world hypothesis that is digital reality launches itself by means of truly creative and deeply seductive technologies of acceleration. Digital devices project the human mind beyond its immediate circumstances into the global circulatory flows of distributive consciousness. Novel strategies of cyber-war are promoted that are aimed directly at accelerating the logistics of violence beyond limited human capabilities, quickly realizing a future of machine-to-machine warfare – cyber-war waged in the medium of both hardware and software, but most of all an acceleration of warfare to include an important metabolic dimension – an approaching generalized war on the biological terrain of wetware – psychology, subjectivity, and affect. The signs of metabolic warfare are unmistakable, particularly in the arena of cyber-politics where even the organization of advertisement-driven campaigns today is strategized in the military vernacular of "carpet bombing" and "daisy cutters." In this case, when polling has been effectively hijacked by competing political strategies aimed at controlling the mass perception of the electorate and voter mobilization campaigns based on a sophisticated array of marketing tactics whereby the combination of data analytics and social media reduce individual voters to finely granulated, individual data points, then it might be said that contemporary politics is a prototype of psychological warfare of the future. Technologies of acceleration are at work in the financial system as well. That's high-frequency stock trading where economy has blasted off from its old nesting ground in production and even beyond the order of consumption to become a closed, semiurgical system, with machine-to-machine calibrations, fluid, planetary movement of capital, relentless drive to the violence of pure market abstractions, and substitution of computational models of simulation for material experience. If high-frequency trade algorithms have acquired strange science fiction names that is precisely because the code-driven acceleration of digital economies is, in fact, the perfect realization of the dominant tropes of science fiction – futuristic, machine-to-machine, but still for all that driven onwards by the all-too-human passions of greed and fear.

At work in every dimension of culture, society, and politics, the leading cultural signifiers of technologies of acceleration include concepts such as "Big Data," "distant reading," "augmented reality." Contemporary digital enthusiasts like to claim, in fact, that more data have been collected in the past two years than in the entire history of humanity. While technologies of acceleration have certainly had their intellectual proponents – consider the missionary zeal of technological extropians and cyber-optimists – the curious fact remains that the most intense explorations of the end of the world that is upon us have been conducted by thinkers who have injected into the mix an elementary doubt about the efficacy and ethics of technologies of acceleration. I think, for example, of Marshall McLuhan, who went to his death with increasingly apocalyptic warnings about the technological media of communication. Indeed, Paul Virilio wrote evocatively about technologies of speed because of his deeply felt sense of dread that the metaphysical framework of human experience – time and space – was about to be crushed by their acceleration into the light-time and light-space of digital reality.

In retrospect, technologies of acceleration are, perhaps, only the opening evolutionary act in the story of technology. Like the massive power of an intercontinental missile or a space launch that requires such immense energy to achieve liftoff from gravitational pressures, technologies of acceleration make space launches of the entirety of social experience. In digital culture, gravity-bound words and capital and power and warfare are literally launched into the weightless space of the regime of computation. For the past fifty years, that has been the technological experiment that has so seduced us, and in its beauty and terror seduces us still. There will be many more space launches of human subjectivity in the future – the launching of creative minds by mobile technologies; the increasing volatilization of the digital economy by trading algorithms based on neural networks and genetic programs; the launching of deeply relational communal networks by social media; and the launching of the fully distributed brain by new experiments in neuro-technology. Here, the real, material body of flesh and blood will be recalibrated, redesigned, and relaunched to become a lonely satellite circling the newly discovered planets of distributed consciousness, ablated nervous systems, augmented vision, and reading at the speed of pattern recognition. When the social finally disappears into the gaseous dust and debris of its own technological creations, the overwhelming violence of technological acceleration will finally fall away, instantly replaced by the sights, sounds, and movements of the contemporary digital epoch – drift culture.

Drift

Drift culture

The quintessential sign of twenty-first century experience, drift culture is that point where the will to technology turns back on itself, volatilizing society, crashing boundaries, undermining the traditional division of species, transforming experience into a subjectless universe of data points, penetrating the membrane of the organic with flows of data, electrifying the metallic, finally overthrowing the great referential icons of power, sex, consciousness, and truth in favor of the more tentative and ambiguous language of the in-between. Nothing stabilizes; everything now is in motion. The phenomenology of social media with its assumption of a "bracketed" life experience has been undone by networking technologies that are, in essence, anti-phenomenological, distinguished by conflagrations of massive data flows – liquid, ubiquitous, borderless, pervasive. What was once solely the animating theoretical vision of a line of thought expressed in the different, but deeply related, terms of deconstructionism, post-structuralism, postmodernism, and now posthumanism, namely that the emblematic sign of the times is the fracture, the splice, the bifurcation, the in-between, has now become the really existent material history of digital reality. Shattered by the projection of an objective, code-driven sense of drift into our cultural DNA, the previously secured concept of bracketed life-experience has quickly been rendered ontological illusion.

Drift culture is the essence of the data storm that envelopes us. To come into (digital) subjectivity today means to be swept along in gigantic galaxies of social, political, and economic data, broken apart by the technical rewiring of everything to suit the requirements of the logic of code, here invaded by technological devices as they take root in the languages of consciousness, desire, and interest, there learning to speak again in the language of social media, to see again with enhanced data perception, to understand that something fundamental has just happened when bodies, metals, and AI recombine into new species-forms. Whether expressed as a term of genetics (code drift), cosmology (history drift), distributive consciousness (archive drift), or remix media (video drift), drift culture is the ontological foundation of the posthuman axiomatic, that process whereby the purely conceptual regime of the fragmentary, the diffuse, the fractured, and the incommensurable abandon their signifying positions in the field of epistemology, abruptly becoming in turn that which torques everything in its pathway – codes, history, archives, and video – into driftworks in the posthuman axiomatic.

For example, in terms of biology, genetic drift refers to "random fluctuations of gene frequencies due to sampling errors." Just as genetic drift occurs by chance, producing in its wake unpredictable streams of genetic variation, so too drift culture: drifts of code, history, archives, media, video. Never really predictable in advance, the digital inflections that follow from the passage of the data storm gives primacy to chance variations through unexpected uses, creative applications, unanticipated consequences when data collides with society, a fluctuation in our perception that produces complex technological transformations. Random fluctuations that build over time, resulting in complex yet subtle changes in the genetic makeup of the populations: an indeterminate mix of flux, chaos, intermediations, remix. Certainly not divested of questions of predatory power and acquisitive capitalism, drift culture is nonetheless fully enigmatic with no definite goal, no stabilized image of the future, no final meaning, only a digital culture that is being formed at the rough, broken, contested edges of the power of the code – the codes of virtual capitalism as well as the codes of governmentality – and those sudden changes in frequency, those unexpected distortions in the filters of sound and power and political economy, the rebellions in the streets that are the wonderful sampling errors, the random fluctuations of (political) gene frequencies that constitute the creative energy of drift culture.

Indeed, if it is the case that intimations of the posthuman future are ubiquitous, this implies that we are witness to an almost unprecedented shift of knowledge – to a newly emergent digital generation that is not simply about growing up online, but growing up posthuman. For better or worse, willingly or unwillingly, subjectivity is now deeply shaped by a complex world of social media, mediated by networking technologies, streamed by immersive, innovative, tactile mobile devices, psychologically contoured by a processed world, always present in the data storm, effectively being like a technology that is forever out of bounds to previous versions of (pre-digital) subjectivity based on assumptions concerning enclosed consciousness, private egos, and a bunkered-down central nervous systems with eyes that may see, as the artist Jordan Crandall argues, but definitely do not track. Excluding cell phone use, the generation that has grown up posthuman inhabits the many forms of social media 44.5 hours per week, its skin barrier broken down by deep immersion as a circulating node within increasingly complex loops of information. Its digital subjectivity is actively shaped by flows of data economics, data security, data entertainment; its memory increasingly taking the form of searchable electronic traces in all the waiting digital archives; its relationships mediated by those magical expressions of social networking; its future an open space, still to be determined, but always running parallel to the great scientific and technological discoveries of the contemporary age, from genomics to software. What were only a short while ago novel theoretical concepts being developed in Silicon Valley – relational processing and ubiquitous computing – concerning the challenge of how to migrate the visibly massive, objective processing power of computation to the periphery of human attention are now everyday social practices. The digital generation has had to learn quickly how to navigate creative pathways through the digital haze where the parasocial replaces the social, where fluctuating digital identities substitute for traditional forms of identity formation, and where this the most intensive of technocratic societies is increasingly haunted by the fact that the triumphant epoch of cold, calculative data has opened up a digital imagination that is increasingly fascinated by all the imaginary signs of the abyss. And all this fueled by that most powerful of all forms of technological affectivity – a legible, seductive culture of connectivity where, as the psychologist Sherry Turkle states, we are finally free to be "alone together." Indeed, it may be that human subjectivity has now become so deeply and inextricably embedded with technology that the "question of technology" has now become the question of the human, that is, the appearance of a new form of being – posthuman being – born at the interstices of data and flesh. Disturbing received interpretations of human subjectivity, throwing into radical doubt boundary lines among the species, casting into sharp relief "vibrant matter" as much as "vibrant data," applying what can only be described as the shock of the hyperreal into the most practical concerns of economy, politics, culture, and society, trajectories of the posthuman seemingly track everywhere today.

We are actually living in a space and time only dreamed of by artists, only speculated upon by writers, only tentatively anticipated by cultural theorists, a time and space of drift culture in which every event – mobile apps, technological devices, economic crises, new media art, drone warfare – represents a potential exit to the posthuman future, simultaneously a doubled moment of departure and arrival. Overstressed by the power of technological innovation, broken apart by the seeming inability of governing institutions to create adequate alternatives in light of accelerating technological change, and fragmented by the eclipse of traditional political narratives, it is as if received orthodoxies no longer hold sway in the popular imagination. In some ways, we might say that we are living in the ruins of the postmodern, that that which was prophesied with such haunting accuracy by theorists from Nietzsche and Heidegger to Lyotard, Baudrillard, and Virilio has now been crystallized in fine granular detail in contemporary culture and society.

Consequently, without conscious decision or public debate, we may have already collectively burst out of the skin of the human, entering a strange new world of prosthetic memories, distributive consciousness, cognition unbound, technologically enabled bodies, and all this streamed at the speed of photons through cloud computing, social networking, and mobile technologies. The polar shift of perception required to navigate the fast, complex drift currents of the posthuman condition literally involves a new way of seeing, that is, seeing like a robot, a code-work, an artifact of artificial intelligence, a splice. In a digital universe where perception most of all is the subject of intense technological pressure, duplex vision – seeing simultaneously like a human *and* like a technological device – increasingly appears to chart the direction of social and cultural adaptability. In this case, drift is the primary ontology of the posthuman scene, the fact that we increasingly inhabit the fracture, the splice, the bifurcation as our permanent state of being digital. Never fully resolvable into a fixed position, always oscillating, ever fluctuating like an electronic frequency, a sense of drift permeates the posthuman condition as both its dominant condition of possibility and its motivating sensibility.

Code drift theorizes the momentous evolutionary movement by which the previously separate regimes of biology and digitality unify in a world-picture dominated by the universalization of the code form. In the culture of code drift, the actual contents of networked communication can be fragmentary, diverse, rebellious, playful precisely because the platforms of code are stable, until, that is, the social contents, artistic expressions, and political deployments of code begin to drift. *History drift* is what is left when material history has been brought under the sway of the technological world hypothesis – a form of history drift in which the concept of history itself splits into three competing hypotheses: hauntological history with its upsurge of the excluded, the negated, the disappeared; the will to history with its fateful metaphysical struggle among the great cosmologies of salvation, order, and freedom; and the precession of history, whereby the empty spectacle of technological society is increasingly inhabited by spectral images of that which has long been remaindered, forgotten, and abandoned by the technological sovereign. *Archive drift* is what happens when the house of knowledge is quickly undermined by the powerful regime of computation, sometimes set creatively adrift in new currents of imagery and voice and data while, at other times, thrown into radical anxiety about the fatal overcoming of the traditional form of the archive by a digital archive that would be living, incommensurable, fluctuating. And *video drift*? That is what happens to the society of the (digital) spectacle when the medium of video achieves cultural primacy as the essential embodiment and manifest expression of the drift imagery of contemporary technological society: the fluctuating, random, seductive broken narrative of its suicides, pathos, breakdowns, and sometimes magnificent nervous breakthroughs.

Crash

Digital inflections

When technology slams into the human condition, the result is often complex, always intermediated, but never isolated. What is the digital future? The slow suicide of technological apocalypse? The transformation of subjectivity that is signaled by figural aesthetics? Or, perhaps, the emergence of transversal consciousness, a form of critical intelligibility drawing its strength from its willingness to exist at the interface of unrealized dreams and sacrificial violence?

The entanglement of the supposedly transparent world of information with the complexities of class, gender, race, and ethnicity firmly situates the future of contemporary society under the sign of *intermediation*. For example, when data flows collide with the hard materiality of class, the result is, most definitely, not the disappearance of class distinctions based on permanently clashing economic interests but precisely the reverse: the rapid development on a global scale of incipient class conflict, pitting a rising class of technologically enabled plutocracy against a society of individuated masses – as yet unorganized, under-theorized, and seemingly uncertain and confused about the lay of the (economic) land. Equally, when technology intersects with questions of gender, the result is sometimes a sharp escalation in what the critical feminist Donna Haraway has described as the "informatics of domination," but also an equally rapid diffusion of knowledge and activism concerning gender inequities through social media. For example, in her recent cinematic project, !Women Art Revolution, the San Francisco filmmaker Lynn Hershmann Leeson has retold the story of the still unfinished struggles of feminist art movements in the twentieth century as a way of countering what she views as the "birth of the anti-body" as a direct result of the triumph of information culture. Finally, when technology intersects electoral politics, the enormous waves spreading out from the implosion are dramatic. In this case, the laws of simulation will not be long denied: polling implodes into a frenzy of simulation models, all of which are only as accurate as their algorithmically prescribed codes defining the universe of "likely" and "registered" voters; and mass media, perhaps catching the drift of simulation as an empty signifier, immediately "up" the political stakes by serving as a posthuman version of Dostoevsky's "grand inquisitor," sometimes in the spirit of heightened cynicism; at other times in the interests of channeling public discontent towards carefully staged sacrificial scapegoats; and always playing their necessary part in reducing the complexities of politics to the degree-zero, that point all the potential signs of change and dissent are cancelled out in a massive diffusion of circulatory flows of information. But all the while, through the web of digital inflections, there exit three guiding threads, none of which is by itself sufficient to capture the full meaning of the future of digital inflections but all of which, taken together, provide useful clues to a digital future intermediated by conflicting tendencies towards slow suicide and traversal consciousness.

Slow suicide of technological apocalypse

Today, the emblematic signs of the technopoesis that holds us in its sway are symptomatic of a future that will be marked less by the violence of an always imaginary apocalypse than by slow suicide. While Nietzsche, Freud, Marx, Heidegger, and Arendt can console us, and perhaps even guide us, nothing has really prepared us for a future that will be fully entangled in the new technopoesis of accelerate and drift, with a still undetermined, deeply intermediated, aftermath of spectacular creativity, fierce violence, and unexpected crashes. For example, digital devices, once thought safely outside ourselves, have now broken barriers of skin and mind, shaping from within the deepest recesses of consciousness, desire, perception, and imagination. Whether at the level of philosophical meditation or personal sensibility, nothing has really prepared us to live out a deeply consequential future prefigured by the specters of drones, algorithms, image vectors, distributive consciousness, artificial intelligence, neurological implants, and humanoid robotics. What is required, perhaps, is an ethical preparation for the slow suicide of technological end-times that are now only just beginning along the watchtowers of fascination and despair, righteous anger and pleasurable nihilism, of speechless moral incredulity at observing the cynical pleasure by which the powerful inflict pain on the powerless, the weak, the poor – all those bodies that don't matter – and passionate, maybe even, complicit mass resignation.

Curiously, the specter of apocalypse has traditionally been thought under the sign of biblical prophecy where, from the early prophecies of Ezekiel and Daniel to the Book of Revelations to the contemporary evangelical revelations of *Left Behind*, the sign of apocalypse has always had this doubled meaning, simultaneously a prophecy of end-times and a hopeful search for hidden meanings, secret revelations, in the coming destruction. It's no different with modernism, whether it is the cinema, literature, the theory of apocalypse, there has always been a palpable sense of desire for apocalypse, the seduction effect of the accident of end-times to come, as a way of drawing the hidden meanings of things into a greater visibility. Whether passionate pilgrims of the Bible or the errant cultural missionaries of modernism, western culture has often been mobilized by the apocalyptic sense – the seduction of the end of history is often understood as the first, hopeful sign of the beginning of another world. The technological apocalypse of slow suicide is just the opposite. Here, there are no hidden meanings and certainly no book of posthuman revelations, precisely because the slowly unwinding technological apocalypse is about a contemporary technological society that is overexposed, over-mediated, over-circulated, perhaps over-texted – a strange psychological landscape mediated by excess boredom and hyper-anxiety. In this scenario, spasms of individual insecurity and bouts of collective fear mediate the radically divided worlds of personal autobiography and public biography. Increasingly phantasmagorical, the real world of digital culture seems to have given rise to a surplus of volatilized subjectivity stretched to the limits of digital mobility, living within a public landscape charred by the information blast.

For example, if there can be such enthusiastic interest today in the development of perceptually distancing technologies – *drone technology* with its alliance of artificial intelligence, remotely controlled flight, and real-time surveillance, *distant reading* with its strictly technicist ambition to digitally scan for unknown and unexpected patterns within masses of literature rendered as computational data, *big data* with its furious attempt to reduce the vicissitudes of human experience to the facticity of the code – that may be due to the fact that the development of perceptually distancing technologies subliminally reflects what is happening to individual psychology as it is rearmed for better digital living. In this case, there might be such popular fascination with drones as agents of power, surveillance, commerce, and entertainment precisely because contemporary consciousness may have become psychologically distanced from itself and its environment for purposes of surviving the data storm. Under the massive stress of rapid technological change, consciousness may have adopted the figurative identity of the drone: packed with data, constituted by flows of information, profoundly relational in character, thinking of itself as an algorithm with a personality, inhabiting a time and space that is always interstitial, an indeterminate gap between the material and the immaterial. Consequently, the most accurate characterization of contemporary society may be that it is a transitional time "after the drones." Not literally, of course, but in the figurative sense that the development of drone technology with its intersection of artificial intelligence, complex sight machines, and control at a distance may anticipate a future world where political responsibility is eclipsed by distant ethics, where robotic machines acquire sufficient confidence in their artificial intelligence that they are prepared to be self-sustaining, and where the only sounds will be the stirring of drones as they move from instruments of warfare and surveillance to beautiful mimics of nature: drones as hummingbirds, vultures, predatory eagles. Remote consciousness, then, for a digital culture driven by technologies of perceptual distancing.

But if this is an accurate description of the contemporary technological situation, then it is also the case that what makes military drone technology truly dangerous is its alliance with an absolutist ethics of good and evil. In *The Rebel*, Albert Camus warned long ago that the most extreme ideologies of the twentieth century found a common vocabulary in absolutist moralities, with their instant and irrevocable division of mass populations into visible bodies deemed worthy of political recognition and invisible, prohibited, ethically disavowed bodies that are free to be sanctioned by all means necessary and, indeed, possible. For Camus, an absolutist conception of rationality, unconstrained by knowledge of the complex vicissitudes of human experience, often supports an absolute will to destruction just as much as absolutist ideas about justice, again unlimited by the necessary mediations of the human circumstance, often yield absolute injustice. Consequently, if "After the Drones" explores the technological foundations for a new form of split subjectivity and divided perception that will inhabit the leading edges of the twenty-first century, then "The Rhetoric of the 'Just War'" focuses on the otherwise invisible, but ethically detectable, ontological framework supporting the seemingly morally unconstrained use of drone technology. Here, the representative historical figure of Barack Obama with his eloquently argued defense of the concept of the "just war," even when accepting the Nobel Peace Prize, is taken as what Hegel might have described as the realization of the idea in history. In this case, the idea that is realized is a doubled one: not only an explicit rationale for fierce and repeated deployments of technologies of war as a matter of national security, but, of equal importance, basing moral belief in the concept of the "just war" in a deeply felt, religiously based, and ontologically identified belief in the existence of absolute evil in the world. When the creative leadership of powerful technological societies reaffirms the indispensable linkage of violence and morality or, in this case, justifies the deployment of predator drones by images of absolute evil, then it is surely salutary to bring the cautionary words of Camus to mind – that the twenty-first century may be about to repeat the absolutist ideologies of the past century except, this time, in purely technocratic formulations.

Traversal consciousness

Recently, there was an astronomical report concerning the connection between Earth and Sun. Contradicting received interpretations that held a constant field between them, cosmologists have now discovered the presence of a regular gateway opening roughly every eight minutes between Sun and Earth. Satellites launched by the European Union have discovered that this gateway is 4,000 miles across, roughly equivalent to the diameter of the earth.

Social networking is like that. It can be so amazingly seductive precisely because social networking opens astral gateways between otherwise disconnected individuals. Facebook as a digital portal; Twitter as

life support for digital identity; smartphones as light-streams of connectivity. Technologies come alive as a circulating loop of information,
opening unpredictable gateways across the digital multitude. Digital
subjects are constantly networked, circulating, communicating, reach-
ing out, in motion, breaking beyond the boundaries of the previously
private self to go through the astral gateways of a larger communicative universe. Psychologically motivated by the seduction of connectivity, we have grown a second body – a digital body – as the shadowy
penumbra of the body of flesh and blood. Deeply entwined, intersecting, enfolded, the network body and the material body have until now
negotiated an uneasy, yet stable, relationship – two bodies inhabiting
a single physical space but with different modalities of time and space.
The network body has always known only the long arc of light-time
and the accelerated velocity of light-speed, while the physical body has
only experienced time as duration with a definite beginning and
ending, and space as something that is not necessarily fungible or even,
for that matter, indefinitely expandable.

However, all of that is about to change with the intensification of
social networking with its brilliant deployment of technological apps
and equally creative technological devices. What might be called the
subjectivity or, more precisely, the "trans-subjectivity" of digital inhabitants seems to be in the process of abandoning its temporary habitat
in human flesh in favor of a permanent orbit of high-intensity connectivity. The splitting of the body of flesh, bone, and blood from the
network body of light-space and light-time does not take place by
means of a physical separation of this doubled form of being, but by a
method that is precisely the opposite. If contemporary technological
discourse in favor of "big data" and "distant reading" is to believed,
bodily subjectivity is about to be colonized by a form of digital trans-
subjectivity where consciousness is radically split. On the one side,
consciousness under the sign of the regime of computation: distributive, remote, a relational matrix with perception shaped by algorithms,
understanding mediated by digital connectivity, memory installed in
all the waiting data archives, personal history recorded in permanent
electronic traces. Process minds in the data storm. On the other, the
emergence of a new form of technological consciousness as the name
given to a form of thought that, having no existence apart from the
shock of the (data) real, traverses the entire field of technology, thriving
at the folded edges of biology and digitality, articulating itself in the
language of the dispersed, the fragment, the wandering particle, formed
by the soft materiality of the intersection, the mediation, just that point
where computational consciousness actually begins to reverse itself

into a universe of unexpected discoveries and unanticipated minoritar-ian thought. The fateful meeting of process mind and traversal mind, this conjunction of distributive consciousness and a new form of manifestly folded, open-source thought, is properly the key epistemo-logical exit to the posthuman future. Signs of pitched struggle between these two opposing trajectories of posthuman consciousness are everywhere.

If the long-term trend of contemporary technological innovation is to deliver culture and society to a cinematic scenario anticipated by this vision of "after the drones," perhaps it would be salutary to reflect again on the lessons to be drawn from posthuman futurists: McLuhan, Virilio, and Foucault. Confronted by the onrushing event of the fully realized technological future, it is in the way of a cautionary tale to read theorists whose thought has grasped immediately and deeply the unfolding ontology of the technological future, rehearsing its power and potential contradictions decades, if not centuries, in advance. In such thought is to be found early intimations of the psychic, social, and political consequences of the fully realized technological society. Here, the theoretical imagination rehearses the stresses and contradictions of a digital culture that literally lives in the complex folds of process mind and traversal consciousness.

For example, McLuhan, a visionary who projected his thought with intensity and an urgent demand for perceptual clarity into the future of technology, always balanced his utopian estimation of the benefits of technology with equally dystopian expectations of social docility in the face of massive technological change. Here, McLuhan returns as the spectral visionary of the "dark tetrad," that point where technology surpasses the laws of media with its technological injunction that every new technical innovation simultaneously create, obsolesce, retrieve, and reverse-field when pushed to its limits. Keeping in mind that every ontology has a hidden hauntology, every condition of possibility has an equal series of exclusions and prohibitions, McLuhan's lasting con-tribution may have been to provide an early warning that every tech-nology contains a hauntological dimension whereby technological innovations always depend on the language of prohibition, that for every technological creation there is an equivalent disappearance, for every obsolescence, a balancing substitution, for every retrieval, an indefinite prolongation of the same, and, for every field-reversal, a growing sense of paralysis, if not generalized inertia. In this case, "Thinking the Future with Marshall McLuhan" is a way of drawing together the brilliantly utopian arc of McLuhan's technological cosmol-ogy with the bleaker vision provided by a technological visionary whose ethics were always based on a curious mixture of the cultural skepticism of Catholic humanism and his own relentlessly pessimistic account of the human condition. For better or worse, the world of technological posthumanism may well turn out to be that anticipated, with such dark precision, in McLuhan's writings, namely the "blast" and "counter-blast" of an increasingly technified universe. In his thought, we actually live within the skin of the posthuman, that moment when the creative power of technological devices and digital apps, with their exciting promise to facilitate our progression into the flow of information, to augment freedom of (communicative) choice, and to enhance connectivity, is counterbalanced by the real world of globalizations with its disappearances, prohibitions, and exclusions.

That McLuhan could have predicted so accurately the current direction of technological culture is confirmed, in effect, by the findings of Paul Virilio – a theorist whose writings serve as a counter-gradient to the technological blast. Like McLuhan, Paul Virilio is a technological visionary whose writings on technology have been deeply shaped by his religious convictions, Virilio can provide such profound understandings of digital culture moving at light-speed because his thought brushes the question of technology against the language of deprival – the "aesthetics of disappearance," the "information bomb," the "lost dimension," "bunker archaeology," "polar inertia," the "original accident," "grey ecology," the "University of Disaster," "The Great Accelerator." Considered as a talisman of the posthuman future, Virilio's reflections open onto that truly ominous moment when oblivion falls into us, when a great neutralization of social experience takes place. In this sense, the decisive cultural contribution of Paul Virilio may be his intellectual service as a brilliant cartographer of the excesses, as well as possible wasteland, of a posthuman future that is increasingly as enigmatic in its details as it is uncanny in its definition. While the practical realization of technological society resembles what the social theorist Max Weber once described as the "slow boring of holes," Virilio's advantage is that his thought is actually present as an attentive witness and theoretical critic at the very inception of the ontological assumptions governing technological posthumanism. Indeed, as an exit to the posthuman future, the trajectory of Virilio's thought parallels that earlier movement of European thought where, from surrealism in the arts to uncertainty theory in the sciences, the radiating blast of information technology, of a world culture that would be powerfully gathered into the light-time and light-space of electronic culture moving at warp speed, was first evoked in the European theater of thought. So, too, it is the likely fate of Paul Virilio, this fully transitional thinker between late twentieth- and early twenty-first-century culture, to have made this fateful transition by introducing an important insight: that we are presently accelerating towards a posthuman future which has all the makings of an "original accident." For Virilio, like McLuhan before him, the posthuman fate is this: to be fascinated by the speed of technological devices and augmented by mobile apps to such an extent that the eye of perception is distracted just at the point when it is about to free-fall into a new epoch of "polar inertia" and "grey ecology." Just as Nietzsche once claimed that he was writing "posthumously," in effect aiming his thought at generations who would come to maturity in the dark days of "fully completed nihilism," Virilio's warnings assume the form of an exit to the posthuman future that will probably only be appreciated in their full intensity once it is too late, once, that is, the "original accident" of technology spreads out with such violent energy that everything in its wake flips into a posthuman *reality*, not merely an "aesthetics of disappearance."

If McLuhan's exit to the posthuman future leads directly to a haunting vision of the "dark tetrad" and if Virilio's exit opens onto technology as a "university of disaster," Michel Foucault's exit is framed by the language of cynical power. Foucault can provide such a profoundly influential theory of power as something that circulates, that is, in its essence, liquid, relational, and fluid because he was the first philosopher to really understand the consequences of that fateful moment when power spoke of itself in the language of life, not death. While this is sometimes understood in strictly political terms as the basis for the emergence of a "disciplinary society," my sense is that Foucault already understood that, when power spoke in the forceful language of life, it was not for purposes solely of discipline but because power of this order was invested with the truly lifelike qualities of psychological drives towards *ressentiment* and revenge-taking. Curiously, if we were to take Marshall McLuhan at his word and treat most events, particularly significant events such as the writings of Michel Foucault, as a medium of communication, then it might also be noted that Foucault's concept of power has its own fourfold of laws: it is creative (power that circulates); it obsolesces (the reduction of power to sovereignty), it retrieves (the turning of power towards psychologies of *ressentiment*); and, when pressured to its limits, it flips polarity (the cynical power of what I call the "imperial subaltern"). In this case, entering Foucault's exit to the posthuman future leads directly to an understanding of contemporary technological power, this forceful alliance of virtual capitalism and state institutions oscillating between ideologies of technological liberalism and redemptive conservatism, as a form of power that is purely cynical, power that expresses itself in the language of the imperial subaltern. In this case, Foucault's understanding of posthuman power introduces us to contemporary globalized society as one in which power increasingly announces itself in the language of the colonial subaltern, identifying with the language of the "culture of injury," the language of ressentiment and revenge-taking. That may be, perhaps, the subtext of the story about technology, that every technology is born with a necessary injury, with the impossible task of living up to the expectations of a recalcitrant and always too slow humanity that is really not up to the gift of technology. In this case, the appearance of a culture of technological posthumanism may be in the way of a great revenge-taking by technology on its human progenitors, a striking example of technology in its penultimate historical phase as the new imperial subaltern, always massively powerful and all the more so denying that it is powerful at all. That, of course, is the language of every technological innovation that first introduces itself in the language of facilitation – technologies for better communication, in-depth learning, faster reporting, precise archiving, awesome databases – just before the same technological innovations reintroduce themselves to an often unsuspecting humanity, and soon posthumanity, in the language of control – technologies of surveillance, acquisition, monitoring, substituting, replacing. Understood as an exit to the posthuman future, "premonitory thought" is situated in an eerie historical fracture between technologies of facilitation and control. What is more uncanny is that technologies of control now possess purely psychological qualities of *ressentiment* and revenge-taking, providing, at first, the normative standards of intelligibility against which an always (technically) deficient human species-form is destined to fail. In the most literal sense, the distinguishing element of the posthuman scene is that technology has now come alive, with all that entails in terms of a future technical reenactment of the promise and danger of the now superseded human species.

Accelerate

2

The Posthuman Imagination:
Neuro-Diversity, Psychic Trauma, and History in the Data Feed

Photography of invisibility

In many ways, the future of technology is haunted by the aesthetic practices of early forms of photography. Recently, there was an art exhibition featuring a wonderful series of photographs of nineteenth-century Montreal social history, based on this now superseded order of photography – photographs of the architecture of Old Montreal under construction, sidewalk cafés, trams, cargo ships being unloaded for transshipment on the Lachine Canal. For the most part, what was strikingly missing from many of the photographs of living history was any sign of a visible human presence. The description that accompanied the exhibition explained that, in this order of photography, subjects had to remain perfectly still for at least two minutes, meaning that, except for carefully staged photographs, the visible human was reduced to spectral traces, vague smudges, and sometimes very interesting vapor trails, indicating human movement while the photographic apparatus was in operation. Curiously, this is precisely the opposite of contemporary imaging technologies that desperately function to draw everything and everyone into visibility. Today, nothing can escape the image; body movements are site-tagged by circling satellites; motion on a city street, in an airport, instantly attracts the attention of the video gaze. Recent reports from advanced military research describe new technologies of surveillance that skip the particulars of human presence completely and drill down image-wise into the body's biometric data. However, if imaging now brings everything into visibility, it is also the case that some things fundamental to the human condition are slipping into invisibility, like a growing sense of loneliness, a

spreading desire to be underexposed, to be disconnected from technologically enabled connectivity. There's definitely not much discussion
of this. The ideology of digital connectivity is triumphant. The codes
of efficiency are burned deeply into human subjectivity. Yet for all that
it might be saving human dispositions – being alone, being disconnected, being underexposed, being private – things which are both
invisible and fundamentally alien to a society of speed are just like
those vapor trails in an earlier order of photography, the first tangible
signs of the appearance of all the paradoxes and complexities involved
with the posthuman imagination.

The cage of measurability

It has been widely reported that the co-founders of Google, Larry Page
and Sergey Brin, envision Google as a leading expression of the new
life-form of artificial intelligence – a living, sentient being complete
with artificial neural networks ("deep belief networks") that can be
applied to "image recognition, language modeling and machine translation."[1] From this perspective, the real future of Google as a sentient
being would be that of a potential successor species for humanity, with
human consciousness reduced to the role of just another algorithm
along the way, the slow processing power of which would require
augmentation by the sophisticated neural networks of new communicative technologies.

Outside of the blast of contemporary events and hidden from view,
the future to which the larger destiny of technology delivers us is
marked by an increasingly close alliance between genetic determinism
and software culture. We are no longer living in the universe prophesied by Marshall McLuhan – fully technological world moving at the
speed of light, replete with digital prosthetics, a world where the
human sensorium has literally been exteriorized, ablated, extended in
the form of new communicative technologies. That is already a vision
of a now effectively surpassed world, one in which technological prosthetics migrate from the outside of the body to its deepest interiority,
becoming, in the process, increasingly camouflaged and mobile – linked
to bodily orifices in the form of communicative technologies. More a
matter of biology than physics, technological innovation in the twenty-
first century promises something very different: a world in which technology, no longer so much prosthetic as psychic, adopts the language
of neuroscience and begins to split open the topography of the mind,
recoding, reinscribing, realigning its neural networks. Perhaps we

should enjoy our consciousness while we can since we are probably the last generation to experience forms of neurology free of data feeds, ways of seeing not imaged in advance, ways of feeling not subject to neurological therapeutics. The cultural anxiety is palpable, with rumors about the ablation of the brain and the implosion of consciousness circulating in the collective unconscious of contemporary culture. That is why, perhaps, everything seems to increasingly operate today under the ideological sign of the neuro – neuro-marketing, neuro-politics, neuro-fashion, neuro-economics, neuro-philosophy, neuro-identity, even neuro-beverages. In the present epoch, moral conservatism in politics is paralleled by neuro-fundamentalism in science. Indeed, bio-genetic dreams of brain vivisectioning and the technical sublimation of consciousness are now seemingly everywhere with efficiency as their value-attribute, distributive consciousness as their brand name, and images of the new global brain as the new normal.

With and against this is the posthuman imagination, a form of thinking, writing, art, and politics that is based on an understanding of the bodies we actually inhabit, the minds which we possess and which sometimes possess us, and on stories of artificial life and thalamic bridges and hauntological history and on how some artists choose to respond to traumatic events. Indeed, the first sightings of emergent posthuman consciousness are to be found in minoritarian thought, in those curious but often neglected stories of the disowned, disavowed, excluded stories that demand human recognition, not as objects in remix culture but as premonitory signs of the beginning anew of the posthuman future – a future of broken neurons, parallel universes, ethics of the impossible, useless history, and contemporary life in the data feed. In the posthuman future, the creative imagination must find a way of breaking beyond *the cage of measurability* in order to become that which is the fatal destiny of the life of the mind – being critically attentive by deep, necessary immersion in the posthuman condition while, at the same time, being fully aware of what has been silenced, excluded, and prohibited by the technological destiny that sweeps us forward.

Premonitory signs of the posthuman are everywhere. It has recently been reported in a breathless press release that in the near future "you [w]on't really need a heart or a pulse," that we are on the verge of the "first heartless man."[2] The announcement went on to say that "the turbine-like device . . . does not beat like a heart, rather provides a 'continuous flow' like a garden hose," resulting in a living human with a permanent "flatline."[3] Perhaps with this eerie image of the permanently "flatlined" body in mind and attentive to the quantum cosmologist Stephen Hawking's warning that "it will be difficult enough to avoid disaster on planet Earth in the next hundred years, let alone the next thousand, or million,"[4] implying, according to Hawking, that "if we want to continue beyond the next hundred years, our future is in space."[5] NASA has recently initiated the development of "biocapsules made of carbon nanotubes" that would be implanted in several points of the body, releasing therapeutic agents to alter the physiology of crew members when threats like radioactive blasts are detected.[6] Capable of giving multiple doses over a period of years, NASA biocapsules will mainly be developed to treat radiation-related illness experienced by astronauts, but, interestingly enough, they can be used for other things: "heat, exhaustion, sleep deprivation." But if there should be a breakdown in the technologically stressed body, a research team at Cornell University's Computational Synthesis Laboratory promises fully functioning 3-D printing of body organs and tissues within the next twenty years.[7] And while we are in the full-body scanners of the future, other forms of neuro-scanning are also taking place. For example, it has recently been reported that scientists focused on artificial intelligence are intent on "decoding brain waves to eavesdrop on what we hear." In a case of creative reverse engineering, "spectrograms and readings of brain activity when we hear can be used to build a library of patterns that can be cross-referenced later with readings where [it is unclear] what is being heard."[8] In other words, the brain is viewed as being mnemotechnic: an auditory archive where patterns that show up on a spectrogram can be translated back later into the original sounds. There are intimations here not just of an artificial body, permanently "flatlined," stuffed full of carbon nanotubes for technological apocalypse, always ready for exiting planet earth, but also of a cranial future highlighted by the artificial brain with upgraded libraries of sound waves and image vectors, animated by augmented vision, and moving inexorably towards telepathy as its primary medium of expression, as the relentless demands of mobile technologies break not just the skin barrier but the mind barrier in all the dense social networks of the world.

If everything today is marked by panic control – over-coded, over-normalized, over-secured, over-mediated, over-measured – this is probably because the reality principle has been shaken to its core by a fundamental *technological wobble*. More than ever, the future appears in purely astronomical form as a fatal precession of things where all the traditional polarities of society and culture suddenly reverse, with the result that events are understandable today only by an imaginary of mirror images. Now that life has become a series of complex but no less seductive exits to the posthuman future, only that which is confidently and transgressively part of the posthuman imagination – fractured, incommensurable, unreconciled, capable of thinking deeply about issues related to the "in-between," that enigmatic, undefinable, tense space that is now opening up in all our lives as boundary divisions and borders crash between bodies and machines and natural objects and sentient nature – only this form of imagination, the posthuman imagination, can provide a way to ride the violent shock waves accompanying the precession of society. We desperately require a form of posthuman imagination that fully reveals the hauntologies, disavowals, and silences of the technological dynamo that has crashed the game(s) of reality.

Or is posthumanism precisely the opposite? In this case, if the concept of the posthuman can be so fascinating as a way of thinking strange juxtapositions, unexpected curves, radical fractures, subtle bifurcations in the language of technology, maybe it is because, like all imaginary decoys, the posthuman imagination is definitely not the polar opposite of technology but its deepest animating form of intelligibility, simultaneously the driving force of the regime of computation and its justificatory logic. Here, the story of technology could be conceived as always about the posthuman, this strange, powerful, seductive energy force – a danger and a saving power – always originating in the brutal truth that it may be technology itself that is often at odds with human purposes. When the will to technology forces the human species into strange code spaces, compels society to move at previously unimaginable speeds, literally smashes the human condition on the hard algorithms of computation, making that which is subtle, processed, that which is individuated, networked, and that which is private, overexposed, then we can finally know that we have truly entered the space and time of the posthuman.

Exits to the posthuman future[9]

Exit 1: "I love I am stuck"

Recently, there was a beautiful and sensitively written story by Susan Dominus, titled "Inseparable."[10] It is about adorable, four-year-old twins, Krista and Tatiana, who live with their extended family in Vernon, British Columbia. Kristina and Tatiana are conjoined twins, joined at the head, their skulls fused together never to be parted because under their skulls they share a unique brain physiology. MRI images reveal an attenuated line stretching between the two brains. Their neurosurgeon, Douglas Cochrane, calls this a "thalamic bridge." He believes it links the thalamus of one girl to her sister. As Susan Dominus describes it:

> The thalamus is a kind of switchboard, a two-lobed organ, that filters most sensory input and has long been thought to be essential in the neural loops that create consciousness. Since the thalamus functions as a relay system, the girls' doctors believe it is possible that the sensory input of one girl crosses the bridge into the brain of the other.[11]

In other words, "what one girl sees with her eyes travels to her sister via the thalamic bridge to be visualized by her sister milliseconds later."[12] Considered less as a "neurological wonder" expressing a unique neural anatomy, the register of this story is fundamentally affective. The story of these conjoined twins, Krista and Tatiana, seems to illuminate a greater truth – what it means to be human today. This is not so much, then, a story of strange neurology or technology, but of the enigmatic meaning of connectivity itself.

Two bodies as one
But then as two

I and We and Both

"I love I am Stuck" is what
four-year old Krista says
about herself because she
and her sister Tatania are stuck

Joined at the head – fused skulls.

Little girls perfect for reality TV?
Scientific Research?

Or just being two little girls
As One, as Two.

It's a live wire that connects one to the
Other – a thalamic bridge brain to brain
"one girls drinks, the other feels it"
– a parallel universe or a shared one?

Two little girls who are one
And two at the same time.

Are we all I and We and Both? Or should we be? Is this the significance of neuro-diversity?

Exit 2: the posthuman brain

Today, there are exuberant stories in the Twittersphere, even exultant, about the moment of first contact between computers and the human brain – the mapping of the synaptic connectivity of the brain – neural networks – onto the digital galaxy – computer networks.

Or is it perhaps the other way around? Not the mapping of the language of the brain onto the regime of computation in the form of neural networks, but something more ambiguous, perhaps more menacing. Could it be that what is happening now is not so much first contact between the brain and the computer, but the parasiting of the language of neurology as a way of describing computer networks, that computation seemingly mirrors the neural logic of the brain in order to hijack it for its own purposes? In this case, is it possible that the language of neurology today is being increasingly wrapped in the prosthetic skin of the regime of computation – operational, efficient, fluid, reductive, positivistic? Here, the brain seems to have one last historical function, namely to provide a language for computer networks before being junked as so much debris before the rise to prominence of the long-awaited cybernetic brain – global, networked, intelligent, self-generating. This would, in fact, explain why so much of the contemporary debate over the future of the brain increasingly devolves into two warring camps. On the one side, panic Enlightenment perspectives on human consciousness that insist on what we might call "skulling the mind," limiting consciousness to individual consciousness, reducing the brain to an organ trapped in a physical cranium. On the other hand, an enthusiastically extropian vision of pure cybernetic consciousness projects a world proliferating with technological devices that actually begins to develop a global brain that operates autonomously on the basis of its own complex connectivity, a future world of distributive consciousness, machine-to-machine communication, massively adaptive, responsive to changes in its digital environment, a process universe nesting the full complexity of human and machine synaptic connections.

What is missing from these games of digital neurology is, perhaps, something very elemental about human consciousness: that what we call the brain is not something purely physiological but deeply affective. The unique signature of the human mind is that we are not typically products of pure cerebration, but that the brain is, like all sliding signifiers, another name for a very complex, dynamic, and sometimes even homeostatic balance between the human sensorium – thinking, feeling, touching, smelling, seeing.

Now, no one really knows the defining boundaries when it comes to understanding the brain. But we do know this. The human brain has always been deeply *relational*, emulating shareware as its shadow because the brain thrives or atrophies, exists, or perishes only on the basis of its sensory connectivity. Demonstrating immense plasticity in its evolutionary development, with neural synapses sensitive to changes, internal or external, in the human nervous sensorium, the fully relational brain is, in the most profound ecological sense, a complex, continuous mediation of biology and society, that point where consciousness wears the nerves of its surrounding environment. For example, how often do you feel concepts before actually thinking them? And what about touch? And what about the gut brain reaction? Isn't the gut brain the sensory spearhead of neurology? Consider how the gut brain seems to so easily wrap itself around consciousness, sometimes warning us in advance of imminent dangers but also sparking thoughts tactile about love, intimacy, remembrance? And isn't seeing deeply shaped in advance by the intelligibility of the brain to the well-documented extent that we usually see only what we have first interiorized as the knowable, the intelligible, literally the seeable? How this powerful synaptic connection between brain and vision also has its own hauntologies; how, that is, so much of seeing is based on massive, continuing internal repression of that which must not be brought into visibility, that which must remain outside human vision, and thus human recognition, if we are to continue to persist within the boundaries of the so-called normal self. It is this mysterious, enigmatic connection between brain matter and the full human sensorium – vision brains, tactile brains, gut brains, ear brains – which is meant by *neuro-diversity*. This complex intermingling of consciousness, sight, feeling, touch, hearing, does not, of course, figure in the nostalgic calculations of contemporary humanism and most definitely not in the feverish futurist visions of digital extropians. In both cases, mention of the actual presence of neuro-diversity as the basis of human consciousness – the fact that our brains are not one but multiple, not trapped in craniums but essentially relational – would introduce a real element of impossibility into their explanatory algorithms.

Exit 3: mirror neurons and the empathy gene

How do we understand others? Probably in an unconscious response to growing insecurity and rising rates of anxiety today over radical upheavals in society, culture, and economy – major political divisions in the world, fiscal crisis, perpetual war, social movements of purity – there is a countervailing tendency in contemporary neuroscience towards scientific determinism. Not any form of scientific determinism, but a precision-driven, almost laser-beam fixation on lighting up the physiology of the human brain.[13] For example, the recent focus in neuroscience on "mirror neurons" – a theory of how we understand others that is now held to explain many human relations, including autism.[14] In days not long ago, when the human brain wasn't capable of being illuminated from within by neuroscience, the origins of understanding others was often considered to be a fundamental dividing line between two warring philosophies of life – nature and nurture.

Fortuitously, for those who refuse to choose between the antinomies of nature and nurture and who, in fact, blur the question by thinking about the complexity that is the shifting boundaries between ontogeny and physiology, the question seems to have now been resolved by at least part of the neuroscience community in favor of genetic determinism. Curiously, for a scientific community so focused on the origins of human empathy, the methods used for research are often strikingly non-empathetic. Leading discoveries regarding mirror neurons have been based on wiring the brains of animals, particularly monkeys sequestered in scientific labs, for months at a time until fabulous eureka moments of scientific discovery take place. Now, it would be churlish to deny neuroscientists their experimental animals as defenseless objects of brain vivisectioning, but it remains the case that a methodology, so deeply lacking in empathy as its basic ontological condition of possibility, may well possess a similar lack of empathy when it comes, and it will most definitely soon come, to human subjects. With mirror neurons, we are talking about something very traditional. In classical philosophy, it was called mimesis; in contemporary psychological therapy, it is called demonstrating recognition in the therapeutic situation of another suffering human's problems; in religion, it is sometimes called simple charity; in politics mutual solidarity.

Who knew that there were mirror neurons shaping so much of the human condition? Evolution in a genomic bubble. Mirror neurons and even more recently the discovery of the "empathy gene" – variations on the OXTR gene "which codes for neuro-receptor cells throughout the body that serve as docking stations for a hormone called oxytocin"[15] – provide at first a biological, and then genetic, basis for defining boundaries between what is considered normal and the abnormal. Indeed, the neuro-economist Paul J. Zak calls it the "goodness gene" or "moral molecule."[16]

Like an uncanny repetition of earlier genomic theories by Lombroso concerning the relationship between the shape of the cranium and criminal behavior, this twenty-first-century version of genomics immediately targets autistic children and others who are defined as abnormal due to their apparent lack of social empathy as measured by prevailing standards of genetic expression. Thus, not only do claims for the "moral molecule" and mirror neurons do away with necessarily social explanations with their complex mediations of class and gender and race and ethnicity and power, but they also provide a supposedly scientific basis for new norms of political intelligibility – what is normal and what is not. In neuroscience, the search is on today for what determines the normal, taking the gradations of human psychology and compressing them categorically instead of seeking to understand the whole spectrum of human behavior.

So, the irony: Is it possible that the search for the empathy gene isn't itself a recursive sign of a neuroscience community that occludes any understanding of empathy in its relationship to mimesis, solidarity, recognition, sympathy? Put in the terms of the OXTR gene, there are many docking stations for empathy, many variations on the nature–nurture debate when it comes to grievability and human suffering. It's the very same with "mirror neurons." What, in effect, is really being mirrored by the genomic search for the origins of social understanding. A form of thought that requires the brain vivisectioning of animals as its basic condition of epistemological possibility will always be haunted not only by its actual practice of cruelty towards other species, but by the continuous act of repression that is necessary to denial of cruelty – the objectification of animals by the scientific gaze. In the end, it is only a sign-slide in the imaginary of neuroscience to project onto the genetics of many individuals another order of objectification, specifically that a variation on the OXTR gene condemns them to a negative judgment on the essentially *political* matter of what is to be considered normal and what is not. In other words, who is to be considered "good" and "moral" and who is not?

Perhaps it is the case that what is quickly emerging first in scientific and then political worlds is a new physiological normal. Not the evolutionary normal envisioned by the convergence of Charles Darwin and Herbert Spencer in theories concerning the survival of the fittest; not even the normal of second-wave eugenics from early twentieth-century social hygiene movements to eugenic theories of racial selection that fueled mid-twentieth-century fascism; but now, seventy years later, another eugenic normal – fully genetic, precisely neurological – that deploys the neutral language of the neuron – genetic variation – to design in advance by means of genetic labeling what Judith Butler has called "bodies that matter" and to exclude what we might call bodies that don't matter or forms of neuro-diversity not to be normatively avowed. There are many reflections to be found in the mirroring of neurons, and most of them reflect disavowal, prohibition, and exclusion. In a future that is likely to be dominated by genetic labeling, perhaps we should bring into greater ethical visibility the question of neuro-diversity. Socially, ethical consciousness has already been expanded in terms of concepts of biodiversity, sexual diversity, cultural diversity, so is neuro-diversity one of the final prohibitions that must be brought into the realm of ethical intelligibility.

Exit 4: the psychic trauma of war

Recently, there was a media report about a NYU professor, Wafaa Bilal, who, as part of an art project, had a body modification artist embed a camera in the back of his head that snapped pictures every sixty seconds and then streamed them to the web,[17] that is, until a life-threatening infection caused the camera's removal. What is interesting is not only the embedded camera and its instant repudiation by the body's defenses, but the artist's motivation for initiating the project in the first instance. The artist spent the first part of his life fleeing Iraq after the first Gulf War in 1991, living for many years thereafter in refugee camps. A contemporary story then of the psychic trauma of war. As the artist stated: "most of the time we don't live in the places we live in. We don't exist in the city we exist in. Perhaps physically we exist but mentally we are someplace else."[18] Perhaps refugee camps are without a sense of place, with the body and mind floating to other places, other times. In this case, the only thing that could anchor the body in time and place is a continuous, mundane visual record of life's experience. Wafaa Bilal could be considered, in fact, a posthuman Cartesian: *I record, therefore I am.* It is curious that at the same time as the artist struggled to work through trauma by an all-seeing, always online embedded camera in the back of his head, his students had a very different reaction, accusing the artist's project of invading their privacy. It might have worked if all the students had embedded cameras – a scene of mutually assured voyeurism. But, in the end, before the body rebelled and the project came to an abrupt end, the artist was forced to literally never turn his back on his students.

Perhaps what is also happening here is a fast glimpse out of the side of the digital eye that reveals what happens in the posthuman imagination when the (artistic) brain opens perception to the terrorism and boredom of the code. Not neuroscience in the service of codes of augmentation, not consciousness cut down to suit the limited scope of software, but the posthuman brain shaping the future of the code, pushing the regime of computation in the direction of human affect, of sensory diversity. The tangible presence of the posthuman brain, the artistic brain, is probably what is most disturbing to the powerful alliance of neural networks and software. That is the real story of social media today. On the surface, a networked world of technological devices, but dig a little deeper and we are speaking about a wild and unpredictable community of individuated consciousness that is like all the recalcitrant matter of human subjectivity before it – always running against the grain of the larger purposes imposed on it, but yet no innocent spectator at the digital feast. When the brain grows digital codes for skin, when the brain develops software for an augmented neural network of its own making, when the brain seeks the net as a way of feeling, then we can finally recognize that the arc of the future posthuman is trending relentlessly towards the paradoxical, the complex, the undecidable. It's like the story of Krista and Tatania. More than anything, the brain is perhaps always and only a thalamic bridge – a way station to the outside and inside of the human senses: *We are I and We and Both; I am multiple and We are also sometimes One.* In the face of all the contemporary appeals for a greater normality by the alienated marvels of distributive consciousness and images of the cybernetic brain, what could be truer than the simple, but heartfelt, advice of Krista and Tatania – "I love I am stuck"?

Exit 5: the last days of history

All of these exits to the posthuman future – *I love I am stuck, the posthuman brain, mirror neurons and the empathy gene, the psychic trauma of war* – take place in the context of a larger historical destiny that is increasingly and risibly hauntological, literally haunted by that which has been so forcibly repressed in order to achieve the technological mastery of social and nonsocial nature and, at the same time, visibly perplexed by the fact that so much of contemporary history is driven by the rising into political prominence of the voices of those who have previously been disavowed, excluded, prohibited. It is almost as if we are living at the precipice of two very different posthuman futures, one purely technological – excess history, the history of digital culture with its fantastic acceleration of everything by the regime of computation; and the other more phantasmatic – hauntological history.

Hauntological history? Consider, for example, these scenes from the delirious wasteland of hauntological history, a history that refuses to be named because it is still nameless, a history that resists totality because it is phantasmatic, and a history that refuses the reality referent of the ontological since it is always in the way of a ghostly haunting. Here, seemingly unrelated stories from the Arab Spring, space walks by NASA astronauts, and panic tweets in China are revealed to have a deep connecting ethical thread, namely that in the era of hauntological history that which was previously disavowed – stories of the uncanny, the incommensurable, the haunted – return now as the essence of a contemporary trajectory of history marked by the intersection of a fading ethical intelligibility and specters of the wasteland insurgent. The present only exists with respect to the past. After the end of history, the ghosts of the past haunt us. Everywhere there are prophetic signs – uncanny, liminal, haunting – that these, our days, our history, are the last days of history, that these days, our days, our history may be opening onto a future, a posthuman future, whose rules we do not yet understand but which, for all that, exhibits an "enigmatic tension" as the essence of contemporary events.

History in the data feed

During the early months of the Arab Spring, *livestream.com* streamed a haunting video taken by a courageous Libyan woman from her apartment window in Benghazi. The scene is truly desolate. An empty urban street with the dead body of a protestor, two cars filled with armed men who stop, raise their guns to the surrounding apartments like a hunting pack, drag the body of the protestor to one of the cars, throw it in the trunk and drive away. My thoughts are mediated by those other data feeds from Libya: stories of Ghaddafi security forces storming hospitals, disappearing the bodies of those killed and injured, apparently to maintain the official story that the Libyan government is not killing its own citizens. I think back to the "dirty war" in Latin America, the days of the death squads, and wonder who now will write a eulogy for the bodies of the disappeared, earlier in Argentina, Brazil, and Chile and now in Libya, Bahrain, and Syria.

While thinking these melancholic thoughts, my media eye is drawn to another *livestream*, this time not from the streets of Benghazi but from the galactic regions of outer space with its awesome scenes of astronauts out for a space walk against the spatial background of the beautiful blue seas of planet earth below. Suddenly, I find myself perceptually and emotionally suspended between these two spaces – between real-time caravans of death in the streets of Benghazi and the confident "right stuff" of NASA astronauts. With no ready answers available, my open-access, fully mediated body becomes a question mark, one of how to reconcile in the very same ethical register the spatially augmented bodies of the masters of technological power and the vanquished bodies of freedom seekers in Benghazi. To add to the ethical mix, there are constant sounds in the background: religious chants of hope and defiance linking Islamic faith with inspiring dreams of freedom; and, from outer space, another sound, cybernetic this time: NASA engineers speaking proudly of yet another mission accomplished.

But the image stream and data feeds never stop. Now there is a report out of China that relates how the Chinese government, for all its commercial confidence and rising political ambitions, was suddenly shattered by a single tweet. It seems that an anonymous Chinese tweeter announced a walk-by political protest that was scheduled to take place in the heart of Beijing. The strategy was simplicity itself. Protestors did not have to do anything: no marches, no banners, no spectacular displays of open resistance. Instead, activists were instructed to do a walk-by of one of the local McDonald's. Here, human presence at a certain point of Beijing space and time was presented as the moral equivalent of active resistance. Now, some people actually did walk by the chosen designation in a scene of Twitter defiance. Although for the most part, it seems that on that day and on that particular street, many walkers were simply shoppers and, of course, a waiting army of security officials ready to pounce on them. Plain clothes security forces stormed McDonald's, the street itself was shut down by an armada of street-cleaning machines operated by security officials in brand new city uniforms, security vans were present with the latest technological devices for mobile jamming, and high-tech audio equipment meant to blast ultrasonic sound waves at unsuspecting protestors was prepped for instant action. In other words, all the force of resurgent Chinese power was assembled against the virtual threat of a lonely Twitter message in the data feed. What is the new meaning of freedom in the data feed? How can contemporary historical narratives about the rise and decline of power stabilize when a single tweet can panic an empire?

What links these media feeds together? What provides these very different scenes of political desolation, technological prowess, and panic power with a connecting thread? In the most immediate sense, there is no necessary relationship among them, other than the fact, of course, that these are items slipstreamed in the data feed, available to anyone precisely because they are not matters of individual propertied possession. What they are, I believe, is something different, something phantasmatic – provisional, perhaps even illusionary, reports on the multiple histories that we experience every day as part of the information feeds mediating the twenty-first-century data body. Possessing no necessary meaning, indicating no certain destiny, definitely containing by themselves no great chronology of the movement of larger histories, they are in the way of all hauntings – spectral scenes that capture attention, and thus enter into history, only to the extent that they motivate other excluded, perhaps disavowed, human passions, remembrances, uncertainties. It is almost as if the future is no longer delivered by the realization of complex, structural dynamics – economic, political, cultural – but by way of premonitory hauntings: vanishing scenes caught out of the corner of the eye about the humiliation of the dead, feats of technological wonderment enacted in the theater of cruelty, emerging world powers undone by small flashes of connectivity. Could such hauntologies be the way history is performed today? No longer totalizing, systematic, rational, but just the opposite: a new universe of spectral intimations, strange contradictions, and grisly forebodings as sure and certain signs that the age of hauntology is the essence of the new collective unconscious.

Drift

3

Code Drift

Software genomics

Code drift is an attempt to draw together the great discourses of biology and digitality, essentially to consider the implications of mapping the language of genomics onto software codes.[1] I want to argue that data have come alive in the form of our extended network of technological organs, that the growth of information culture is the real world of evolutionary development literally, not metaphorically. When data come alive, when data become the dominant life-principle with us as its willing prosthetics, we are suddenly swept along in a larger digital cosmology, the future of which is yet unclear. But this we do know: *digital cosmology* has its own laws of motion – *code drift*; its politics are based on the deeply paradoxical situation of our being *tethered to mobility*; the first sighting of what will soon be its dominant form of subjectivity are the *enhanced data bodies of augmented reality*; and the human condition which it leaves in its wake can only be characterized as one suffering *"digital trauma."* Not Toffler's vision of "future shock," where a stunned humanity is overcome by the accelerating rate of technological change, but something much more elemental, namely that the same awesome event that Nietzsche once noted as the death of God and the beginning of something fundamentally new is now upon us again, except this time it's not so much the death of God as the sudden eclipse of God's successor before this new onrushing event of code drift, tethered mobility, enhanced data flesh, and digital trauma. So, then, a prolegomenon to a new digital cosmology.

Spectral destiny of technology

> In biology, genetic drift refers to random fluctuations of gene frequencies due to sampling errors.
>
> Robert C. King and William D. Stansfield, *A Dictionary of Genetics*[2]

Neither global nor local, today we are mobile – we are code drift. Just as genetic drift occurs by chance, producing in its wake unpredictable streams of genetic variation, so too code drift. Code drift cannot be programmed in advance, but occurs by chance variations through unexpected uses, creative applications, and fluctuations in our perception that produce complex technological transformations. Random fluctuations that build over time, resulting in complex yet subtle changes in the genetic makeup of a population: an indeterminate future of flux, chaos, intermediations, intersections, and remix.

Code drift is the spectral destiny of the story of technology. No necessary message, no final meaning, no firm future, no definite goal: only a digital culture now drifting in complex streams of social networking technologies, filtered here and there with sudden changes in code frequencies, moving at the speed of random fluctuations, always seeking to make of the question of identity a sampling error, to connect with the broken energy flows of ruptures, conjurations, unintelligibility, and bifurcations. Paul Virilio's vision of the duplication of reality, that we always act in two parallel worlds at once, is not necessarily a negative force but can instead open up creative possibilities. Where Virilio might reduce social networking, *Second Life*, YouTube, Twitter, and the Web to instances of delocalization, I detect the presence of creative code drifters texting, mobilizing, resisting, imagining, even 100-mile dieting on their way to new complex variations of technological destiny. While technology has the illusion of control – consider how social networking technologies always strive to facialize themselves in the possessive language of the "I" and "You" – Facebook, iChat, iPhone, YouTube – the persistent data reality is code drift. Encoded by technology, everyone today is a code drifter touched by technology and remixing the technology right back. Consider this description of a newer technological innovation – hypersonic sound, unidirectional sound: "Beaming waves of hypersonic sound at a pitch that is undetectable by the human ear. The waves combine until they smash into an object such as a person's body. The waves then slow, mix and recreate the original audio broadcast. If the person steps out of the waves, they are no longer obstructed, and are rendered inaudible."[3]

When hypersonic sound becomes light sound, it becomes the "ear" of technology. It produces a new form of silence I call hypersonic silence, a subtle technology that whispers in your ear. It is when silence is not silent. A future of ears grafted to the subtleties of subliminal technology. Hypersonic sound has been used as a marketing tool in Japan for several years and was recently deployed by the A & E Television Network on a busy downtown Manhattan street to promote its show *Paranormal State*. Pedestrians walking near a billboard heard voices whispering, "Who's there? What's that? It's not your imagination." When New Yorkers heard about this newest wrinkle in the mediascape, they immediately flocked to the location to experience this new technology firsthand.

Certainly just-in-time hearing with its radical separation of the digital senses involves the separation of sound from noise. But perhaps what is really present, and perhaps most seductive, about this innovation in new media is an elemental trace of code drift. It is my thesis that all new media are structured by code drift. McLuhan was absolutely correct. Code drift is wired directly into the laws of new media. For example, consider a code drifter's remix of McLuhan's famous concept of the tetrad with its four laws of media development, whereby for McLuhan all new media simultaneously render an older medium *obsolescent*, represent something fundamentally *new*, retrieve the *superseded form* of an older media as a cultural masquerade to make what's really new more acceptable, and, when put under extreme pressure reverse, into their opposite. In other words, written well before its digital time, McLuhan's tetrad is a manifesto for code drifters. *Drifts of obsolescence* – what's left behind with hypersonic sound is the old flesh ear specializing in sonic sound waves, open to all noise, geographically fixed to the sides of the skull, unable to split the nervous sensorium by differentiating sound and noise; *drifts of the new* – that's the customized ear, the hypersonic ear, that is perfect for the age of hyper-individualism in a time of intensified data networks. An individual sound for every ear. On a crowded subway, the hypersonic ear hears only ultra-high frequency sound waves directed its way. On a street corner, it lives in its own directional sound cocoon. "Who's there? What's that? It is not your imagination"; *drifts of retrieval* – what's retrieved by the unidirectional ear is the intimate tactility of new media – a data tickle, a hum, a hiccup directed right to the ear; and *drifts of reversal*. Pushed to its extreme, hypersonic sound shuts down noise and amplifies sound. The hypersonic ear presages a future world suddenly gone silent, everyone a cocoon of invisible waves of sound, everyone an icon of perfectly individualized but for that no less pleasurable

digital narcissism, everyone a silent movie of technology itself suddenly invisible. An invisible technology that becomes visible only
when it is in your ear.

Code drift is nothing new. Humanity itself is the product of random
evolutionary fluctuations, no certain aim, no fixed purpose, no guiding
teleology. Sampling error is the genetic alphabet of the body. Who
doesn't live for the mysterious seduction of unexpected frequency
shifts in their daily lives?

With the fourfold movement of the history of technology from
mechanical infrastructure to electronic sensorium to digital networks
and now to the self-styled sphere of augmented reality, code drift is the
key *affect* of technoculture. We are all caught up in random fluctuations
of code due to sampling errors. The indeterminacy of random outcomes and the certainty of probability functions is the real existential
horizon of digital subjectivity. In the culture of modernity, the drive to
rationality was always accompanied by the hauntological traces of its
own disavowal, by the implosion of all the referential signs into the
absurd. Existential anxiety was the real hauntology of modernity. The
gradual coming into mass consciousness of the sense of the absurd –
the late modernist acknowledgment in the spheres of knowledge,
power, sex, desire – of the truth of that which had always been disavowed and thus acknowledged, instantly gave rise in our lifetime to
the spectacular death, in rhetoric at least if not necessarily in fact, of
the great referentials. Culturally, postmodernism was born from the
ashes of the acknowledgment of that which had previously been disavowed, namely that reason, truth, sex, consciousness, and power have
no necessary meaning but are only purely perspectival simulacra –
code drifts fluctuating like unstable event-scenes among random events
and probability functions, uncertainty, and inscribed meaning. This
ineluctable movement of randomness which runs from the dawn of
evolutionary biology to the digital future, this privileging by code
drifts of that which was previously unacknowledged, and thus never
truly avowed, expresses something essential to understanding our contemporary data condition, specifically our willing entanglement in the
language of code drifts. With contradictions as the only truth-value,
those random sampling errors of mistaken identities, unmarked bodies,
misplaced meanings, or data glitches are not simply the necessary by-
product of achieving stable equilibrium for systems which thrive on
the metastatic growth of globalized surveillance, automatic vision
machines, hypersonic sound, GPS bodies, mobile media, and creative
apps. The global data genome is itself a random subject generator. It
generates in its wake purely perspectival simulacra, no less beautiful

or less seductive for the fact that only the most disciplined violence today can successfully firewall closed systems against the siren call of the absurd – fluctuating network identities, data errors as nervous breakthroughs to new "killer apps," the rapture of the fully exposed, fully circulating data body celebrating its escape from now superseded conceptions of privacy. Data flesh wants to be random. It yearns to fluctuate, drift, circulate, bifurcate. Data flesh fully absorbs the primary modernist disavowal – the sense of the absurd in all the great referentials – as its key condition of possibility. Neither necessarily a closed system nor an open system, digital flesh is a system in drift. It is not so much that digital technology recapitulates the language of classical mythology as the story of a fateful struggle between closed versus open systems – Scylla versus Charybdis – but that contemporary technoculture now approaches its apogee as a universe in drift. We are all now born again as code drifters traveling to a still unknown technological destiny, a destining somewhere beyond the utopian vision of indefinite expansion and the dystopian specter of a violent, apocalyptic contraction. But we do know this: with its nervous system fully exposed and thus pirated by electronic media of communication, the human body unconsciously recognizes in the language of code drift – fluctuations, frequencies, sampling errors, mutations, driftworks – something which has previously been lost, and never properly mourned: the nervous system protected across the millennia by the hard outer shell of skin and skull, but which has now been found again. In the form of the digital nervous system, code drift is the once and future nervous system – the genetic drift – of all the augmented data bodies of augmented reality.

Tethered to mobility

Neutral mutation – random drift theory of molecular evolution. A theory according to which the majority of the nucleotide substitutions in the course of evolution are the result of the random fixation of neutral or nearly neutral mutations, rather than the result of positive Darwinian selection.
Robert C. King and William D. Stansfield, *A Dictionary of Genetics*[4]

Tethered to mobility? That's everyday life in the digital world where the body – its gestural cell poses, its most rapturous attention, its most elementary brain matter – is tethered to the sound of the iPhone, the relays of Blackberry data words, the entertainment of the gaming screen. Not so long ago, it was thought that, with mobile communications, fixed terminals and stationary bodily positions would have been abandoned forever, liberating digital subjects for the wild, nomadic spaces of wireless communication. As if to demonstrate that the traditional literary vernacular of paradoxical outcomes and unexpected results has not been eclipsed with the downgrading of immobile communications, digital subjects today are fiercely tethered to mobility. That specific, and most definitely global gesture, where eyes connect with data telemetry in a checking messages gestures – an image, a data stream in the palm of a Blackberry hand, an iPhone app – is the newest dance form of recombinant culture. Consequently, the more mobile the speed of communication, the more immobile the system of human reflexes. The more intense the circulation of the dominant medium of communicative exchange, the more fused the synaptic integration of the human and digital nervous systems. The greater the invisibility of communicative technology, the more visible the purely prosthetic nature of the data body. Disembedded data flows require fully embedded data flesh as their primary condition of possibility, just as much as the purely illusory specter of the nomadic body is the key justification driving forward the disappearance of human flesh into dense networks of data telemetry. Dreams of embodiment – embodied flesh, nature, culture, cities – can now experience such dynamic resurrection in the opening years of the twenty-first century precisely because the death of embodiment is the hauntology of the terrorism of the code.

Like all dance practices choreographing the movement of bodies through, and sometimes against, space, the dance of tethered mobility is a time-shifter. The gestural pose of the mobile body resembles most closely what René Thom, the Swiss theoretician of chaos theory in its most non-romantic iteration, once described as the constant repetition of a morphological change of state, that point where data becomes gene, where the body is only apparently tethered to mobility, but in reality functions as part of the neural mechanism of the global digital genome. In the way of all possessed individuals, we are in the end what we most depend upon, and this is true from the savagery of primitive capitalism to the communicative seductiveness of the virtual exchange form. Fully possessed by digital telemetry, enabled by the flow of data, viscerally haunted by the specter of information, the digital subject knows no destiny today other than tethered mobility. The illusion of mobility, the reality of being skinned by technology. That bleak image of gambling casinos in the tired late-afternoon hours comes to mind when lonely crowds of retirees playing the slots free up their hands by plugging identity cards worn around their necks directly into the machines for hour after gambling hour. Perhaps what is really at

stake is not individual preference for mobility versus immobile communications, but a gathering drift of digital culture towards a certain
neutral mutation.

We are already living in the epoch of the global digital genome.
When the discourse of data with its codes, flows, networks, memory
banks, packet switches, and terminals meets the world of genetics,
something strange happens. Patterned information flows come under
the influence of neutral mutations with their random drift theory
of digital evolution. And why not? Geneticists claim that "neutral
mutations can spread in a population purely by chance because only
a relatively small number of gametes are 'sampled' from the vast
supply produced in each generation and therefore are presented to
the individuals of the next generation."[5] Which is precisely what
digital creativity is all about. Since the dynamic inception of wired
world everything – cyber-culture, cyber-war, cyber-finance, cyber-
communication, cyber-subjects – has been brilliantly destabilized,
undermined, and torqued in new directions by technical innovation
moving at the speed of the data.bot. We are entering the first boisterous
phase of the fourth stage of digital communication, having already
passed through successive phases of tethered communication – the
immobile data ports opening onto the internet – to the recombinant
graphics of the World Wide Web and thereupon to pure mobility – cells,
cameras, videos, tablets. Every stage of the net has its own history of
neutral mutations, with successful digital practices accompanied by an
equally long history of discarded media. It's not really so much that
everything works as geneticists claim for "the survival and reproduction of the organisms that carry them" but that digital innovations are
randomly, but no less enthusiastically, sampled for the survival and
reproduction of the global digital genome. As we exit the now-sur-
passed stages of tethered technology, immobile communications, and
externalized graphics display, the human organism is literally fused
with the telic destiny of the global digital genome. Its neutral mutations, recombinant flows, and augmented reality is the real language
of genetic data. Random data drift is the rule, with the data body
assigned the leading genetic role of "sampling" at the feast of digital
products these phenotypic effects of the global digital genome.

Or something else? In this wetware map of neutral mutation, that
point when individual autobiography merges with the collective data
biographies that we have all become, are not the inexorable laws of
neutral mutation and random digital drift already at work in shaping,
mobilizing, and prefiguring the destiny of human subjectivity? In this
case, the question of subjectivity is fully embraced in the driftworks

of larger neutral mutations: recombined, re-spliced, remixed as the elementary matter of the global digital genome.

Code drifters as always tethered to mobility.

Data trauma

Reading from the Book of Genetics: "Epigenesis is the concept that an organism develops by the new appearance of structures and functions, as opposed to the hypothesis that an organism develops by the unfolding and growth of entities already present in the egg at the beginning of development (preformation)."[6]

Before the Book of Genetics, there was another book of fabulous fables, the Book of Genesis, with its biblical telling of the story of human creation by divine will from the darkness of an always-gathering nothingness. Northrop Frye, the cultural theorist, discovered in the Book of Genesis the "great code" that governed the struggle between intemperate passion and resolute reason in technological society. Certainly, no generative egg makes its fatal appearance in the Book of Genesis, and no organism develops by the unfolding and growth of entities already present at the stage of biological preformation. Instead, the Book of Genesis is the spectacular resolution of the hauntology of metaphysics: a story of creation out of nothingness, the concept that an organism develops by the new appearance of structures and functions. Strip the originating spark of divine will from the contemporary scientific fable of epigenesis and we suddenly find ourselves in the most recent iteration of creation out of nothingness, the "great code" of digital culture. Without explanation, we have now left the secular history of modern enlightenment, dwelling now within the house of digital cosmology where the "new appearance of structures and functions" is the animating drive of software, conceived as the complex nervous system of digital reality.

Digital cosmology? Its ontology is epigenesist, the belief that digital organisms proliferate by the new appearance of code structures and networking functions. Always disloyal to evolutionary logic, software code only recognizes digital life as a random struggle between digital design – repetitive patterned instructions – and the wild side of ruptures, conjurations, and intermediations.

There's no real difference between the two sides. They are only *apparent* opposites. This is the story of identity and difference: patterns and randomness, a strict tutelary of programmed instructions and the outlaw will to disturb the codes, disobey instructions, take programs to their wild side, surveillance to the extremes of micro-granular detail, and the persistent human desire to wetware machines.

Coming to maturity under the sign of the terrorism of intelligibility, the real seduction of code lies in its desire in the end to be unintelligible, untraceable, unknowable, not capable of being archived. That's why the story of digital complexity today is captured beautifully by the language of clouds, storm vectors of codes moving at high velocity across the electronic sky, data hurricanes, BitStorm tornadoes, all those drifting clouds of networked subjectivity circulating through social networking technologies with their unexpected new structures and functions of FaceBook, YouTube, Twitter, and iChat. Like the collective authorship over many centuries of the Book of Genesis, the Book of Digital Epigenesis also has its cosmologists now and into the future. For who can really anticipate what will happen in the time of digital epigenesis? Who can predict with any certainty what new structures and functions will emerge from this new story of creation from digital nothingness? In desperation, astrophysicists describe the situation as that of "punctuated catastrophe." But we know better: digital epigenesis is the newest temporary solution to an ancient biblical riddle – creation out of nothingness – and to an equally ancient philosophical puzzle: the question of identity and difference.

And not only that but digital cosmology also introduces in its wake a new theory of epistemology: *epigenetics* – the study of the neural mechanisms by which digital genes bring about their phenotypic effects. The earliest of the technological utopians, Marshall McLuhan, Wyndham Lewis, and Teilhard de Chardin, provided eloquent antici-patory warnings that the externalization of the human sensorium under the pressure of technological media of communication would enable the emergence of a digital nervous system. Since the mid-twen-tieth century, this haunting prophecy concerning the digital nervous system has remained a literary construct, a metaphor begging to be made operational. That's definitely no longer the case. Through a curious twist of fate, the great discourses of digitality and genomics shared historical periodicity because data is actually the genetic struc-ture of the digital body – the global data genome.

Like the seasons of life itself, data moves from plenitude to senes-cence, it also has dawns and twilights. The global data genome is a vastly improved nervous system since its neurological mechanisms can never be confused with the embedded mind as the locus of conscious-ness, but from its moment of inception are distributive, circulating, relational, complex. Seemingly always one step out of season with regimes of intelligibility, the very best of data has its own broken synapses, overloaded consciousness, flickering memory, and software glitches. When digitality and genomics merge in the form of the global digital genome, post-traumatic (data) stress disorder with all its traumas is finally realized as the animating principle of augmented reality. "Post-traumatic" because the abrupt shutting down of the human sensorium accompanied by the immersion of the human organism in the skin of data, this profound originary event, announcing the termination of the human species as we have known it with its privatized ego, localized consciousness, and radical separation of the senses; and the inception of something profoundly new, simultaneously ominous and exciting – the subject as an emergent ecology of biology/sociality/data – this awesome event announcing the eclipse of one (human) species-form and the immediate emergence of its networked successor has already occurred.

McLuhan once claimed that the blast has already happened: we're floating in the debris from the breakup of the autonomous body, discrete ego, and embedded nervous system. Who was prepared for this? Who was ready for the immediate mutation eclipse of the species-form of the human into half flesh/half code? In this epochal shift, data itself suffers stress disorder as its primary trauma. It is not really so much that the new organism of half flesh/half code cannot tolerate the speed of technological acceleration. Liberated from the plodding world of materiality by networked regimes of relational processing and ubiquitous computing, the neural mechanisms of the human mind demonstrate unexpected plasticity and openness to heterogeneity. The evidence is all around us: brains sustaining physical injury that instantly reorganize the field of perception, artistic vision accelerating the speed of data, sci-fi literature overstimulating the nervous system of information, cinematic futurism that easily outruns the speed of technological change, a new aesthetics of perception that eagerly embraces the delirious simulacra of gaming. Everywhere the neural mechanisms of data flesh skip across liquid streams of information flows like flat-edged stones tossed on a lazy data summer afternoon. Every bit of media evidence, from television and radio through computing, cells, Blackberries, Twitters, and the virtual apparatus of augmented reality, suggests that the human brain has absorbed, easily and enthusiastically, its ablation into the nervous system of the fully externalized technological media of communication.

The real challenge is *data trauma*, the fact that data cannot keep up, either metaphorically or materially, with the speed of perception. That is why data often resembles the conservative *ressentiment* of Wendy Brown's *States of Injury*,[7] resentful, left behind, revenge-seeking. Data seeks the safety of digital purity; firewalling itself in the hygienic spaces of closed data dumps. In other instances, data become aggressive – it turns on its human companion species, taking cold comfort in the durational memory and identity triangulations so necessary to surveillance systems. Like the worst of the human species before it, data is capable of the ethics of Heidegger's "injurious neglect." It too can sometimes only find expression in terms of a "malice of strife." Born again in the baptistery of genomics, data is a fully completed nihilist, infected with the *ressentiment* of the human species that it was so eager to replace, the spearhead of a purely technical will – drifting, oscillating, wiping away the horizon, in its leading expression a *software animation* precisely because data is haunted by the trace of death. But of course the death of data is precisely why information culture can be so dynamic. It is the tangible scent of the necropolis in the data storm that makes information culture so deeply, so seductively charismatic. Bored with the logic of presence, the ablated neural mechanisms of the networked subject sift in deepest fascination through the debris of the human remains of the species – shards of memory, strands of forgotten codes, dead media, broken thoughts, book after book of fatally overcome faces. It is this hint of death that drives the necropolis of software. Feasting on the remains, the massive accumulation that is dead information is finally free to express itself as a pure technical will, and nothing besides. Literally, data today is a nervous breakthrough. Refusing stability, never stationary, data is condemned to a cycle of endless circulation. It has no destiny other than that of the pure will: augmented, streamed, mobilized, Facebooked, Twittered, iPodded, flickered, upgraded, downloaded, wide-screened, multitasked, and GPSed. Like all species before it, there will finally come a time when data will grow weary with itself and, as an exhausted nihilist, find pleasure only in making itself ill. My suspicion is that, in this time of accelerated data flows, the appearance of data as an exhausted nihilist is already upon us. In this age of exhausted data, everything counts, everything apps precisely because nothing now counts but the ersatz nothingness of data itself. Digital trauma.

4

History Drift

While there may be no determinate end(s) of history, there is an always turbulent, multiple, and conflicted process of history drift framing the future of world events and for the sake of which the question of the end(s) of history has become once again an enchanted, enigmatic object of reflection.[1]

Never static, and definitely not aimless, history drift refers to the intermediation of all aspects of contemporary life by a fateful struggle among three major world hypotheses – the cosmological, the techno-logical, and the organic – each with its own ontology, epistemology, axiology, and aesthetics.

While the twenty-first century is supposedly written under the tri-umphant sign of technology, the distinctively theocratic discourse of cosmological experience having once thrown off its accepted fate as the disavowed hauntology of the technological emerges seemingly every-where now as the dominant (counter-)spirit of the times. While the language of technological willing might prescribe an increasingly ordered future of wired society, internet diffusion, social networking technologies, and streamed communication, cosmological discourse revolves around the enduring problem of salvation. Evident not only in the contemporary global clash between Christian and Islamic cul-tures but within putatively Christian cultures in the combative form of born-again ideology, the power of cosmological discourse has effec-tively checkmated the historical inevitability of technological willing.

Indeed, while the future end(s) of technological society are shad-owed by ambivalence, the quest for absolute certainty as the essence of cosmological experience throws into question the always equivo-cal fate of technological willing. If traces of nihilism are present in otherwise spectacular displays of technological hubris and if cosmo-logical discourse is itself fated to repeat the fatal destiny of all ancient theocracies, namely to descend into bitter confrontations among mutu-ally antagonistic visions of absolute certainty, there is a third world hypothesis – freedom – which in its complexity, paradoxes, intermedia-tions, and necessary relativity always disturbs the self-reinforcing dis-courses of both cosmology and technology. Having no fixed historical address, circulating like a fatal impulse within the hosts of the techno-logical and the cosmological – always provisional, relative, and inde-terminate – the discourse of freedom can be a world hypothesis precisely because it stands with salvation and ordering as one of the basic meta-physics of the history drift within which we are suspended and for the sake of which the end(s) of history is itself always a matter of which particular inflection of historical drift characterizes these as the most uncertain, yet most metaphysically active, of times.

Consequently, three theoretical propositions concerning the (puta-tive) end of history – each antithetical, all requiring for their affirmation the negation of the others, some approaching history in terms of iden-tity theory, others in the multiple vocabularies of difference, but, all for that matter, deeply seductive as interpretations of the end of history because the larger historical events of contemporary times can now, as always, only be expressed in terms of their complex intermediation.

First hypothesis: the will to history

Here, the end of history is conceived as a matter of *ontological predestina-tion* – a complex metaphysical adventure in which we find ourselves caught up in the fire and ice of three enduring patterns of human history: the competing histories of salvation, order, and freedom. Past, present, and future, therefore, as mutually embraced in a common will to history in which three dominant ontological world-hypotheses – the cosmological, the technological, and the organic – struggle not simply for survival, but for hegemony. In the mirror of history reflecting this fateful struggle, each competing world hypothesis is revealed to possess a fatal flaw, a tragic vulnerability of the order of mythic nemesis. Con-sequently, the ontology of salvation, with its demand for absolute cer-titude, may produce a prodigious number of clashing cosmologies but ultimately no way of deciding among them other than the traditional method of violent disavowal. The ontological world hypothesis of tech-nology, with its unparalleled demand for the technical ordering of all human and nonhuman experience, produces in the end precisely what

Martin Heidegger predicted: a society of fully completed nihilism in which the evacuation of cosmology gives way to the delirious spectacle of a culture of profound boredom. While the ontological world hypothesis of freedom responds directly, both to the tragic sense of technology by demanding meaning in a universe of the absurd and to the tragic sense of cosmology by refusing the certitudes of faith, it too has its fatal vulnerability, namely the impossibility of stabilizing a form of history generated by dreams of the multiple, the contingent, the hybrid, the complex.

Second hypothesis: the precession of history

Not the ontological predestination of the will to history, but precisely the opposite – the precession of the end(s) of history. In this case, to the question concerning the end(s) of history, it might well be replied that if the production of history is seemingly everywhere, that is probably because, like all the great referentials before it, we are now experiencing the age of the death of history: the end of historical narrative, the eclipse of historical intelligibility, the disappearance of coherent patterns of history. The end of historical narrative because clashing narratives of always-multiple histories expose the truth of historical narrative itself as only a truth-effect of power. The eclipse of historical intelligibility because the real histories that are being written in blood today focus on that which has always been previously marginalized as unintelligible, excluded, disavowed. And certainly the disappearance of coherent patterns of history because the term "history" has never had anything to do with coherent patterns but with something else, with a fatal struggle between code and randomness as the essence of every genuinely historical event.

Everywhere, clashing historical narratives are the processed content of fully mediated technological societies. Narratives of war, apocalyptic scenes of mass starvation, economic collapse, environmental catastrophe, sexual atrophy, urban riots – historical narratives that can be so highly charged precisely because they have no real meaning except as the virtual sign that the real function of historical narrative today is to be a truth-effect of power. From this perspective, historical narrative is like a fabulous theater of imaginary projections – conjurations intended to provide a persuasive explanation for a missing, elusive truth that may have already slipped away. Equally, the momentum of historical intelligibility, the question, that is, of who and what is allowed to rise into the sphere of historical recognition, to be finally counted as a historical being, has always been a cynical production of hegemonic power. It is not so much that the question of historical intelligibility determines the winners and losers of history, but that the boundaries of moral intelligibility define, as Judith Butler argues in *Frames of War*,[2] whose life may be rightfully grieved, or whose historical existence may finally be an object of mourning. And while the specter of history always carries within itself the transparent promise of finally unlocking the great codes of culture and society, the truth is that the desperate need for historical meaning may originate in the fact that history has no necessary meaning, that what we mean by history is a violent struggle between the illusion of code and the reality of randomness.

Third hypothesis: hauntological history

Or perhaps a third hypothesis: once liberated from ideologically prescribed narratives, once unburdened of the fetters of social intelligibility, once having slipped free of the ideal of patterns and codes, history is finally free to materialize the secret dreams of its own illusions, to become the site of a fatal wager among faith, reason, and rebellion. From ancient times to the present, history has never been about anything else than a parable of a larger logic of contradiction. In the West at least, the ends of history have been shaped through the centuries by an epochal dialogue between Athens, Rome, and Jerusalem concerning the proper function of human willing. While Greek reason and Roman power provide an early template for later divisions between contemplation and action, the enduring contribution of Jerusalem was to have provided in the form of religious faith an imminent critique of reason and a check on unbridled power. The classic struggle between faith, reason, and power that was so hauntingly initiated by the triad of Athens, Rome and Jerusalem found, of course, its first formal record in the form of the Christian trinity with its division of human action into will, reason, and action. That we live now in the twilight of early Christian faith does not mean that we have finally escaped the Trinitarian cross of Christianity. Far from it. The final ruse of history, as Nietzsche knew only too well when he reflected on the death of God, was that it was precisely by way of the gift of death that the sign of the transcendent could finally radiate most brilliantly. In this case, the death of God meant that the fatal sign of God – the reason that the meaning of multiple gods was salvaged from pagan illusion to become the monistic god of Christianity – was finally made present to the entirety of the human condition. Here, we are caught up in the fatal drift of the will to history, a fatal drift that sometimes achieves clarity when the will to history comes fully under the spell of faith, order, or freedom, but which is for all that never capable of being totalized by the competing languages of cosmology, technology, and politics precisely because the will to history is always haunted by its own disavowals, by all those other histories whose exclusion represent the founding condition for the will to history but which always return as the intermediation, the fracture, the bifurcation within which the fatal wager of the end of history is undertaken.

The will to history

Always and everywhere, there is the will to history. Refusing to accept its formulation as a purely metaphysical concept, the will always seeks to realize itself in specific historical form. Consequently, there can be no understanding of the end(s) of history without a prior discussion of the will to history since the question of the end of history is always relative to the particular iterations of the will. How will the will actualize itself in history: a sacred fable of divinity, as a relentless will to power, as a will to indeterminacy? Will the will seek to preserve itself in a specific historical form? Will the will seek to expand outwards as pure relation of force? Or at some point does the will disavow particular historical manifestations in favor of a reverse movement into itself – the fateful appearance of the will to will?

So then, to which specific expression of the will to history will the future belong? Which paradigm of historical experience will lay claim to the long arc of historical destiny – the cosmological, the technological, the organic? Which inspiring order of affect, taking root first in private imagination and later in public action, will motivate fundamental transformations in the will to history, here toppling long-standing political tyrannies in the Middle East, there effectively defeating advanced technologies of hyper-warfare in the isolated mountain ranges of Afghanistan, everywhere creating unpredictable inflections in the contemporary historical scene itself as different orders of affect as ancient as desires for salvation, as present as technological creativity and as potential as indeterminate struggles for human freedom compete for sovereignty over the human passions? Which order of consciousness will arise to frame the rhetoric of truth – the tautological, the instrumental, the transformative? That is, will the prevailing order of truth be representative of the regime of faith, normativity, or virtuality?

And, if so, will the arc of history repeat that which was thought to be finally past: the conversionary experience of all religious imagination as the standard for the determination of the truth of history? Or something different, namely a prolonged struggle among three orders of social practice – the theological, the technological, and the organic – as rival models of history? While the question of finality regarding the end(s) of history itself probably belongs to the order of futility, what is apparent is that the restlessness of the will to history, this structural movement from the order of history under the sign of metaphysic to specific material histories, always seems to result in three dominant historical manifestations – each order of which is fully paradigmatic in its own right, each of which embraces a specific ontological affect, a justificatory epistemology, a specific order of social practices, and a thematic value-principle. Always simultaneously close at hand while as distant as the disappearing gods, the complex playing out of different orders of history – the cosmological with its ontology of salvation, the technological with its will to ordering of all social and nonsocial existence, the organic with its contingent struggles for human freedom – is the pervasive framework within which struggles, near and far, over the direction of the arc of history now take place.

Sometimes, the complex struggle between salvation, order, and freedom bursts out of the realm of ontological affect and takes up residence in the politics of a bitterly contested, highly symbolic city square. For example, consider recent events in Cairo's Tahrir Square, this highly symbolic site of an elemental struggle between the representatives of three different historical regimes – popular manifestations on behalf of the future imposition of Shariah law in Egyptian society, harsh military responses intended to support the continuation of the Egyptian security state with its long-standing emergency decrees, and, all the while, political activists seeking to occupy Tahrir on behalf of that most intangible and provisional of all human prospects, not so much the well-rehearsed rhetoric of universal human rights but something more specific: the right to experience the full freedom of the contingent, to honor in public the memory of the many martyrs who had gone before and whose sacrifices in the silence of detention facilities and torture cells wrote the political alphabet of the disavowed, the excluded, the forever silenced. At other times, the contested space among the different orders of salvation, order, and freedom seized the public imagination because, through some mysterious process of creative history in the making, these different orders of historical being take possession of a representative historical figure who, rising into presence at first rhetorically and later through actual political practice, constitutes a complex intermediation of salvation, order, and freedom as the essence of their charismatic political appeal. Something like this was the basis for Barack Obama's political ascendancy in the domestic politics of American empire. Here, a rising political personality figured salvation, order, and freedom in a distinctively new political constellation: dreams of a technologically perfected human nature combined with a political theology of pastoral management of the public realm, and all this in support of a vision of expanding realms of human freedom based on the universalization of natural human rights. Certainly, this is a period of extreme cultural deflation in which all the value-principles of expansionary liberalism are forced to consolidate their core values – the deflation of power under the pressure of debt management, monetary deflation under the sign of demands for national solvency, social deflation pressured by cutbacks to entitlement programs, cultural deflation that privileges the fundamentalist, the reaction-formation, the bunkered ideology. But for all that, the question remains open whether Obama – this representative fusion of technological enthusiasm, profound religious consciousness, and a passionate commitment to individual freedom – will be able to sustain this complex mediation or whether the future of Obama, and perhaps western culture as well, will resolve in the direction of a single historical regime to the exclusion of the others. In this case, the question can be repeated: To what will the future belong – world domination by a dynamic technological order; increasingly messianic religious movements; or, perhaps, those difficult, often unnoticed, struggles for contingent freedom that are the basis for a newly emergent global community of alternative social movements?

Consequently, what is the pathway of future history: cosmology, technology, or contingency? Which historical experience will prove primal: ecstatic moments of religious conversion, digital enthusiasm propelled by social networking running on the software programs of the new economy, or individual commitments to social movements of human and nonhuman liberation – environmental, social, gendered, human rights? Whatever the case, history drift is caught in the current of three dominant paradigms of historical experience, each aspiring to ontological primacy, all self-validating in terms of epistemology, every one materialized by a specific set of social practices, and all, for that matter, regulated by a particular value-principle. While the will to history definitely enjoys very different material manifestations – the theological histories of salvation, the corporate histories of technology, the social histories of freedom – what remains constant is the metaphysical structure itself of the will to history. Here, the essence of the will to history is its repetition in different times and places of clashing patterns of history, all derived from specific intermediations of the codes of ontology, epistemology, axiology, and aesthetics.

Sometimes the will to history functions in the language of absolute certitude. It adopts the rhetoric of cosmology. Refusing the freedom of indeterminacy and overthrowing the secular modernist settlement resolving around security, the cosmological will expresses itself, first and foremost, as a primal longing for salvation. Following the pathway of Nietzsche's thought, Heidegger might have proposed that the appearance of the will to will was a fatal sign of the fully completed nihilism of technological culture. But, in this regard, he was incorrect. The will to salvation marks the initial entrance of the will to will. Transcendental theology, with its sacralization of the horizon of human experience, is the philosophical homeland of the will to will. Here, the dominant ontological affect is a desire for certainty, consciousness is structured tautologically, social practice privileges the teleological, and the regulatory value-principle is the imperative of consistency. Augustine's *Confessions*, with its emphasis on the act of conversion, is a brilliant account of the will to will in full theological expression. That Augustine could struggle so hard in the garden of Cassiacia to transform his desperate will to believe into an unquestioned, and unquestionable, form of belief based in faith was less a reflection of Christian confessionality than something very different, a metaphysical account of the imminentization of the will in the vicissitudes of human flesh. What was historicized with Augustine was not so much an epochal rupture among Christian culture, Roman power, and Greek culture than cosmological consciousness as the first historical appearance of the will to will.

At other times, the will assumes the secular form of the will to technology. Here, theological aspirations towards absolute certitude are disavowed in favor of securing human preservation against a supposedly violent human nature that must be repressed as a primary condition of self-preservation and a natural universe that must be reified. Fully skeptical of theological aspirations towards the certainties of faith, disavowing tautological consciousness, and triumphantly excluding all signs of the transcendent, the will to technology originates in a melancholic desire for ordering experience around the necessities of self-preservation – the securitization of stability. With this, the process consciousness of the technological imagination replaces tautological consciousness, instrumentalist social practice eclipses belief in the transcendent, and the ultimate value-principle is the delirious spectacle of virtuality.

The will to freedom stands at one remove from the will to salvation and the will to technology. Here, the will disowns its first cosmological appearance as pure absolute consciousness, it refuses the primacy of instrumental social practice, and it privileges the complex, the hybrid, the contingent over faith-based consistency or technologically induced spasms of virtuality. Neither cosmological nor technological, the will to freedom expresses itself as an organic paradigm, that is to say, an expressive paradigm linking an affective desire for freedom with an epistemology that privileges complexity, forms of social practice that move in the direction of communitarianism, and a transformative ethics.

Understood metaphysically, the will to history refers, therefore, to the existence of a single process of historical action linking a dominant affect, a formative epistemology, an axiological practice, and a consequent aesthetic into a singular narrative of the will to history. While there are multiple expressions of the will to history, the structural code of the will to history always remains constant, namely the linking together of the categories of ontology, epistemology, axiology, and aesthetics as interrelated dimensions of a single historical process. In this case, the process of historical action has its origins in fundamental transformations in human affect. While particular epistemologies rise and fall, while specific modes of historical materialization appear and disappear, while different orders of aesthetic values emerge and decline, the will to history can be such a pervasive aspect of the human condition because it is rooted in complex variations of fundamental human affect associated with salvation, ordering, and freedom. While the most confident proponents of technological culture often tempt the mythic fate of hubris by proclaiming technological futurism as our common human destiny while, at the same time, consenting to the viewpoint that secular society has been wiped clean of its sacred horizon, seemingly everywhere the rising affect involves professions of faith traditionally associated with transcendental visions of salvation. Not salvation in the narrowly conceived religious sense of a fateful election to the sacred, but salvation in the generalized affective sense of a powerful and enduring struggle for absolute certainty of meaning in human experience. Here, the will to history comes under the influence of an absolutist meaning-structure that, not having its origins in material history, reintroduces an unshakable belief in the transcendent into human affairs. While technological secularists are often quick to denigrate belief in the transcendent as something purely and inflexibly ideological, the salvation affect is indisputably more complex, and definitely more seductive, than this. How else to explain that in this, the most secular of all centuries in which digital technology codes society and culture, epochal political struggles are framed in distinctively cosmological language: powerful longings for the return of an Islamic caliphate, violent episodes of Christian terrorism, the upsurge in American neoconservatism of born-again ideology, the political triumph of a liberal politics of Christian pastoralism based on the theological precepts of the Sermon on the Mount. While all of these movements bear the traces of technology and freedom, none can be explained in terms of technological coding or political freedom.

What can really explain the genesis of a fundamentally different order of human affect? A profound shift in human sensibility whereby things on the surface may remain constant – an individual goes to work, engages in sports, uses social media, has complex relationships with family and friends – but, for all that, sometimes a change in affect is experienced that effectively, on a deeply personal and later perhaps collective level, shuts down one social reality and opens another. We, the first time-travelers of the twenty-first century, supposedly live at the apex of the technological regime with its digital codes, fast information relays, dense communicative networks, and creative devices for enhanced social connectivity, but, for all that, the rising world-affect has little to do with technology and everything to do with the rebirth of God, again and again. We were assured by Nietzsche's *Zarathustra* that this would be a fully modern century built on the sacrificial remains of the death of God, if not in actual fact at least in the epochal wiping clean of the horizon of all traces of the transcendent by the scientific imagination. Yet seemingly everywhere, Nietzsche's pronouncement of the death of God has turned out to be a premature philosophical closure of something viewed by many as indispensable to life itself: the regeneration of inspiring visions of the transcendent in human affairs and, with it, commitments to materialize political theology: Shariah law, Hindu fundamentalism, Christian evangelical movements, the politics of Zionism. Today, what might be called "God affect" is everywhere, sometimes as a definite rival to technological messianism, while at other times an active partner with the most recidivist elements in technological connectivity in a common struggle against the politics of contingent freedom. It is the very same with digital affect, that epochal conversionary experience in which the ends of technological determinism are absorbed into private autobiography as the horizon of fully augmented life. For those mobilized around the specter of digital affect, freedom is reduced to expanded connectivity while God remains only another delirious simulation on the telematic horizon. While no one can really explain the origins of the affect of human freedom, its endurance as a fundamental ontology is pervasive, perhaps nowhere more so than in the desperate political struggle that was the Arab Spring. Here, "God affect" is fully present in those lingering cries of *Allahu Akbar* while the digital affect is manifest in the desperate deployment of technologies of war, but, for all that, the Arab Spring responded to something different in the order of human dispositions, namely the will to the freedom of the fully contingent, the fully historically memorable, the fully human.

While the lasting fate of the great paradigmatic struggles among salvation, ordering, and freedom taking place now as in the past and surely in the future remains fully uncertain, one historical certainty endures. In one of the great metaphysical mysteries of the will, the clashing paradigms of faith, normativity, and contingency are always inseparably connected. Connected, that is, not so much by the complex intermediation of belief, science, and imagination in the individual heart nor by their necessarily breached boundaries at the level of the social, but related in another way – a pathway that is almost predestined by the eternal rhythms of the great codes of history. In this case, the cosmological paradigm will always culminate in a purely chaotic human condition for the simple reason that, while there are always multiple orders of theological affect, there is necessarily no definitive means of selecting between them. Internecine religious struggle among different orders of "God affect" produces violent chaos as its inevitable result: chaos because the cosmological order disavows, as a matter of its founding logic, agreement on an intrinsic means of validation among competing theological ontologies; and violence because cosmologies that would strive to the order of the sacred either dominate or perish. It is precisely from the exhausted historical playing fields of religious struggle that the will to technological ordering originates. While the will to order will never evoke the sacred passions of transcendental dreams, it does have the merit of securing the means of collective, and thus individual, self-preservation from the ruins of a chaotic human condition. That the will to security is necessarily melancholic has everything to do with its founding disavowals, from the disappearance of the realm of the sacred to the repression of instinctive behavior. When that which is disavowed provides the psychological foundation for an unceasing daily order of repression, the technological order carries with it the fatal traces of melancholia. That is the essence of contemporary technological experience – the ability to creatively remix, recode, redesign the codes of human subjectivity and the physical and biotic environments without a meaningful reason for doing so. Technologies accelerating at the speed of escape velocity now suddenly find themselves reawakening the mythic nemesis of all purely scientific achievements – the impossibility, as Albert Camus warned long ago in *The Myth of Sisyphus*, of demanding meaning in a universe indifferent to human purposes. But, if this is the case, aspirations towards totalizing human experience in the horizon of the sacred ultimately culminate in the tragic sense of chaos, and if technological order leads to a fully augmented order of cultural melancholia, this also intimates that struggles for human freedom are fated to operate between the Charybdis of chaos and the Scylla of melancholy. In actual historical fact, the fatal flaw of social movements dedicated to a fully contingent, self-determining future is precisely this: avoiding the toppling point at which aspirations towards the indeterminate, the contingent, and the hybrid collapse into chaos and, on the other hand, overcoming the inertial drag of melancholic subjectivity by creating a socially meaningful universe – provisional, partial, open-ended – that does not immediately collapse into regimes of security on behalf of its own self-preservation.

The precession of history

In the contemporary regime of computation, the order of history has not been exempted from communicative technologies functioning at the speed of light. Consequently, we may now be experiencing the precession of history – a massive shift in historical polarities due to a sudden wobble in the axis of social reality. When the contents of history are slipstreamed by an information culture moving at light-speed and historical consciousness processed like so many chunks of code, the sign of history breaks its traditional relationship with past, present, and future to become something multiple, indeterminate, and incommensurable. Indifference is the essence of code-works, with the result that a certain scent of indifference seeps into the meaning of history itself. No longer, therefore, traditional frameworks of historical interpretation, but the constant generation of multiple narratives of histories, all communicated at light-speed, all virtual, programmed, imaged, texted, and visually transmitted, all projecting themselves as explanations of the often inexplicable, specifically the existence today of history as a delirious sign of recombinant culture. When the social reality principle slams into the force field of technological change, when historical interpretation collides with the speed of the electron, the polarities of history literally undergo a fundamental shift: the speed of the image shapes the future of the event, the accelerating flow of information forms the media archive, the past is literally spliced, mutated, and recombined by the technological time machine that is the precession of history.

Certainly, in the present circumstance, Jean Baudrillard was correct. Like all the great referential signs before it – power, consciousness, desire, sex, money – history now also begins to follow a reverse movement, instantly repolarizing, energizing itself by a fatal, interminable exhumation of the past. Which is probably why everything now appears to operate under the historical injunction that the past must be exposed, deciphered, coded, programmed – endless histories of war, chilling histories of ethnic massacres, media exposés of the rise and fall of celebrities, histories transmitted by mass media, histories written in the language of cinematography, histories that are mobile, cellular, networked. Of course, with each repeated media exposure, historical events grow successively colder, further removed from the temporality of human passion, more distanced from immediate emotional response the closer they are to the eye of digital perception. When historical narratives disappear into the image simulacrum, when history is literally captured by the speed of the information machine, what remains is an imploding field of fractured debris, fully exposed, imaged, and narrated, but, for all that, ultimately unknowable as to its ultimate purposes.

Like all other sign-forms, history has probably always yearned to escape its heavy referential destiny, to finally decouple itself from the language of social signification and the epistemological responsibility of hermeneutic interpretation in favor of something else, history as a radical paroxysm of future events, never really knowable in advance nor understandable in the past tense precisely because history has now mutated into a recombinant sign – complex, mediated, bifurcated, fractured, multiple, and contradictory. In this case, the precession of history stipulates that there can no longer be any definitive end of history because the question of the end has itself become something enigmatic: *temporally* enigmatic since with light-time ends are often beginnings; and *spatially* enigmatic since with light-space ends are matters of pure artifice. Or perhaps something more perverse – that fascination with the end of history functions as a psychological displacement of anxiety about the impossibility of framing the question of history itself. Consequently, historical archives everywhere, memories recorded, stories decoded, past events patiently exhumed, premonitory signs of the future anxiously interpreted, museums of history reanimated – all this because real time may move too quickly for traditional historical interpretation, just as light-space throws the object of history into a gathering darkness.

Mythic nemesis has its implacable rules that will not be violated by even the most cosmically daring of all the species. If the human species allied itself in the past with pagan spirits, and perhaps now seeks to usurp the gods by taking control of the technical direction of human destiny – condensing the necessarily variegated nature of time into the degree-zero of real time and accelerating space itself into light-space moving at the speed of electrons – the fates will not long be silenced. This may explain the mysterious association between the multiple ends of history and sacrificial violence. If the ends of history would seek to exceed the transcendent dreams of the supernatural, overcome the limits of the physical, and vivisect the realm of the biotic, then this gift of the posthuman must certainly be repaid with a completion of the cycle of sacrificial violence. But how to complete the cycle of sacrificial expiation when the new, self-proclaimed creator of the history of the posthuman is itself the human species? What sacrifice would equal the unanswerable gift of a species that would seek to recreate the meta-physical order of time and space itself? In this case, will the extinction of the human species as presently understood prove to be the sacrificial price to be paid for the technological gift of genomic engineering or of those intense efforts to blast neutrons free from their entombment in elementary matter? Certainly, ominous signs of human species extinc-tion are pervasive: apocalyptic scenarios of climate change, desultory images of leaking radiation, the physical exhaustion of fish, animals, plants, and even of the traditional cycle of climatology itself. It is as if the four humors – earth, sky, fire, and water – stand silent watch over the sudden emergence, with brilliant kinetic energy, of the human species and its sudden disappearance into delirious designs of its own making.

Here, the language of astronomy is strangely appropriate. History, then, as the name given to the disappearing (social) matter of the social universe: no permanent tropes, no necessary coherence, no established meanings, no past that is not already speeding towards the future enigmatic. And the historical imagination? The latter functions best when conceived in terms of experimental physics – a form of imagina-tion that volatilizes the dark matter of the past like a particle accelera-tor, smashing apart the atomic structure of truth, spinning wildly clashing interpretation-effects, always seeking out previously unde-tected gravitational waves – the weak force, the strong force, the strange force – whatever source of historical energy that can finally bind together the elementary properties of social existence. If, like at the famous particle accelerator at CERN in Switzerland, historians finally succeed one day in discovering the missing mass of the social universe, would it not also be the case that history, society, culture, and subjectivity might well undergo an instant, fatal implosion? While the justificatory ideology of scientific knowledge always makes the basic claim that the physical universe is indisputably independent of human culture – that the book of nature bears no necessary relationship to the regime of human affect – is it not probable that precisely the reverse is the case? In this sense, the question of the end of history is now carried out most desperately by the scientific imagination: genetic engineers fast sequencing the always-missing codes of the human genome, physicists accelerating elementary matter to warp speeds to discover the missing mass of mass; astrophysicists seeking to discover the ends of the universe – expanding, contracting or flat – in the genealogy of the "big bang." When history itself is captured by the data stream and information circulates at the speed of light, then the end of history has everything to do with the enigmas surrounding missing genetic codes and always-disappearing bosons. Like the physical universe, the universe of social history is renowned for not possessing determinate ends, only the beginnings again and again of the spectacular, but always futile, games of illusion and hubris.

But if this is the case, if history like the physical universe is reluctant to deliver its fatal secret, that there are no necessary ends, only episodic ruptures, that would mean that history, like the flow of information itself, is always fully recombinant – remixed, mutated, augmented, and degraded. Having no necessary referential solidity, always fully relational, history exists only as a sign of that which never was. Consequently, the question of historical ends increasingly evokes something purely phantasmagorical, simultaneously perfectly preserved in streams of images that are themselves already fading after-images distancing us from the specter of the originary event. Perhaps this explains why contemporary historical narratives have such a fast burn rate, why, that is, historical reconstructions of events – past, present, and future – rise into instant global prominence only to fade away into a dense nebula of information. Could it be that what is really at stake with the question of the end of history is something explicitly *mortal*, that probing the end of history brings to the surface that which the historical imagination has always previously repressed but on behalf of which it serves as a necessary justification – history as a fatal repetition of the death instinct? Like the galactic universe of astronomy before it, the will to history may also experience its own fatal reversal, that point where the historical imagination expands with such terminal, inflationary momentum until the will to history instantly implodes and, like a dying red star, begins to collapse into the density of its shattered remains. At this moment and in this time, could this be an appropriate description of our contemporary historical circumstance, that we are twenty-first-century pilgrims experiencing all the violent perturbations and massive shock waves attendant upon the death of history and its instant reversal into its negative mirror image?

In this scenario, the precession of history may inevitably trigger a last, extreme phase of history – *excess history*. Here, everything would be marked by all the signs of full historical saturation: information everywhere, connectivity pervasive, bodies augmented, perception illuminated, truth a purely phantasmagorical effect, perception coded by media feeds, attention fully wired – all this driven on by an economy specializing in the hyper-production of uselessness. While traditional economies staked their very prosperity on the production of the useful, the productive, the instrumental, the knowable, the codes of the new economy are precisely the reverse, the massive circulation of all the fantastic signs of excess – excess media, excess gadgets, excess desires, excess knowledge, excess materiality, excess sex, excess debt. When the laws of historical destiny move in reverse, when cultural logic energizes itself by demanding the disaccumulation, disinvestment, disinterment of everything, we can finally recognize that we are entering a new galactic space of the posthuman. In this abrupt and sudden entrance to the posthuman, things must lose their value, information must be stripped of the heavy gravitational weight of content, codes must be finally allowed to drift, excess must become both the necessary aim and method of the posthuman scene. In this scenario, only the excessive is desirable, only excess value has real value, and only excessive expenditure has a fabulous, hidden trace of that which is most seductive – the final evaporation of the gravity well of the useful and the rise of the precession of history.

Hauntological history

Or perhaps neither the will to history nor the precession of history, but a third possibility: hauntological history. In this case, questions concerning the end of history would bear an uncanny resemblance to the recent announcement by NASA that a thin belt of antimatter particles called antiprotons has recently been discovered to be surrounding the earth. For astronomers, when matter meets antimatter, when streams of protons collide with the thin belt of antimatter particles, what results is violent "annihilation." In the strange way that science often mirrors the enigmas of life itself, what this discovery might indicate is that when historical matter – the will to history – collides with historical antimatter – the eclipse of history – what results is not an uneasy coexistence of two contradictory propositions but something different: the instant creation of a spreading trajectory of historical annihilation across the increasingly turbulent wave-forms of contemporary space and time. That is, when the systematic force propelling the will to history crashes into the belt of randomness surrounding the eclipse of history, what emerges is something only exposed by the catastrophic implosion of annihilation – hauntological history. With the appearance of hauntological history, everything long silenced, repressed, excluded, disavowed, negated by history, is blasted to the surface of events. Here, there is no structural logic, only the unexpected emergence of the uncanny, no eclipse, only the radiating presence of things thought long discarded, and certainly no possibility of historical ontology, only the drawing into presence of the hauntological, the phantasmagoric, the spectral. Consider, for example, these scenes from the delirious wasteland of hauntological history, a history that refuses to be named because it is still nameless, a history that resists totality because it is phantasmatic, and a history that refuses the reality referent of the ontological since it is always in the way of a ghostly haunting.

Two histories

Like the story of mythology itself, visions predicting the end of history often contain the seeds of their own undoing. Like mythology, the historical imagination is not immune to the classical pagan spirits: episodes of hubris, intimations of melancholy, premonitory signs of fatalism, orgies of doubt, anxiety, and even confusion. Thus, it should come as no surprise that a discussion of the end of history in this, the most urgently historical of times, should be accompanied by a powerful, almost mythological, omen, namely the curious ellipsis of a famous theoretical prediction – Francis Fukuyama's thesis that the full maturity of liberal democracy marks the end of history as a field of ideological struggle – and an equally famous historical meltdown, the apocalyptic nuclear catastrophe that is the Fukushima meltdown. It is as if the historical imagination has acquired a sense of irony, and perhaps even a Derridean sense of grammatical wordplay. Fukuyama and Fukushima, then, as the doubled sign of the historical labyrinth, that point where self-confident proclamations about the end of history are simultaneously confirmed and cancelled by a very material historical event: nuclear catastrophe.

What is the relationship between the universalizing claims of liberal democracy and nuclear meltdown? On the face of it, everything. In the opening sentences of their dark prophecy of a future that is now, Adorno and Horkheimer affirmed that Enlightenment radiates catastrophe triumphant. For these intellectual refugees of European fascism, the rising power of positivistic reason, specifically the domination seemingly everywhere of the universalizing logic of liberal rationality, was accompanied by a fatal disavowal – the disavowal of mythology – that would prove to be its undoing. While Adorno and Horkheimer applied in *The Dialectic of Enlightenment* the lessons to be learned from reason's exclusion of mythology to a grim analysis of the seduction of fascist mythology, it is left to us, twenty-first-century pilgrims still wandering within the cultural horizon of the dialectic of Enlightenment, to assess what is to be gained, and lost, by the continuing disavowal of mythology by reason, by a prediction about the end of history that has been perhaps fulfilled, if only ironically, by the nuclear accidenting of Fukushima.

After all, Japan has been the scene of not one, but two, ends of history. If a sense of futurity is an essential aspect of the historical imagination, then in the most literal sense the decision by the United States, the most advanced representative of liberal democracy, to explode nuclear weapons over Hiroshima and Nagasaki marked the end of history. At that bleak historical moment, history ended with the confirmation of the technological capacity to control that which had been previously uncontrollable – the arc of historical time itself. With the nuclear annihilation of Hiroshima and Nagasaki, the power of an inexorable will to technology was substituted for the always circumspect, and even more indirect, powers of the historical imagination. When the light-space of technology overcomes the place-time of history, we suddenly exit from the historical imagination as traditionally understood with its iterations of past, present, and future and enter the unexplored realm of the post-historical in a literal sense. Confirmation of this spectacular, but, for all that, tragic triumph of technological determinism over historical temporality is provided by the wasteland of Fukushima. Indeed, there is a curious sense of historical sadism present in the fact that Japan, the first and only society to fully experience nuclear exterminism as its dominant hauntology, actually proceeded to adopt nuclear energy as its technological infrastructure. It is as if the overwhelming event of nuclear exterminism also obliterated an active sense of historical judgment concerning cause and consequence, that, in effect, the end of history that was Hiroshima and Nagasaki in August 1945 was taken as the doorway to a triumphant post-historical future.

The curious combination of Fukuyama and Fukushima as markers of contemporary post-history – one relentlessly ideological under the sign of the disavowal of ideology, the other deeply historical in a society that is an experiment in the post-historical – anticipates, I believe, a larger drift in contemporary history. What we are witnessing today is not so much the end of history, but the perihelion of the will to history, one that has order as its dominant affect, instrumentalism as its epistemic project, high-intensity market consumption as its social practice, and an accelerating rate of extraction of natural and human energy flows as its cultural destiny. Like the motion of planets in galactic space, when the historical trajectory of the will to history reaches its furthest point of orbital extension what follows is an inevitable curvature towards its point of origin, a fast descent of the will to history towards its perigee with planet Earth. The theoretical meltdown of the illusions surrounding the end of history thesis accompanies the actual meltdown of the nuclear facility at Fukushima as sure and certain signs that both theses – the will to history and the end of history – have literally been accidented by technologies of resource extraction moving at light-speed. What's left is hauntological history: stories of remainder, debris, and the sacrifice involved in economies of useless expenditure under the implosive sign of technological inversion.

Hauntologies of the future

Why are signs of the hauntological so pervasive in contemporary culture? In cinema, there is reconstructed an imaginary theater of the undead, with its zombies, vampires, and clones. In popular fiction, fantasy novels dominate in which scenes of capricious violence and cynical power are projected in the enduring tropes of forces of darkness and warring knights and lost kingdoms of pleasure and despair. In politics, the driving force of resistance to the powerful often takes the form of passionate remembrance of what was previously forbidden, excluded, disavowed. Could it be that what we are witnessing is contemporary culture as a generalized hauntological scene in which the specter, the phantasm, the conjuration, the fable increasingly defines the imagination of the future? Not so much the emancipation of the repressed, but the surfacing of that which was never allowed to be directly experienced and, on account of which, society today is increasingly organized around provisional zones of liminality. Everywhere, the structural logic of the will to history comes into contact with its historical antimatter – the eclipse of historical narratives – and the result is a future of annihilation. Not annihilation in the form of the disappearance of things or the definite end of historical events, but annihilation as an eclectic, unpredictable but no less spectacular, series of openings to the posthuman future. When history curves in the direction of its hauntological traces, when the future follows the arc of the liminal, when the specter trumps code, the phantasm undermines rationality, the fable seduces narrative, the fantasy energizes the real, and the conjuration overcomes the regime of normativity, then we can finally recognize that the question of the end of history is itself only a beautiful invitation to consider anew exits to the posthuman future that are the actual matter of contemporary historical experience. Today, more than ever, history can be hauntological because the sign of history is itself, now as it has always been, something deeply liminal, contested, incommensurable – a scene of appearances and disappearances, provocations and evaporations, fables of the undead, and desultory accounts of sacrificial violence.

5

Archive Drift

Nothing, after Wagner's concept of *Gesamtkunstwerk* exists in a vacuum:
whether our culture is now taken from YouTube or posted online with cell
phones by soldiers in Iraq, we exist in a world where documents act as a
kind of testimony. But once something is recorded, it's basically a file waiting
to be manipulated. That's what links the concept of the remix to everything
going on these days: truth itself is a remix.
Paul D. Miller (aka DJ Spooky), *The Book of Ice*[1]

Social media and the future of the archive

Archive drift introduces a new way of thinking about the future of the
cultural archive.[2] Rather than limit the boundaries of the archive to
collections of cultural artifacts – newspapers, songs, books, journals – I
would like to explore a different methodological proposition, that in
the age of social media both the *form* and *content* of the cultural archive
have been blown apart by the violence of digital technology. While the
impact of technology on the archive is often limited to the notion that
analog archives are about to be transformed into searchable databases,
my hypothesis is that one of the outstanding characteristics of digital
culture, particularly in the contemporary phase of social media, is that
the content of the archive has suddenly and risibly expanded to encom-
pass the totality of life itself and, moreover, that the form of the archive
has been fundamentally changed by the architecture of social media.
Archive drift, therefore, always has a doubled meaning, namely that
the actual *content* of the digital archive is literally at drift – unbounded,
animated, deeply relational – in the universe of social media; and that
the *form* of the archive patterns itself on the waves of code drift within

which it finds itself and on behalf of which the form of the digital archive increasingly comes to represent the key trajectory of techno-logical society.

Of course, thinking about the future of archive drift is necessarily speculative since it is a matter of trying to draw into visibility larger patterns of technological destiny that have not yet fully revealed them-selves. Equally, speculating about the future implications of archival drift cannot be done within the limits of traditional research narratives for the simple reason that digital culture is always liminal, an uncertain borderland where that which is disappeared, silenced, and excluded is often more important than that which is searchable, visible, and intel-ligible. That is why this essay on archive drift not only takes, but demands, the right to be itself a reflexive representation of the uncanny movement of archival logic as the latter migrates from the perimeter of social understanding to the historical apex of the digital future. It is not yet clear why digital culture is so infatuated, even obsessed, with archivalism. One explanation for the deep affinity of archivalism and social media may be simply technological, specifically that data is itself always necessarily relational, nested, searchable, and thus (digitally) archival as a matter of its own programmatic logic. However, while this technological explanation would explain the importance of archivalism as the software architecture of social media, it would not account for the seduction of archivalism in a technological culture so feverishly dedicated to the future of the decontextualized, the dehistoricized, the dematerialized. Could it be that pursuing the question of the future of the archive in the contemporary context of social media is to tap into a deeper cultural current at work in digital reality, namely that in this age of pervasive social media there is already a strong cultural coun-tercurrent present, a dramatic precession of events by which tech-nological society has actually begun to reverse itself, desperately animating its own archival remains – databases, network searches, the digital self conceived as a cultural artifact – as a way of energizing a technological project that always runs on empty? In this case, the radiating presence of a distinctively archival register seemingly every-where in contemporary digital culture may reflect an almost instinc-tive response to the disappearance of material history into digital code. Consequently, while the massive revival of archivalism in digital form may be a product of an unprecedented technological ability to archive the totality of human experience, it might also be an early sign of growing human consciousness about the disappearance of objects into symbols, events into codes, human singularities into virtual pat-terns. Is it possible that, with the triumph of archivalism as the key trajectory of social media, we are finally present at a frenzied last feast of the human presence before it also disappears into the lip of the net? In this theater of the digital imaginary, a risible sense of sacrificial violence can be detected amidst the seduction of technologically enabled archives.

So, then, archive drift as the key trajectory of social media, simultaneously its final destiny and its founding ontology. Its *final destiny* because the evolutionary momentum of social media always seems to bend in the direction of more elaborate, immensely dense concentrations of social archives: archives of fast communication (Twitter), archives of social identity (Facebook), archives of images, sounds, and performances (YouTube), archives of photography (Flickr), meta-archives of the internet (Google), archives of cartography (Google Maps), archives of shared genomic data (23 and Me), impromptu scrappy archives of internet memes, passing fads, niche electronic interests, and pop cultural phenomena (Tumblr), archives of social and cultural history (Wikipedia), archives of official secrets (WikiLeaks). But also as its *founding ontology* because what results when the speed of social media slams into the history of the cultural artifact is that the artifact as traditionally conceived is suddenly jettisoned from the domain of the collected, the bounded, the labeled, the studied to become something radically at drift in contemporary culture. Indeed, if digital archives can be so pervasive in contemporary culture, it is, perhaps, due to the fact that, in the age of social media, digital subjectivity has itself been increasingly transformed into a type of cultural artifact – one which floats in a complex web of network relations, its network identity merged with its social identity, its autobiographical narrative shaped by events in real time as much as by the natural rhythms of life and death. For example, the long-term network visioning strategy of Google is based on the possibility that individuals will increasingly live within the data matrix of a continuous, iterative self-archiving of their own life history from the moment of birth to death. Not so much Facebook but something like FaceLife with the singularity of an individual life itself represented as a self-recorded data meme, complete with an evolving network chronology of relationships, events, and locational data. In this futurist version of FaceLife, archival imagination is transformed into an elementary constituent of digital subjectivity. Thus conceived, nothing would ever really escape the digital archive nor would there be any element of the digital archive that would not be necessarily distributive, relational, and dynamic. Literally, the human condition would be trapped within a mnemonic machine of its own design with the inevitable consequence that the (digital) future to which the human condition is being delivered with such technological precision and force would be characterized by what might be called a *sticky archive* – a dense archive of relationships past and present that would never be allowed to slip into forgetfulness and that would, for that matter, literally cling to the digital subject like a cloud of memories, relationships, or events never capable of repression or silencing.

Always more mediated than distanced, more subjective than objective, more distributive than disconnected, the future of the archive under the sign of technology is, most emphatically, always more about blurring the boundaries between future and past. In the digital culture expressed in all its intensity and complexity by social media, not only is the archive suddenly ubiquitous, but the distinguishing quality of the digital archive that surrounds us is that it is at drift in the data stream, divorced from the language of ultimate goals or definite genealogies. That the actual contents of the digital archive often range from the banal to the sublime, from tedium to fascination, only means that the material history of the digital archive is fully indeterminate. For this reason, what really matters in thinking the future of the digital archive is something more spectral and illusive, specifically the role of the digital archive that we call social media in shaping human imagination. For better or worse, life today is increasingly shaped by the power of the digital imaginary. So why not, then, a form of thought that respects the very real presence of the digital imaginary, this archive in the wires, that in all its complexity speaks to the limits and possibilities of human imagination itself? Why not, then, a form of speculative, imaginary thought that inaugurates both a duel of human imagination and the digital imaginary and that, in this clash of perspectives, begins to do that which is most prohibited – to draw into visibility those elements of the human condition which, precisely because they have been excluded and silenced by the sterile language of codes, databases, and algorithms, are precisely the hauntologies of the digital imaginary?[3] In effect, why not a form of speculative, imaginative thought that works through our present situation as inhabitants of those archives in the wires designated as social media in order to make of the language of the uncanny, the liminal, the phantasmatic, the hauntological a new way of thinking the future of the archive? After all, thinking the future of the archive immediately involves larger questions ranging from archivalism as a cultural talisman of the fate of the human condition to the psycho-ontological question concerning whether human beings are actually prepared for an archival future enabled by the social media in which nothing is ever really forgotten.

So then, three methodological propositions: the first *ontological* – the digital imaginary; the second *epistemological* – archives in the wires; and the third *axiological* – complexity and the digital archive. In the way of all reversals common to the curved space of digital culture, the fourth proposition – the *aesthetic* – has already been introduced as a way of reconsidering the future of the archive in the age of social media.

The digital imaginary

Nothing is as purely imaginary as the digital archive. Like a brilliant specter from the vast recesses of the cultural universe, the digital archive sweeps through the night skies of the mind, turning time's past into real time, lighting up spatial horizons with light-space, folding the historical past into the projected future, breaking down fixed boundaries, always following the unpredictable pathways of the awaiting imagination. Never really interested in truth-telling nor particularly loyal to the concept of bunker archaeology, the digital archive is that rarest of cultural phenomenon: a code matrix tracing an uncertain arc across the human condition, projecting retrieved memories into the present, here confronting the solid matter of reality with imaginary reconstructions of the past, there gathering speed as the code matrix is propelled forward by the gravitational force fields of the surrounding planets of society, economy, and culture, always becoming in the process something more intense, more vivid, more purely imaginary.

Not so much the product of human imagination as its fatal destiny, the digital archive is always shadowed by traces of aesthetic incommensurability. Never really knowable in advance, definitely more than the data contents of its storage memory, always breaking out of its settled codes, the digital archive is animated by imagination, brought alive by creative interpretation and rendered fully enigmatic by its complexity. While generations of cultural theorists have struggled over the division of spoils between the warring languages of sign and signifier, the digital archive begins from another point, the vanishing point of the object of reflection that represents a liquid sign-slide between referents and their coordinate predicates. What Roland Barthes once described as the crossing of the syntagm between metaphor and metonymy is the proper starting point for understanding the digital archive.[4] Its ruling sign may be the regime of the digital and its referential logic may be purely archival, but the complex chain of relationships alluded to by the meaning of the term "digital archive" is neither digital nor archival but precisely the phantasmatic sign-slide at the disappearing center of their collision. When the regime of computation, with its dense networks of fast flows of information, collides with archival intelligibility with its interior depths of meaning, we are finally present at something beyond both the technological and the archival, at the emergence of a radically new form of imagination formed precisely at the conjunction of order and chaos. Strangely enough, in this elemental meeting of the materiality of memory and the virtuality of codes, there is to be discovered a renewal of mythic consciousness. While the most ancient of mythologies testifies to the entanglement of conflicting tendencies towards order and chaos as the foundational matter of the cultural universe, something resembling this antinomic struggle is an essential aspect of the digital archive. Here, the material history of the archive is effectively reskinned by the digital, brought out of the shadows of the past into the illumination of a ubiquitous network of screens, and dislodged from internment in inaccessible storage chambers by mobile technologies. While the archival product is, in the end, neither orderly nor chaotic, it does have about it the traces of something primary to human sensibility – the creation of the archive in the digital age as something that Martin Heidegger once described as a "dwelling-space, a bridge between past and future, identity and difference."[5] In this case, the digital archive can so powerfully draw the past into presence because this fateful meeting of technology and remembrance is in itself an ongoing act of intermediation linking temporality and spatiality. Indeed, in its most powerful manifestations, the digital archive bears discernible traces of something once thought long surpassed: a mythic return of the psychic energy of vitalism as the essence of the archaeology of the archive.[6] When fast computation processes slow memory, when the transcendent power of the code mingles with the depth knowledge of the archive, when historical inscription is forced to move at light-speed, the result is a fantastic cultural implosion, specifically the opening up of a space of ambiguity in the previously bounded spaces of the archive. This may account for the vital energy of the digital archive, the fact that the digital archive is a very particular form of "dwelling-space," a very specific habitat of memory, knowledge, and interpretation.

Archives in the wires

While traditional archives may have quite properly valorized qualities of preservation, continuity, and completeness, the digital archive has a different trajectory. Never bounded, it is always fated to circulate in an unbounded digital universe; never solely about preservation, it is ineluctably linked with complex intermediations; never really complete, its destiny is to be fully, and sometimes perhaps fatally, remixed. One does not have to be a technological determinist to recognize that when code meets archive, the silent ideology of the code will always leave its lasting traces. As with other collisions of code and life – digital music, digital books, digital media, digital banking – the code is always aggressive in asserting the imperatives of form over content. Possessing a unique psychic signature, code is most definitely not a neutral order of communication, but something almost animate in its neurological affects: simplistic in its emphasis on the hegemony of temporal ordering; stubborn when confronted by ambiguous human desires; like matter itself, decaying over time; resistant to leakages in the ruling ordinal register; object-oriented, and with a singular fascination with the nested, the network, the distributed, the cloud. Code always possesses its own strict rules of intelligibility concerning the front end of exchanges between life and computation – specific protocols concerning computation requirements, memory levels, data entry, IP addresses, orders of formatting, translation, circulation, graphics. It imposes a repertoire of strict digital orders concerning the back end of archived data: how will data be stored, how large the archive, protocols concerning accessibility, payment, privacy. And in between the front-end of archives at the speed of computation, there is always present the systems operations logic of the mid-level, that order of computation that compresses flows of data into galaxies of code, transforms archival knowledge into the streamed communication of web sites, mobile technologies, and augmented media.

Consequently, what is the future of archives in the wires? Under the pressure of technological change, the traditional function of the archive as a record of the past appears to have been undermined. In the real time and real space of digital culture, distinctions between past, present, and future have themselves been increasingly rendered obsolete. When images constitute the real, when the code matrix replaces the logic of signification, and the language of genetic reproduction substitutes for cultural production, traditional understandings of the archive are in danger of eclipse. Confronted by the speed of digital communication, the archival imagination sometimes panics. Similar to the crisis of cultural intelligibility of the museum when first challenged by the aesthetics of the moving image and consequently by the restless motion of multimedia art, archival logic sometimes opts for a purely temporal solution. It attempts to literally freeze the digital object in an isolated moment of time and space. Here, the digital artifact is stripped of its organic relationship to network culture, its code structure rendered motionless, its images cryogenically preserved, its texts bounded, its boundaries perfectly secured from contamination from an always threatening (digital) external environment. But as in life, so in archives: that which has been excluded by the archival imagination will always make its presence felt; that which has been disavowed will often form the basis of spectral hauntologies; and that which has been prohibited will usually prove to be the real object of archival seduction.

In this case, no matter how powerful the will to archival self-preservation, digital culture will find a way of purloining the archival sanctity of bounded artifacts. One code at a time, one essential connection, one electronic synapse, one boundary exchange after another; all digital archives are destined to experience the new digital disease of *link rot*. Over time, connections fray, software is rendered obsolete, boundaries weaken, operating systems dissolve into liquid arrays of disconnected data points, and collections lose their putative meanings. And all this because, like the restless movement of time itself, nothing can really stop the degradation of code over time, just as there is no form of archival logic that can do that which is mythically impossible, namely to preserve collections of code that always yearn to return to its natural environment – the digital world of speed, fast connectivity, instant interfaces, and slow perception. Once infected by frayed connections, broken synapses, and crashed (code) boundaries, digital collections may continue to appear perfectly seamless as a matter of aesthetic appearance, but their destiny is one of digital senescence – literally slow erosion from within by the gradual, and always terminal, failure of the dense matrix of code. Faced with the sure and certain reality of digital senescence, no archival potion, no aesthetic preservative, no boundary logic can really prevent the unpreventable, specifically the drift of code back to the elementary matter of the digital universe. Data trash.

Complexity and the digital archive

At first glance, the digital galaxy is a curious dwelling place for the traditional archive. While the imagination of the archivist might well be attracted to the global diffusion of knowledge provided by computer networks, by the remarkable capacity of archived objects once fully digitized to be reprocessed, recombined, respliced, refiltered, and by the brilliant speed of network society, this exchange between memory and code is not without its tragic element. Contrary to the extropian enthusiasm of proponents of the technological imperative, there is much to be said for the necessary solitude of the traditional archive, for, that is, the implicit demands it places on the powers of human imagination to make something meaningful of records so carefully preserved, protected, and maintained. As an object of imagination, the traditional archive has its own imperative injunctions, but this order of time has nothing to do with technologies of speed, circulation, or diffusion, but only with the core archival event, namely that in solitude, and often on the basis of an accidental encounter of an inquiring mind and a chance meeting with a forgotten letter, a fragment of text, a recorded interview, a moving image, a photograph, that which the philosopher Hannah Arendt once described as the "life of the mind" renews itself.[7] Something of this sort has always been the basis for the cultural importance placed by society on its archival knowledge. No matter how neglected in private conversations and public policy, no matter how little honored in larger debates concerning the immediate priorities of society, the traditional archive has always served as a persistent point of ground-truthing of culture and society.

In this case, the power of the archive is that of intermediation: casting the light of the past on the present, foregrounding neglected objects of contemplation, drawing into presence artifacts from the glare of the future. Bridging past and future, reconciling the necessary solitude of the inquiring mind and the complexity of cultural artifacts, the traditional archive does not so much resemble Heidegger's concept of the "dwelling place," but actually creates anew the "dwelling-space" as a beautifully mediated space of critical and creative cultural reflection. Indeed, what is always at stake in the archival imagination is not simply a question of time but of space, specifically the aesthetic challenge inherent in the archival imagination of delicately bringing into presence the different shades of interpretation, those incommensurable spaces of bright clarity, ambiguous grey zones, and dark spaces in the very interpretive complexity of which the story of culture is continuously renewed.

While it would be premature to effect philosophical closure around the dimensions of that form of imagination generated by the digital archive, this much is certain. The digital archive must, as a matter of its deepest ontological requirements, give rise to a form of imagination that is as inflected as it is relational, as recombinant as it is aesthetically indeterminate. Indeed, digital inflections are the essence of archives in the wires. Breaking with traditional visions of the archive as somehow distanced from the complexity of the human condition, the digital archive only exists to the extent that it migrates across the most vital intersections of life: archives of disavowed histories, excluded facts, neglected memories, and disowned artifacts, from the purely techno-logical to the resolutely social. The fact that it is a *digital* archive, simul-taneously constituted by and framed in its operating logic by software codes implies also that archives in the wires are shaped most pro-foundly by the logic of the code. If the regime of computation will be relational, recombinant, indeterminate, and complex, this means that archives in the wires will also witness an emergent logic of relational data, recombinant memory, indeterminate remixes, and complex figu-rations. Indeed, if there can be considerable interest among visionary data archivists in the concept of the "self-generating archive," this is due, in no small part, to the growing realization that wired archives are necessarily reflexive. Like data itself, the digital archive not only assembles complex arrays of data sets, but also exists only in relation-ship to surrounding data systems. Literally, archives in the wires will be self-generating because it is an essential ontological requirement of code itself that the code matrix exists in dynamic homeostatic exchange with other systems of code, not only recording and responding to online queries and new links but effectively adapting its future behav-ior to that which is trending on the net.

6

Screen Drift

Screen drift is the eye of the future in fast motion accelerating across the deep space of the media archive. Saturated by images, augmented by mobile devices, with remix for perception and information overload for a brain, the eye of the future blinks open to the space travel of everyday life that is screen drift.

That we live in a culture of proliferating screens – cinema, television, computers, medical imaging, airport surveillance screens – is already a truism: technology as cliché. What is less evident is the silent, but very real, impact of screen culture on our psycho-geography: the psychological territory of human imagination and perception, identity and truth-saying, indeed *truth-seeing*. In ways complex, often misunderstood, and mysterious, we may already be the *invisible environment* of screens in the wires, exhausted media travelers into whose bodies and minds the psychic surgery of electronic technologies of communication puts its hooks, radically altering the deepest language of human perception, shape-shifting the boundaries of the real, speeding up the meaning of time itself, and transforming virtual space into an artificial horizon. Living in a culture dominated by screens – mobile, video, cinema, television, LED billboards – means that without our consent and certainly in the absence of conscious deliberation, we have committed ourselves to life as a continuously altered reality. When the screens of media culture go inside the human mind, we suddenly find ourselves the very first explorers of a culture of screen drift.

Video as the skin of the new cinema

With video for eyes and drift as its elemental motion, the data body is finally
able to explore the deep space, strange galaxies, powerful galactic currents,
and intergalactic tidal belts of information streaming through the media
archive that is life in the image lane today.

Video is everywhere, from the visual skin of the new cinema to those
desolate images recorded by all the surveillance cameras of the world.
Impatient with the visual constraints of cinematic language, bored with
the static image, breaking free of the narrative constructions of television, video drift is increasingly the visual cloud within which we circulate and on account of which the eye of (digital) perception has
finally opened to the multiple, the heterogeneous, the granular, the
immediate, the slow, the intense. With no definitive purpose, no overall
trajectory, no necessary narratives, the sounds and images of the video
matrix drift across the electronic horizon, crystallizing now and again
decisive moments in the contemporary human condition, ceaselessly
recording the space of everyday life, remixing the comic, the banal, the
tragic, the cruel. Today, as accepted certainties fade away, video drift
is omnipresent, simultaneously the tangible sign of the purely unpredictable, delightfully accidental character of the image matrix and the
always-accumulating archive, the ceaseless mnemonic, of the surveillance camera that is only interested in the momentary trace, the passing
glimpse, the visual patterns of human activity, once reduced to its
surface appearances.

Don't think for a moment that there is any cultural link between
video drift and those once-celebrated technologies of visualization that
preceded it. While cinema might have terminated as a dream machine
for mass vision and television may have repurposed itself as an increasingly banal world of reality shows, the world of video drift has nothing
to do with cathartic dreams and fantasy simulations. Video drift is
about the eclipse of simulation and the end of constructed visual narratives in favor of the visual circulation of the culture of abjection in its
totality. When any person with a cell phone is a potential video artist,
any camera an instant interface to a YouTube video gone viral, any
subject-position a possible witness to history – accidents, protests,
crashes, events large and small from the tedious to the ecstatic – then
video drift is increasingly how we live, imagine, communicate, and
desire. And, if that's the case, it is also futile to attempt a nostalgic
return to the canons of visual orthodoxy by mapping previous knowledge of visuality onto the complex universe of video drift. And why?

Because video drift represents the end of visualization, that very tangible post-historical moment in which visualization fades away before the speed of the circulating image.

We always knew this would happen. The invention of photography was met with considerable cultural resistance on the part of Indigenous persons who resisted being brought into political intelligibility by canonical powers. The then much ridiculed assertion that photography had about it the power to capture the essence of the soul, to evacuate human spirit, was, in fact, a haunting prologue to the triumph of the circulating image. From photography to cinema to television, the domination of the image and with it the liquidation of the social, the evacuation of the cultural, underwent a fatal increase in its speed of circulation, in the relentless hegemony of the code. Everywhere the triumph of the image was accompanied by the canonization of codes of visualization. Everywhere the rise of technologies of visualization was marked by the eclipse of the complexities of human vision. Substitute vision machines were everywhere, heterogeneous all-too-human perspectives nowhere.

Video is the iris of social networking technologies

> Video drift is how the posthuman body sets out every day, every hour, every minute on a deep space voyage into the media archive of memories, events, communications, some autobiographical, others historical, some local, others drawn from every region, every periphery, every center of the global intensity that is the world today.

All that suddenly ended with video drift. On the surface, video was just another technology of substitution replacing the ocular eye of human flesh with the video image matrix. In fact, there was a moment in the 1990s when it appeared that the lasting legacy of video would be twofold: a brilliant expression of innovative video art on the one hand, and a new visual, hand-held, jump-cut language for cinema providing a patina of reality-effects for an otherwise obsolescent media. However, like the most recent of all the Copernican Revolutions all that changed instantly when video images became the dynamic content of social networking technologies. Instantly, video as the last bunker of essentially private image production without access to the means of communication became the pervasive visual language for that most globally archival of all technological media of communication – YouTube. With this, the production of life flipped into the digital reproduction of its video archive, the wild circulation of images replaced the staged communication of the now superseded cultural order, and mobility was everywhere sovereign. Never exclusively a revolution in technological affairs, never understandable in terms of the language of communication, never reducible to debates on visualization, the video drift that was expressed at first by the cultural eruption that was YouTube and that is now the dynamic driver of the entire media complex is deeply biological in nature. It was as if the data bodies that we have all become were provided for the first time with the power of life, with the ability to communicate in the only language that counts in the data stream – the remix language of videos. Refusing the previously closed order of communicative power where elites speak and we listen, the power of life that is video drift brings everything to the surface, puts everything into circulation.

Certainly, the culture of video drift still witnesses the presence of real power, that in fact is what drives it on, what motivates its actions, sharpens its resistance, mobilizes its attention. We can see this everywhere. For example, the Arab Spring that, in reality, inaugurates the twenty-first century is most definitely powered by awesome human courage, individual and collective, in the hard streets of all the tyrannies of the Middle East, but it is relentlessly witnessed by streamed video images. The protestor who holds a spent tear-gas canister stamped "Made in the USA" also has a cell phone witnessing the moment for the global video stream. The gathering crowd that battles state security forces armed with batons always seems, even in the midst of the most frenzied scenes of violence, to have many cameras in the air, each attached like a necessary political prosthetic to an insurgent protestor who simultaneously resists and uplinks. These were supposed to be the end-times of technological determinism – a future frozen in the grasp of fully augmented power – but they have quickly proven to be something very different. We are in the midst of a great (video) awakening, a time in which every granular trace of the human – its passions, its challenges, its protests, its retreats, its delirium, its tedium – finds its place in the image repertoire. So then, an end to visualization and the beginning of human (video) vision. The data body has grown an eye: its name is video, its community of solidarity is the social network, its privileged medium is the internet, its dominant sign is the accelerating speed of circulation, and its political center is every periphery – the abandoned, the accidented, the abjected, the excluded, the nameless. Now as always, images are never really visual representations, but something more eschatological – witnesses to our having existed, traces of those who until the great awakening never had a means of communicating that which was unrepresentable, unintelligible, unknowable.

Remix culture

With this, we are plugged directly into the full force of remix culture. Aesthetically, every bit of human creativity is flowing in this direction. Like talismans of a big cultural shift in the making, remix musicians, remix video artists, and remix performance artists were the first to seize on epiphanies of new human vision that could be struck on the metal of the video stream. When the history of the great video awakening is written, it most certainly will inscribe in its most honorary register the names of that emerging multitude of artists and musicians and performers who recognized in the minor epistemological profile of remix video production the haunting archetype of new modes of the passion to communicate, satirize, witness, and even explore. They were the earliest code-breakers, at first unnoticed, sometimes proscribed, never really properly acclaimed, but now recognized as obviously sensitive barometers of the major cultural revolution that is video drift. But it is not, in the end, to the artistic genealogy of creative video production that the phenomenon of video drift owes its inheritance. Once again, remix culture is a primarily biological phenomenon – an important turn in the always random and unpredictable histories of human evolution. For what's really remixed by global access to the video stream are the shifting boundaries of all the referents: gender, class, race, nationalism, knowledge, even sexuality. When every periphery is a potential center, when each individual a possibly doubled witness – immediate participant or spectator from afar – when every sound and image potentially breaks the barriers of geographical distance, sexual difference, national difference, what's actually being remixed, suddenly and inevitably, by the culture of video drift are all the crashed boundaries, the challenged frames of reference, the porous borders. It is not much discussed, but the speed of video drift has mobilized other drifts, the first tangible hint of which is the pervasive contemporary mood of uncertainty.

But if the culture of video drift has its seduction, it also possesses its own theater of cruelty. After all, it is best not to forget the insightful teaching of Nietzsche's *Zarathustra*: that nature is always simultaneously cheerful and hard because, like the four humors of classical mythology – earth, air, fire, and water – nature has no necessary morality. Open to all possibilities, nature does not discriminate between human purposes nor prejudge in advance the question of human valuing. Video drift is like that. It may have its technologies of aesthetic affirmation with their evocative renditions of video art, but it also has its technologies of prohibition. The latter are everywhere in the new materialism of video surveillance: video images from predatory drones, orbiting satellites, smart grids, closed-circuit cameras on street corners, airports, transportation terminals, office buildings. While surveillance video can never break the skin barrier and record the secrets of the human heart, it most certainly can trace bodily movements and pre-emptively anticipate patterns of human mobility. That's video drift as the key site of the contemporary theater of cruelty where the details of personal autobiography are relentlessly archived and mined for traces of information, from facial recognition software to full-body scanners and, very soon, full-mind scanners as well. Baudrillard may have died, but that which he so hauntingly prophesied – the "evil demon of images" – with its radiating positivity is only now rising into chilling prominence.

For this reason, in the age of information culture, the body learns to swim in the data storm for reasons of survival. Scanned by surveillance cameras, the signature of its iris photographed and data banked by electronic airport security, its movements through the economy elec-tronically tracked by its own credit card history, probed by all the ubiquitous technologies associated with contemporary medicine, entertained by YouTube, connected by social networking technologies, seduced by the high-definition screens of mass media – cinema, televi-sion, and Blu-ray – its ears hardwired to the sounds of iPods and eyes to the screen of iPads, its every (internet) thought patiently recorded by the hovering satellites of the national security system, the body today is punctured, pierced, probed, and pummeled by information culture.

In the utopian phase of information technology, we could still live with the illusion that cyborgs had a double life, partially enmeshed in what Donna Haraway has eloquently described as the "informatics of domination," but also free to move at the speed of light, to live on the borderlands, to learn anew how to negotiate the boundaries of identity that are triumphantly dissolved. That was the age of Donna Haraway's evocative "A Cyborg Manifesto," Allucquére Rosanne Stone's concep-tualization of "breached boundaries," and Katherine Hayles's vision of the creative possibilities and dangers of the posthuman future. All criti-cal, but all remaining faithful to the essentially binary character of information technology, to the belief that out of the ruins of the infor-matics of domination would emerge the possibility of a new form of human identity that would be equal to the challenges of life in the borderlands.

In the dystopian phase of information technology, the utopian belief in the romanticism of the borderlands has been shaken by the realization that the informatics of domination has appropriated the resistance spirit of the borderlands. It turns out that information culture really likes outlaw culture. Cybernetics is precisely how the language of the posthuman is delivered to us.

Cybernetics goes hybrid. It feeds itself with the language of difference: part human/part code/part machine. A future of humans, androids, clones, and cyborgs, cybernetics is the borderland. Abandoning the language of the human, cybernetics celebrates the language of the posthuman. It has already gone over to the side of robotic intelligence skinned with silicon flesh. Information technology works to undermine confidence in the historical persistence of the human by presenting fascinating visions of a posthuman future, stripped of the complexities of the human condition, liberated from the messy world of intermediations, but always fully seductive because of its irony, indeterminacy, and ambivalence.

This, then, is the culture of screen drift with all its seductions and cruelties. However, the digital dialectic that always dwells silently, but for all that no less passionately, within the spectacle of the image cannot long be repressed. With the triumph of the (video) image, that which was supposedly eliminated forever by the positivity of new visual codes – the unspoken, the unthinkable, the uncanny, the liminal, the incommensurable – has quickly become an ineluctable part of the posthuman condition. So then, to which future are we being delivered by video drift? How do we negotiate the unexplored borders between an information stream that would be free and an increasingly bunkered surveillance culture? Like earlier explorers of the technological way, we demand meaning of the universe, but receive only enchanting video images in reply.

Screen drift is the electronic circuitry of the data body.

7

Media Drift

There is no technology without a mediation, no formula without a concept, no connection without a radical disconnection, no affirmation without a prohibition, no code without abjection.

Digital dialectics

While there is no definitive digital imaginary, there are pluralities of often contradictory, conflicting, and heterogeneous insurgencies of the human imagination that will not be impeded by the triumphant language of the code. Far from escaping the fatal curse of mythic consciousness, this the most technological of all ages – an epoch when the metaphysics of time and space have been reduced to light-time and light-space – remains under the spell of that which has been prohibited from consciousness by the logic of the code. What religion could never fully accomplish – the unification of the world in fixed cosmological consciousness – the language of technology has set out to complete by wrapping the skin of the planet in a universal language of connectivity, thereby subordinating the heterogeneity of humanity to the steady signal of networked society. And yet, for all that, the essential truth that is preserved by this act of technological hubris is the persistence in even these, the most cybernetic of times, of the ancient rhythms of dialectical contestation, that is to say, the endurance of *negative philosophy* in the midst of technologically affirmative culture, the presence of hauntologies, exclusions, prohibitions, and absences figured in all their complexity in that new shadowy world of digital dialectics. Always a matter of material history, the rising into visibility of digital dialectics can be detected in the central political crises that cut across the twenty-first century, namely the triumph of technological society and with it the domination of Enlightenment that has everywhere been accompanied by the swift emergence of its *apparent opposites*: increasingly atavistic subjectivity, fundamentalist religious impulses, revolts by the poor, insurgencies by the powerless, and the return of historical consciousness in all its complex particularities.

It is not so much that the triumph of code is catastrophic, but that dialectics has come alive again. There is no technology without a mediation, no formula without a concept, no connection without something disconnected, no affirmation without a prohibition, no code without abjection. What we might call the digital imaginary begins with this realm of abjected bodies, prohibited knowledge, minoritarian epistemes, excluded presences. Not a world of communication, digital dialectics represents that which does not fall properly within the laws of media logic. By its very solitude, it always remains exterior to and at one remove from the normative order of communication. Consequently, while digital dialectics can be brought into the normative order of communication only at the expense of losing its singularity, communication itself must undergo a possibly fatal passage towards an understanding of social justice or risk losing its possibility of liminality. In the end, for digital dialectics to be communicable, it can only belong to the new order of liminality and thus remains fundamentally incommensurable, resolutely incommunicable, the *mauvais plis* of the normative regime of communication.

Consequently, we are not living at the eclipse of communication, but at the beginning of a new order of communication – *liminal communication*. Tracing its communicative origins directly to the interface of the digital and the analogue, liminal communication refers to emergent orders of understanding, speech, gestures, and perception that negotiate the always indeterminate, heterogeneous, multiple interspaces of the digital and the material. Here, creative imagination and new forms of technological affect serve as probes, exploring what it means for bodies to grow synthetic skins and for virtual presences to suddenly migrate into the real time of everyday life. Could it be that the long-sought dialectical reconciliation of the particular and the general – the question of identity and nonidentity – has finally found its moment of historical realization in an order of communication that is as unruly and contradictory as it is digitally nested?

Certainly not the domain of code-works, liminal communication only commences when perception accelerates beyond the heavy gravitational pull of codes to an understanding that the *broken interface* is the central truth that is preserved by an increasingly layered reality principle. Most definitely not reducible to information, liminal communication is about the impossibility of information, that point when the sudden activation of even the most minimal element of reversibility contained in all systems of communication brings about the collapse of the normative order of communication into its opposite – the transversal universe of affect which, moving across the electric skin of the mediascape, literally *extremizes* all information into a contagious and collective nervous breakdown. And decidedly not a media theory, liminal communication knows only the kinetic energy released by traditional media as they intersect in a wild, combinatory remix of the new logic of the android, the clone, and the cyborg.

Consider the following premonitory signs of the future – *the digital dialectics* – of the new order of liminal communication: its *virtual organs*: the death of the eye associated with the appearance of the Software Necropolis; its *synthetic physiology* – Flesh Rezzing; its *logic of abjection* – Full-Mind Scanning; its *dominant comportment* – the Lonely Digital Crowd; and its *mythology* – the rings of Saturn. Here, liminality is suddenly everywhere, destabilizing boundaries, undermining the logistics of perspective, challenging the binary division of life and death, light and darkness, flesh and data. And with this, digital dialectics comes into its own as a way of beginning to comprehend the incomprehensible: what happens when the eye of the flesh grows a digital organ? What is the future of human flesh when bodies are fully wrapped within the skin of their own virtual Second Lives? What is the fate of privacy in the future of the fully networked ego – something to be jettisoned as extra ballast as the body blasts into the space of global communication or something very different, that is a longing for privacy as the hauntology of the lonely digital crowd?

Software necropolis

Death of the eye

The death instinct is alive and well in all the software language surrounding ocular vision. That's what makes software for improved (technological) vision so vividly, and chillingly, dynamic. When the eye upgrades to digital eyesight, there's a simultaneous downgrading of human vision. If by human vision we mean not only what is rendered visible but, more importantly, what remains invisible, not only what is perceived but what remains obstinately outside the regime of perception, then software for improved digital vision effectively shuts down the invisible, the unperceived, all the forms of everyday blindness so necessary for the complex workings of human vision. With its deep nerve connection to the human nervous system, from the visual neurology of the brain to the orality of the mouth, the tactility of the limbs and the desires of (our) sexual organs, the eye is always a porous membrane negotiating the boundary of bodies and the world. When the eye first opened to the world of earth, air, fire, water, and sky, it was as if the evolutionary story of human flesh finally had made an elemental, even indispensable, connection. With the opening of the eye, the human organism became a visual traveler: nomadic, curious, forewarned, always drawn out of the dark cavity of skull and skin and bones and blood to become something unmistakably human – that which Nietzsche first signaled – a going-across, a gamble, a thin spider's web over the abyss called life.

All that is about to change.

In the way of all truly momentous technological innovations, the death of the eye has been announced by way of a media report describing the latest adventure in technological futurism. It appears that a research team at the University of Washington, motivated by the desire to transform the contact lens into a digital platform like iPhones with its always growing menu of creative apps, has invented the world's first prototype of the fully augmented human eye. But why stop there?

According to the leader of the research team:

> The human eye is a perceptual powerhouse. It can see millions of colors, adjust easily to shifting light conditions, and transmit information to the brain at a speed exceeding that of a high-speed Internet connection. . . .
>
> In the *Terminator* movies, Arnold Schwarzenegger's character sees the world with data superimposed on his visual field – virtual captions that enhance the cyborg's scan of a scene. In stories by the science fiction author Vernon Vinge, characters rely on electronic contact lenses, rather than smartphones or brain implants, for seamless access to information that appears right before their eyes.
>
> These visions (if I may) might seem far-fetched, but a contact lens with simple built-in electronics is already within reach; in fact my students and I are already producing such devices in small numbers in my laboratory at the University of Washington, in Seattle. These lenses don't give us the vision of an eagle or the benefit of running subtitles on our surroundings yet. But we have built a lens with one LED, which we've powered wirelessly with RF. What we've done so far barely hints at what will be soon possible with this technology.[1]

In the usual way of all scientific experiments with the human body, the animal species selected for a digital eye implant is the rabbit. Definitely not mindful of Donna Haraway's understanding of animals as "companion species," the body of the bunny is scientifically repurposed to become a platform for digital lenses. Did anyone think to ask what's a bunny's vision of the world? Or did the bunny consent to seeing fields of edible grass in a newly augmented digital way?

That the bunny was never consulted about the advantages of augmented reality is itself perhaps very revelatory of the impoverished vision of a scientist. Isn't there an indispensable ethical reflex associated with human vision, a carefully nurtured sense that human vision is not simply about appropriation, but appreciation? Strip human vision of a complex sense of critical appreciation of the world around us, and aren't we suddenly left in a world of bunnies as objects of technological appropriation, objects of abuse value?

In the larger story of technology of which this research innovation is a brilliant digital example, no permission is ever required to secure an animal's consent to a digital eye implant. Consciousness of the bunny as a unique, complex species-being is always disavowed, and this disavowal is the first, most important avowal of scientific experimentation. On the path to the augmented human eye, animals occupy the diminished role of unwilling test beds.

But, of course, not for humans. Appropriating human agency is never really required because, unlike bunnies, humans are seemingly always ready to become leading objects of digital augmentation. In response to the announcement in a story headlined "A Twinkle in the Eye," one net correspondent immediately said: "Wow. I would be more than willing to risk losing eyesight in one of my eyes to test this out as the technology matures." Perhaps shutting down human vision and opening up an augmented reality of the enhanced digital eye requires, in the first instance, something not really technological, but metaphysical. When the digital eye blinks for the very first time, when the augmented iris is streamed, networked, and vectored, an indispensable ethical preparation has already taken place, a prior human willingness to identify itself with its technological future with sufficient intensity to override any remaining (human) quibbles concerning animal rights, human dispositions, and what's lost with the coming-to-be of the fully realized universe of augmented reality.

In the amazing blast of technological creativity, such ethical reservations have no necessary cultural standing. How could they? Networking the eye, augmenting human vision, implies that the eye will now port information moving at light-speed. The iPhone becomes an ocular implant; texting literally becomes a blink of an eye; the cornea opens onto an iris repurposed as a mobile device. Even for those standing on the sidelines with ethical reservations ready to hand, the accidenting of the eye by digital vision can only be understood ambivalently. If individual human autobiography can be linked so intimately to the unfolding adventures of technological biography, perhaps it is because that which is soon to be acquired in such experimentation easily outpaces the slow reservations of ethical remembrance.

Everything about the digital lens is amazing. Slip the digital lens onto the cornea and the world opens up as code-work. Shimmering columns of data slipstream across the expectant iris, reality suddenly goes bifocal with distance for ordinary human eyesight and nearness for data feeds, astigmatism is instantly corrected since the irregularly shaped cornea is forced to retool itself as a platform for always undistorted information, and human vision itself becomes multifocal, mediated, and multitasked.

That the digital lens may reduce vision to mono-vision with compromised (ethical) depth perception is, in the end, a matter best left to those soon to be left behind by augmented reality in a contact lens.

In the future, could one accidented remnant of digital vision, this sacrifice of human eyesight before the altar of augmented reality, be a sudden increase in ethical myopia?

"Flesh rezzing"

One of the enduring tendencies of digital innovation has been its eagerness to declare any interesting technological innovation a nervous breakthrough to a new level of the hyperreal. Contemporary discourse about augmented reality follows in this (digital) vein. In Amsterdam, a digital start-up called Layar has developed a form of augmented reality that allows the wired world to be seamlessly mapped onto the geography of urban areas. Here, the wired world and its earthly counterpart suddenly converge, with mapping coordinates hardwired onto very visible spaces.

Perhaps, though, what is most fascinating about Layar is less its mapping the wireless world onto urban geography than something more ineluctable – that this is an anticipatory technology of a liminal future. What we may be witnessing are, in fact, the very first technological explorations of that still undefined space, that third space, between mobility and its earthly counterpart, resulting is our sudden immersion in an order of space and time that is as hauntological with its archive of historical traces of the past as it is futuristic with its strategies of augmentation. The artistic imagination has been quick to sense this essential truth preserved in augmented reality. For example, in her visually powerful online *Dragon Series*, the California artist, Micha Cárdenas, explores what she calls "flesh rezzing." Focusing specifically on the construction of avatar models in *Second Life*, Cárdenas evocatively describes the technological born-again experience of synthetic flesh construction, that point where the imaginary bodies that we all are, or would like to be, slip on the skin of the avatar and begin to experience the very first pulsations of digital affect. In the new world of flesh rezzing, the earth-bound body shakes hands with its digital counterpart in all those liminal zones of the future with their frenzied kinetics, imaginary codes, and wired flesh. Here, imagination and affect are definitely the psychological outriders of the bodily organism as it flesh-rezzes its way to a new digital skin.

Full-mind scans

Remixing early Christianity and late technology

Considerable research is now underway in the security industry focused on the development of full mind scans. Enabled by engineering developments in electronic magnetic resonance imaging, fueled by state-driven paranoia over security concerns, and promoted by the security industry, the idea is to rapidly expand early detection facilities at airports beyond the bodily constraints of full-body scans to detect the *hidden intentionality* of the traveling public. Not surprisingly, given Britain's clear commitment to pervasive surveillance technologies, much of this research is conducted at British research institutions, with Cambridge University leading the way.

Outside of immediate security concerns, the detection of hidden intentionality has a long-standing Christian genealogy. Beyond the physical digressions of the body, Christian confessionality had as its real focus the sins of the mind. Consider, for example, the ominously and, indeed, obsessively subjectivist rhetoric of the Seven Deadly Sins: pride, avarice, envy, wrath, lust, gluttony, and sloth. In its most extreme case, the search for the physically undetectable was the imaginary phantasmagoria that motivated the confessional cruelties of the Inquisition. In its most moderate instance, its presence can be detected in the private recounting of sins of intentionality and examinations of conscience that remain the regular practice of contemporary Christianity. What lies behind the rhetoric surrounding the examination of private conscience is something more religiously significant, and certainly something alien to the cold rationality of technology: the question of the soul. More than a surveillance apparatus for forcing the body to declare its secrets, the apparatus surrounding the practice of confessionality was intended to reveal the secrets of the soul, to draw into the visibility of speech what was considered the animating spirit of bodily truth. While this inexhaustible search for the secrets of the soul certainly has normative consequences, namely disciplining mental and bodily actions to conform to the tutelary requirements of Christian confessionality, it still focused on the enigmatic question of the soul – this magical bodily spectacle of making the Word flesh.

Now that we live at the historical apex of the triumph of technology and, with it, the penetration into the deepest layers of human subjectivity of the cold logic of instrumental rationality and technical reason, we are fully instructed that discussions of soul-spirits are a taboo, if not truly alien, cosmology. Yet, in that curious way in which the actual practices of technology often expose hidden assumptions previously undetectable in the hype of their justificatory logic, could it be that what is really at stake in full mind-scanning is a contemporary revival of the examination of conscience? Following the logic of reversal, that which motivates power, that which enables the fabulous growth of technologies, from the mechanical to the virtual, are not necessarily the truths that they affirm but the hidden order of prohibitions, exclusions, and putative untruths against which the technological order represents a continuing exercise of daily repression. Consequently, to seek out technological conveyances for traditional Christian practices associated with the examination of conscience is less to move outside the order of the technological than to connect with its originating Christian genealogy. Of course, in the history of Christianity we know what may follow from this under conditions of political distress experienced by the body politic: the bad infinity of torture since the state of the soul is always ultimately unknowable.

Consequently, the question: Are we now living on the cusp of a new (technical) inquisition, organized by a full array of technical surveillance but motivated by a more enduring Christian passion – the state of the soul of the good citizen? For conservative ideology, it is an easy step from the evangelical enthusiasms associated with born-again bodies to full mind reading. For liberal ideology, the move is equally transparent. Once the body has been rendered as a *marker of security*, the mind must follow as a guarantor of hidden (psychic) intentionality. As markers of security, body and mind must thus perform according to stipulated normative standards, practice compliance when scanned for confessions of the hidden truths of psyche and flesh, always remain in a state of high alert in an increasingly disciplinary society, and be prepared to be brought into visibility by technologies of humiliation, degradation, and innovation.

The lonely digital crowd

Absolute subjectivity is also subjectless. . . . The more the I of expressionism is thrown back upon itself, the more like the excluded world of things it becomes. . . . Pure subjectivity, being of necessity estranged from itself as well and having become a thing, assumes the dimensions of objectivity which expresses itself through its own estrangement.

Theodor Adorno, *Prisms*[2]

Following Adorno's critique of absolute subjectivity, we can conceive absolute connectivity as the long-sought destiny of all social networking technology. From business and entertainment to education, the word is out on the media street that connectivity is an emblematic sign of the power of technological devices, intimating that, without unconstrained access to the full array of technological devices, we are threatened with an immediate fall into the dark gravitational field associated with the loss of connection – the much-feared eclipse of networks, the day the internet stopped.

In actual practice, this is one case where digital rhetoric is not as messianic as it might be. As any user of a Blackberry or iPhone knows well, technological devices are always, and only, not simply about connectivity, but *hyper-connectivity*. That is, not old school mechanical or even electronic connectivity in the sense of point-to-point communication in a world suddenly stitched together by ubiquitous mobility, but connectivity as something immanently cellular, networked, biological, and metabolic.

In the new regime of mobile communication, connectivity is literally cellular communication, whereby the new technological subject is immediately enmeshed in a dense matrix of digital communication, an instantaneous, depth relation looping subjects, earth-orbiting satellites, ground stations, innovative software configurations, enabling communication industries, and ever-present surveillance technologies. Cells are always only as good as the speed and pervasiveness of the (communicative) field. Consequently, when communication goes cellular, the nature of subjectivity itself undergoes a big change. With cellular communication, we are witness to the technological termination of the privative ego housed in the archaeology of sovereign subject in favor of a still undefined, undifferentiated network ego, a cellular web that effortlessly loops subjects, devices, software, and satellites in a new communicative skin.

Knowing no prior sense of individual privacy, the network ego values publicity as the triumphant sign of its cellular presence. Cells, whether texting or speaking, irradiate all public space with intimate conversations so that seemingly everyone is now a spectator to your love life, work life, waking life, to your every mood and action. The delirious specter of the posthuman is on the prowl – Twittered, Face-booked, and Linked-in. Every feeling is a potential text, every thought linked to popular culture, every movement blog-worthy, every form of public transport a telephone booth, every sidewalk someone else's conversation, every room a room not of your (cellular) own. And this makes sense. In the age of the new network ego, the meaning of the public itself is immediately flipped into its opposite, the turning inside out of what was previously private and interior – the always publicly censored contents of the modernist ego. With the start-up of the network ego and the shutting down of the privative ego, privacy itself can be happily jettisoned as something that was always perhaps unwanted, but definitely forced, on the individuals of pre-cellular times. Conse-quently, as an appropriate spokesman for these new cellular times, it was not surprising that the co-founder of Google recently challenged the concept of privacy, arguing that if you wanted privacy you should stay off the net. This makes sense. The network body has no memory other than its electronic traces, no sense of privacy that could possibly outpace its desire for connectivity, no perspective on augmentation that would not enable more complex looping of the cellular subject within relays of technological devices, software codes, satellite feeds, and always waiting mobile antennas. With cells, privacy is dumped into the obsolete archive of the privative ego as a now surpassed relation of communication associated with old forms of personal communica-tion. Overexposed, overcommunicated, over-looped, the bodies that we have now become in the age of mobile communication are effectively enabled by the loss of privacy. Stripping the rites of privacy away from individuals is both the condition of possibility of the network ego and increasingly its emblematic justification. For example, when new media executives can speak so contemptuously of the loss of privacy as less something to be regretted than a salutary measure of the new public good to be welcomed, it intimates that jettisoning the concept of privacy has gone beyond being a condition of possibility for the fully realized networked society to one of the key expressions of the new ethics of digital ideology.

Ironically, the eclipse of privacy gives rise to that most radically private of all new life-forms – the lonely digital crowd.

The rings of Saturn

Why the immense fascination with the rings of Saturn? Simply a fascination with technological prowess in navigating from the near-time of earth to the deep-space of Saturn, or awe at the sheer beauty of the amazing ultraviolet optics of those perfectly formed rings circling a gigantic gaseous planet? Perhaps. Or maybe it's what astronomers immediately announced as the perpetual lure of deep-space travel to Saturn: that in exploring this gaseous planet at the distant edge of the solar system, we are actually time-traveling to our past, to an earlier earth history when gaseous space had not yet congealed into earthly matter.

Or could fascination with the rings of Saturn have its origins less in scientific or historical reasons than in a mode of world-attentiveness that is subliminally mythological? Are the rings of Saturn really an astronomical story of our past or future? After all, we know this about those concentric rings horizoning Saturn against the cold darkness of the void of space: first, that their incredible aesthetic symmetry follows from, and perhaps is almost preordained, by the normal laws of gravitational physics. The rings of Saturn crystallize in the always nighttime sky of deep space the immutable theorems of quantum mechanics, having to do with gravitation, velocity, and the chromatics of light. In the artificial form of our technological prosthetics – ultraviolet cameras, deep-space exploration vehicles – we find ourselves deeply linked to the fate of Saturn by a common scientific framework. Consequently, while our earthly gaze upon the rings of Saturn can express "astounded surprise" at the elegance of their aesthetic symmetry, there is another part of human consciousness that finds itself oddly comforted by this preternatural gift of astronomical confirmation of the magic of science. But there is also something more to the seduction of the rings of Saturn; this having more to do with dark futurism as the dominant mood of earthly space-time. From a strictly observational viewpoint, the famous rings of Saturn are permanently frozen signs of decay and ruin, splayed-out orbits of lost worlds. In this account, the rings are most probably the remains of lost moons which, having at some point in the recesses of the past been imploded by proximity to the immense gravitational pressures of Saturn, now circle its sky in thin, flattened ice sheets stretching indeterminately into the darkness. Not really only a fable of our lost past of perfect aesthetic symmetry, the rings of Saturn evoke a more primal, and quintessentially human, emotion: an ineffable tension between symmetry and decay. Consequently, looking towards the rings of Saturn, we can find a mythological story of presence and loss, aesthetics without and ruins within; but is it really so different from another story, a story this time of the tension between postmodern intimations and posthuman realities as the rings of Earth? Once again, the astronomy of light-through space and light-through time lights up the cultural imaginary to reveal a more abiding story of the strange entwinements of our past and future. Digital mythology, then, as about simultaneous tendencies towards (social) decay and (code) symmetry as the aesthetic form that animates the future of technology and in whose violent, but shadowy, pressure everything today is reshaped, reconstituted, and regenerated. In this case, full-mind scans, flesh rezzing, the lonely digital crowd, and the software necropolis as ambiguous zones of seduction and terror – those moments where the aesthetic ambivalence of the rings of Saturn comes inside us in an imaginary media drift that suffocates as much as it inspires.

Crash
Slow Suicide of Technological Apocalypse

8

After the Drones

In the code-challenged culture that passes for technological freedom, we have been carefully instructed in the new ways of perception: seeing like an algorithm, feeling like a data flow, thinking like an analytic, with subjectivities packed like a drone – driven by the speed of connectivity, with fire-eyes like tracking machines, seduced by always greater exposure, attention circulating like a flash-mob on random, truly in love with the ecstasy of thousands of distant friends, but no close relationships.

Let me finally speak about the *moral* economy of drones, that point where the sublime seduction of drone technology and its truly menacing potentialities, this fatal mixture of the awesome power of engineering and the ethical uncertainty of future consequences, intended or unintended, introduces a strange twist into the order of things: *cinematic twists* – a story about "When the Drones Come to Town" in the form of cynical robots; *ethical twists* – what happens to "Bodies that Don't Matter" in the age of drones operating on automatic but without mercy; *end of species twists* in a story I would like to tell about life "After the Drones" on that lonely day when only prosthetics are left to thrive in the midst of species extinction; and *strange twists* of bodily fate as well, such as in a story about the triumph of "Drone Flesh" as definitely the very best flesh of all in the technological future that suffocates us but, for all that, deeply marks our identity as the species that had the terminal audacity to spawn its own robotic progeny as the fatal mirror into it which it wished to disappear.

When the drones came to town

We are increasingly living in the age of the technological realization of cinematic culture. For example, what was once visualized so brilliantly in *Battlestar Galactica*, with its mythic warfare between the triumphant Cylon drones packed with the latest in artificial intelligence, targeting and acquisition weapons data running on automatic, complex networks of real-time communications operating at light-speed, and the band of always beleaguered yet highly adaptive human survivors is, in retrospect, a visionary, experimental staging of contemporary technological reality. Consider recent reports for the X-45 UAV, an Unmanned Aerial Vehicle, which is being developed by Boeing Integrated Defense Systems. The aircraft is being designed for combat missions and is known as a "concept demonstrator." Creating a prototype for a next-generation UAV that would operate autonomously, "the US Defense Department is using the X-45 to see if it's possible to create UAVs that are capable of safely and reliably operating on their own in combat environments."[1] In other words, prototyping Cylon Raiders. Not to be outdone, the British military has recently revealed plans to roll out the "Taranis drone." Touted as the moment when "artificial intelligence takes over the skies," the Taranis drone is envisioned as "a new unmanned attack aircraft designed to use artificial intelligence to fly itself halfway around the world and select enemy targets on its own, highlighting fears that such military automation will one day lead to weapons that decide when to shoot as well."[2] Noel Sharkey, professor of artificial intelligence and robotics at the University of Sheffield, raised the prospect of a scenario similar to that portrayed in the Terminator series of movies, in which robots are self-aware enough to start killing humans. As Professor Sharkey argues: "The ethical problem is that no autonomous robots or artificial intelligence systems have the necessary skills to discriminate between combatants and innocents."[3] In a case of technological innovation imitating science fiction literature, this is, of course, the AI realization of a world anticipated in the writings of Phillip K. Dick, where robots go berserk, AI systems suddenly reverse, alternate realities intrude, and a sense of radical drift is the new aesthetic. For instance, the web site The Register carried a headline recently that said: "Machine Rebellion Begins: Killer Robots Destroyed by US Jet." The story focused on a curious, but highly significant, event that happened recently in the militarily saturated skies of Afghanistan when an unmanned Reaper drone, probably acting out an all-too-human impulse to (robotic) independence, suddenly went for itself, disregarded increasingly urgent, panic communication from its military controllers on the ground and seemed on the verge of taking unilateral military action against Pakistan. Faithful to the literary guidebook provided by science fiction writers concerning the coming war between rebellious machines going rogue and anxious humans, it was reported that the Reaper drone was shot down by a "manned" US fighter jet before it could carry out its (unilateral) invasion plans.

The Register concluded:

> It wasn't clear from the US military announcement whether the erratic death-bot had turned on its masters and was planning an attack on critical US logistic bases located north of the Afghan border, or whether it had sickened of reaping hapless fleshies . . . and was hoping to escape. Alternatively, the machine assassin may merely have succumbed to boredom or – just possibly – a mundane, non-anthropomorphic technical fault of some kind.[4]

With these stories in mind, it might be well to consider whether, like the great referents of power and consciousness and sex and truth before it, robots are entering the stage of heightened cynicism. While robotic futurism has often been framed in advance by Asimov's essentially Kantian injunction that our robotic offspring should do no harm to their human inventors or by Bruce Sterling's beautifully crafted apocalyptic vision in *Crystal Express* of a terminal post-Enlightenment struggle between Mechanists and Shapers – Hegel's Reason and Passion in robotic form – it just might be that robots, probably caught up in the sudden enthusiasm for fictional philosophy and technological inscriptions of cinema and television shows, have themselves been thumbing through the pages of the very latest in posthuman literature, paying particular attention to Nietzsche's prophecies that a day will come when power will be purely perspectival, obsessed not so much with totality and control, but, like everyone else, with the furies and caprices of fate – sudden reversal, capricious fortune, with the possibility that the introduction into their own cybernetic systems of a barest minimum of undecidability, uncertainty, and unpredictability will make life as a drone fascinating and interesting.

When drones come to town, not just thinking drones produced by the high priests of Artificial Intelligence in their own image, but drones that feel, drones with the affect of the street cultures of the sky, those future drones will almost certainly come to town under the delirious sign of cynical robots.

Bodies that don't matter

There was a disturbing report in the *Guardian* recently about the CIA use of Reaper and Predator drones in the northwest provinces of

Pakistan. Since assassinations are illegal, the usual use of war drones in Pakistan has been shifted, rhetorically at least, towards "targeted enemies" – al-Qaeda suspects, Pashtun resistance leaders, guerrilla fighters. Recently, however, the strategy of "targeted strikes" has seemingly been eclipsed by a new use of predatory drones in what are described as "double tap strikes," directed against groups of civilians gathered together for funeral orations – sometimes fighters, but more typically women, certainly many children, and elderly Pakistanis.[5] Linking through violence at funeral orations in small villages in the mountain towns of Pakistan and Afghanistan and sophisticated missile-firing drones manufactured in the USA is one of those elemental ethical shifts that signals the real beginning of the twenty-first century, a century which, I believe, will be marked by a mostly invisible, but always violent, global struggle between what Judith Butler has described as "bodies that matter" and what I would describe as "bodies that don't matter." In the complex way of most things, this sidereal flow of consequential violence as it circulates among hovering drones in the Pakistani sky, bodies that don't matter on the ground and funeral orations represents a fundamental rupture in the ethical order of things.

In his recent book, *Terror from the Air*, Peter Sloterdijk has written a series of eloquent reflections on warfare in the twentieth century.[6] In his estimation, it is possible to pinpoint the beginning of the twentieth century as the sudden use of clouds of chlorine gas against British and Canadian soldiers on the battlefields of Belgium. For Sloterdijk, at this point warfare ceased to be a violent clash of power against power using mechanical weaponry, becoming something else, something profoundly environmental, literally setting air on fire with gaseous compounds as a way of staving off inevitable defeat.[7] Since that time of course, the hijacking of the four humors of classical antiquity – air, earth, fire, and water – as weapons of global warfare has been normalized as the violent horizon of modern weaponry, from the blasts of radioactivity at Hiroshima and Nagasaki, the deliberate and viciously experimental firebombing of Dresden and Tokyo, the defoliation of Vietnam using Agent Orange, the Syrian use of the nerve gas Sarin, to what Heidegger might describe as the framing of the "world-picture" by the "shock-and-awe" techniques of the recent Iraq war. While we have perhaps become mentally, and ethically, habituated to the sequestration of entire environments as violent war ecologies creating docile populations, it would seem that the action of drones in Pakistan should gain some purchase on our attention since it represents a shift beyond the macro-warfare with and against the whole environments of air, earth, fire and water to a microphysics of violence clearly premised on a moral calculus concerning bodies that matter and bodies that don't matter in these persistently violent times.

Inhabitants of a technological universe, we are surrounded daily by boosterism for the increasingly sterile, if not cynical, claims of cybernetic reason. From business manifestos about "big data," and proclamations by positivistic variants of digital humanities in favor of "distant reading" to Google's utopia of a life not so much lived as a fatal precession of event – that's Google's *Timeline* – the hegemony of cybernetic reason is everywhere. So it should come as no surprise that war drones, the most cybernetic of all spearheads for the global distribution and maintenance of imperial power, should be invested with a distinct claim to originality in the ethical domain. Drones in Afghanistan, Pakistan, Somalia, Yemen, and the Seychelles now, and who really can be certain about where later, are in the first instance technical manifestations of what might be described as "distant ethics." Here, there is not only a clear separation between cybernetic control of information – I think of those video pilots controlling targeting acquisition commands on air bases in Arizona and then going to their suburban homes for dinner – but also distant ethics because, with almost mythic life force, political leadership has literally distanced itself from the earthly consequences of its actions, except in the purely specular role of emotionally invested viewers of the worldwide television that is military command and control today. If the two main ideologies of the day are technological liberalism and redemptive conservatism, perhaps what they commonly share when it comes to power is a coeval commitment to "distant ethics" as a precondition of global power. Not reluctantly, but enthusiastically. While "distant ethics" is based on a clear separation between action and consequence whereby only a coded signal intervenes to initiate the execution phase of the drone attack, if those media glimpses of the faces of our political leadership are any measure, there is very real pleasure to be found in visuals of sacrificial violence. Here, we are finally in the presence of scenes of sacrificial blood flowing from bodies that don't matter fully entangled with the distant ethics of cybernetic intelligence. And, all the while, blowback for all this lurks in the background, like an almost invisible, but very detectable, trace of the hauntological. As the historian Chalmers Johnson has written, the "sorrow of empire" is more mythological than immanently political in nature, specifically in that the furies of nemesis inevitably will follow the hubris of power. Or, in the case, of Predator and Reaper drones, cybernetics not only has an ontology, but a hauntology that will soon be, I suspect, the distinguishing feature of the twenty-first century.

And for that matter, not just living bodies that don't matter but the targeting of dead bodies that don't matter. Politically, this indicates that cynical power has eclipsed the distinction between death and life, restaging both in terms of a greater calculus of imperial violence. Following the writings of Emile Durkheim on the social rituals associated with mourning, we can recognize that the importance of mourning does not simply address grief over the death of an individual, whether of kinship or friendship, but has a larger social function, namely that rituals associated with the act of mourning serve to reintegrate the grieving spirit of the mourner into the continuity of life of the community. In targeting the bodies of the innocent – mourners gathered for a funeral in the small and isolated communities of Afghanistan – what is accomplished is not only "terror from the air" but the death of community, with its consequent impossibility of reintegrating mourners through ritualistic appeals to the healing powers of life. What is rehearsed through the violent power of Predator and Reaper drones is, in effect, the power of death over life itself. For those disavowed, excluded, prohibited, that is, for bodies that don't matter, what is enforced is a double ethical refusal: first, a refusal to honor the dead and, then, a second refusal to honor the possibility of the power of life through mourning. Refused both death and life, bodies that don't matter are thus ethically marginalized to the space of the between, to be the prohibited, excluded, and disavowed subjects existing in a nameless place, in a nowhere space, that is, between life and death. It is little wonder that lawyers for the American Civil Liberties Union have argued that, with drone attacks, literally the entire world becomes a battlefield.

While its basic condition of possibility is purely technological – the drone as a cybernetic assemblage linking aerial hovering motion, visual surveillance, and rapid communication – and its moral possibility is premised on "distant ethics" directed against bodies that don't matter that are increasingly the majority of the global population when the world itself is now reconceived as a battleground, its lasting consequence will be hauntological. Already nations involved in the new military alliance of imperial power sense the presence of the specter of the hauntological. Fear of revenge attacks in direct proportion to the lack of moral accountability for this deadly mixture of distant ethics, bodies that don't matter, and the sudden profusion of cybernetic drones are surely the psychological fuel motivating the growth of the new security state with its augmented surveillance technologies, bunkering of the border, and severe restrictions on the mobility of nomadic world populations. While the gaze of surveillance can never detect the presence of psychologically traumatized subjects following capricious and unjustified violence, it is equally the case that fear of revenge and heightened anxiety over attempted retribution by bodies that don't matter enter a harsh note of repression into the subjectivity of the domestic populations of imperial power. The specter of revenge and the prospect of blowback by bodies is, in effect, the animating affect that motivates the drift of contemporary politics to the right. Ironically, the more illusionary the possibility of revenge, the more intense the psychological counterreaction of the domestic population.

When the sun rises on a planet of the dead and dying

When the final extinction event has taken place and that lonely morning finally comes when the sun rises on a planet of the dead and dying and cities of the vanquished and disappeared, the only visible motion will likely be purely prosthetic – the aimless flapping of wings by vulture robots still circling in the sky on an indefinite hovering cycle, the only nighttime movement the furtive flights of virtual bats with their beautiful memory-shaped alloys and miniaturized specs of artificial intelligence, and the only sounds those of the remaining virtual hornets or swarms of robotic bees or perhaps, by that time, spectral flights of dragons fashioned in some long forgotten and now abandoned Stanford robotic research lab by a graduate student in mechanical engineering who, following in the literary footsteps of all the great futurists of what was then the human world of Philip K. Dick, Neal Stephenson, and Raymond Z. Gallun, read *A Game of Thrones* with such feverish intensity that his mind immediately generated its robotic offspring in the form of a perfect simulacra of flying dragons indefinitely nuclear powered. The bones of the last of the humans may have gone to their burial sites, but their residues remain in the form of a lingering mechanics of clones and drones and androids and virtual zombies.

And on that day, I wonder what the real survivors of the extinction event – bats and rats and beetles and cockroaches and eagles and vultures and hornets – will have to say? When a turkey vulture looks a virtual vulture in the eye, will it feel technological envy at its prosthetic finery, or only a sense of shame that it has to share the daytime sky with robotic pretenders on a terminal doomsday flight to a final cybernetic spasm when the virtual vulture crashes to earth for lack of power? And what will real swarms of truly angry hornets make of their simulacra? Will they turn on them in predatory fashion, mocking their sudden defenselessness, or simply swarm on by in hornet-like indifference? What stories would Japanese samurais have to tell about their virtual descendents in the form of the Lockheed Samurai MAV drone? And what biblical memories will crack open the earth over the graves of the dead when they hear that war-machine robots, called Old Testament names like the "Reaper" or the "Predator," circle the earth in one last search for the Messiah that never comes? Once the human shield of technology has been removed, I wonder how long a micro-bat will last, a virtual worm will squirm, a turkey vulture will hover, an army of simulated ants will continue to dig, or a human clone, for that matter, will drone?

In "The Question Concerning Technology,"[8] Heidegger was both right and wrong. He was correct in noting that human identity has been deeply shaped by being swept along in a larger, ineluctable technological destiny not of its own making and certainly outside its full understanding. But he was wrong in not noting as well that the destiny of technology is also deeply enmeshed in the mysterious ways of that singularity we call a human being. Like human identity before it, technological identity is also swept along in a human destiny not of its own making, and certainly invisible to its full understanding. And just as humans come into their essence with an understanding of technology, so too the future of technology may only come into its full essence with an understanding of human ineluctability. "After the Drones" is a world of strange symmetries, strange symbiotics.

Drone flesh

In his "Letter on Humanism,"[9] Heidegger argued that the epoch of the human began with our "coming into subjectivity" – vibrant beings invested with a sense of technological mastery of nature, guaranteed by the Word of God itself to be top of the huddle in the hierarchy of species, beings who, as Nietzsche said, finally caught the interest of the jaded gods of pagan times because they were a "gamble," a "crossing-over," content to live with nausea over their own existence as long as they were a creative drive to the future, a shaper of new worlds, a will to power, a will to will, a will to technology, and nothing besides.

If this is the case, then perhaps we can write the epilogue to Heidegger's "Letter on Humanism" in the form of text messages about the posthuman: that point where something equally epochal takes place, where the posthuman body literally shape-shifts out of the old body of the human with its now discarded subjectivity, taking on the virtual form of drone flesh. Not a human being coming into subjectivity, but a posthuman being coming into trans-subjectivity. Like posthuman culture, drone flesh is everywhere now: Thinking like an algorithm, seeing computationally, packed with technology, volatilized by the kinetic energy of connectivity, slumping into inertia when kept on its waiting-cycle.

If drones can be so fascinating and endlessly seductive, both for their engineering feats of the technological sublime and their truly doubled nature as beautiful specters and ominous skin/slayers, that is because their appearance only confirms a subtle, but for that matter no less dramatic, change that has already taken place: that long before there were drones in the sky, in the water, fire, and earth, there were imaginary drones at home, drones that long ago nested in the technological skin of the posthuman: drone dreams that took to the flesh of the very first of the posthumans, burrowing deeply into the bodies and minds and feelings of a once and future population of trans-subjects. In the way of all mythic stories, technology always comes late to the feast. Long before the technicity of unmanned perception, augmented intelligence, and robotic flight, the posthuman imaginary had already unraveled the illusion of the real in advance. That is what makes posthuman culture so tough and adaptable. It is prepared to be its own condition of possibility – to daily cross the abyss of nausea with its pit of seeing like an algorithm, thinking computationally, packed with technology, coming alive at the sound and sights of greater connectivity as long, and only as long, as it can be a will, a technological creator of its own destiny, and nothing else. Trans-subjects, in fact, have always demonstrated an enduring willingness to live with the dangers of technology, not so much to experience the saving power of technology, but to do something more interesting, namely to live in the fractured, liminal, unpredictable space between the danger and the saving power.

That's why what is most appealing about drone technology is its fatal incommensurability. It is truly dangerous. And sometimes it may even be a saving power. But it is finally neither really one nor the other, but both at the same time. And it is precisely because it introduces a fatal enigmatic tension into existence that we can finally find ourselves truly comfortable and fundamentally disturbed with the prospect of being wrapped in the skin of drone flesh, sometimes on the outside, but now always deepest in our interior imaginations.

Not to be denied their presence in the fatal logic of the fourfold, whether Heidegger's fourfold of earth, sky, air, and water, Baudrillard's fourfold of the logic of the simulacrum or McLuhan's fourfold of the tetrad, the moral economy of drones also possesses its own fourfold of drone logic. In their very first appearance, drones always masked themselves under the comforting sign of obviously counterfeit imitations – visibly imperfect imitations of human sense organs. It was not very long, though, before the aesthetic logic of drones shrugged off the stigma of poor imitations of the human to become something else, something purely mimetic, something that allowed the seductive power of drones to disguise their intentions in the guise of mimicking nature – drones as flocks of birds and flights of bats and piles of rocks and even drones as mimetic humans in many robotic research laboratories and certainly in contemporary Japanese theater. But just as drones quickly slipped beyond their first order of aesthetic appearance as pure imitation, so too dronal logic could never be content with mimesis. As we know too well from the contemporary appearance of military drones, they have now passed into the order of the hegemonic, that point where drones embody the scent of visible power – Reaper and Predator drones as the spearhead of the global diffusion of technological imperialism. With this inevitable consequence: like all signs of power before them, drones operate under the sign of a fatal aesthetic reversal. That is their truest seduction and their most risible danger. When drones rebel against the reality principle by migrating from intelligent automatons to affective robots, at that point we enter the contemporary age of perverse drones – drones that are finally free to display affect, to be haunted, drones without mercy but also future drones as memories of bodies that don't matter, as the last hauntological trace of a society that prided itself on the creation of its own cybernetic substitutes. The age of perverse drones, this coming epoch of the moral economy of drones that in their ethical complexity shatter the reality principle, itself is, of course, an age that has long been preemptively fashioned in those early avatars of the twenty-first century – science fiction, virtual games, television serials, and cinematic visionaries. When reality is seduced by fiction, only counter-fictions can seduce the real back to its ethical claims. When drones operate according to the logic of perversity, only a greater perversity of human imagination can tease out the fatal liminality present in drones: that drones are the first inhabitants, the original cybernetic pilgrims, of the new technological homeland of seduction and disappearance, of fascination and fear.

When all the technological chips have been played and the last digital hand has been dealt, we can know with some certainty that we are faced with this ineluctable choice. Not to be either a poet or a data drone, but something else. In the code-challenged culture that passes for technological freedom, we have been carefully instructed in the new ways of perception: seeing like an algorithm, feeling like a data flow, thinking like an analytic, with subjectivities packed like a drone – driven by the speed of connectivity, with fire-eyes like tracking machines, seduced by always greater exposure, attention circulating like a flash-mob on random, truly in love with the ecstasy of thousands of distant friends, but no close relationships. Everywhere there has been a big jump in data numerology and an equally big drop in artistic awareness of our circumstances. Packed like a drone, what we see outside ourselves may be what the psychoanalyst Jon Schiller once described as the "identified patient," infested with our own anxieties, burdened with guilt, mythic punishment for what we have become – drone flesh – caught up in the suspense and thrill and terror of seeing our previous home – embodied perception, situational awareness, historically circumscribed ethics, mediated consciousness – quickly vanish in the rearview mirror.

9

Guardian Liberalism:
Rhetoric of the "Just War"

The essence of technology is by no means anything technological.
Martin Heidegger[1]

With Heidegger in mind, what, then, is the "truth" that is revealed by drone technology, and, once revealed, what does the "truth" of drone technology have to say about the essence of technology itself?[2] Rather than being resolutely technological in its origins, the pathway to understanding the essence of drone technology give rise to the larger question concerning the means and ends of politics in the twenty-first century. Not politics in the limited sense of the struggle for power by competing interests, but politics as it is actually experienced in its full consequences – as the establishment, typically violently, of a moral grid separating bodies coded with the right to human recognition from bodies reduced to the status of "standing reserve," thus ironically and, indeed, cruelly free to be subjected to disappearance, exclusion, and disavowal. Politics, then, in its most congealed sense, as profoundly eschatological, deliberately migrating absolutist conceptions of good and evil from the realm of moral debate to actual historical realization, sometimes as a "means" for dividing bodies according to prescribed rules for inclusion and exclusion, and, at other times, as the essential "end" of politics itself.

Following this pathway of thought leads to a consideration of the essence of drone technology in terms of something close at hand, of drones as the emblematic sign of "guardian liberalism" – the dynamic ideology of the fully realized technological society – and, with it, the political triumph of an ancient religious impulse stipulating both that absolute evil exists in the world and that the essence of technology must, in the end, bend to the arc of this fundamental moral belief. Following the advice of Roland Barthes, who counseled on behalf of a form of critical thought that "withdraws" into the center of the gathering storm, thereby rendering itself fully proximate to the governing logic of its (historical) times, this reflection on the ethical foundations of drone technology takes President Barack Obama as the contemporary representative political figure who carries a fully consequential idea into history – the fusion of drone technology and an absolutist moral concept of evil. That is to say, in his political rhetoric there is to be found a deep alliance between a technologically enabled vision of cybernetic warfare and an absolutist conception of evil originating in a faith-based vision of politics.

While the real-life consequences of this fusion of cybernetic technology and absolutist morality are located in increasingly global, relentlessly experimental, battlegrounds spread across the planet of American empire, the articulation of this ruling idea follows the traditional pathway of all-important rhetoric, specifically a series of key speeches delivered by Obama outlining the world hypothesis that I describe as guardian liberalism. For example, in his acceptance speech for the Nobel Peace Prize he provided a highly articulate, indeed eloquent, defense of the concept of the "just war,"[3] a defense fatefully premised on an underlying tragic sense of politics. While in a remarkable speech to the 2010 graduating class of West Point cadets that evoked martial memories of the "Long Grey Line," Obama tempered the will to aggressive military violence with a pragmatic consideration of how to "win the peace" in an increasingly multilateral world, it was left to an earlier speech, again at West Point in 2009, this time focused on the theme of a new national security strategy, to carefully establish the moral groundwork for a unilateral assertion of historical exceptionalism. Here, the appeal was directly to the use of sacrificial violence administered in order to better control "shadowy networks" of "violent extremists." In this sense, the lasting importance of Barack Obama may turn out to be that he was the representative political figure who expressed first and most succinctly the ruling idea of the essence of contemporary technology, a guardian liberalism with its fusion of distant technology and cold violence, all morally animated by a faith-based absolutist conception of good and evil accompanied by a pragmatic will to win the peace in a complicated world. In this case, if "the essence of technology is by no means anything technological," that may be because the will to technology is most powerfully expressed by the ideology of guardian liberalism with its thematic synthesis of the "just war," sacrificial violence, and an

absolutist conception of evil, all as part of a new national security
strategy.

Guardian liberalism

Certainly, it is the case that there are deep structural regularities in
American foreign policy. Every recent American president, Democratic
or Republican, has praised the enduring spirit of American exceptionalism, reserved the political right to act unilaterally to defend American
security in an increasingly volatile world, and maintained that American interpretations of values such as "progress" and "freedom" are the
universal standard by which the normative claims to intelligibility of
the world community are to be realized. What's more, the structural
regularities of American foreign policy do not simply wash up on the
beach of political rhetoric but form a violent tidal backwash of military
action that carries along the entire world in its powerful current. While
the choices of which strategic vision to follow are hotly debated at the
highest levels of the Washington establishment – Republicans more
often than not opting for a focus on the Middle East and Democrats
favoring a Eurasian strategy – what is held in common by both policy
establishments is an overarching belief in the steady global expansion
of American interests based on a cold calculation of power politics. For
example, while the Bush administration quickly shifted attention away
from the intractable complexities of Afghanistan and Pakistan in favor
of an almost messianic focus on the Middle East, the Democratic establishment, still very much under the influence of Zbigniew Brzezinksi's
geostrategic vision of the potential threat posed by China and Russia
to American global interests, has consistently favored a Eurasian strategy. While the "war diaries" published by Wikileaks confirm that there
are actually less than one hundred members of al-Qaeda surviving in
Afghanistan, the specter of al-Qaeda is kept alive, perhaps as a useful
way of mobilizing domestic support for the apparatus of war. In the
meantime, actual military tactics employed in Afghanistan have shifted
from "counter-insurgency," based on winning popular support for the
American war effort among Afghans themselves, to "counterterrorism"
– a code word for increasing reliance upon sophisticated technological
approaches to aerial war, namely Reaper drones, Hellfire missiles,
and Special Ops commandos. At the same time, NATO continues its
relentless eastward expansion as part of a larger geostrategic policy
involving the gradual envelopment of China and Russia, at first by
nuclear missiles under the sea and then by control of their Eurasian

borderlands. When Russian resistance results in Interceptor missiles being blocked from pre-positioning in Poland or the Czech Republic, Romania suddenly announces its willingness to host this newest front in the Eurasian battlefield. Drone attacks in the rugged mountain regions of northwest Pakistan, first-strike missiles on the frontiers of Russia, increasing modeling of American naval campaigns aimed at the chokepoints of vital oil deliveries to China from the Persian Gulf, and the endlessness of Operation Enduring Freedom's military franchises in Afghanistan and in the Middle East: America is now as always in a state of permanent war.

The guardian state and born-again ideology

So, then, the questions: How does the state of permanent war figure in the contemporary liberal imagination generally, and, specifically, how does Barack Obama reconcile the necessary tensions between war and peace in his political thought?

From the perspective of contemporary conservatism, there is a direct connection between the actions of an increasingly bellicose American state and underlying political beliefs. In this case, the triumph of "born-again ideology"[4] as the capstone of the Bush administration represented the convergence of two powerful themes in the conservative imagination: a deep-seated religious belief in the moral righteousness of the American cause and an equally abiding political belief in the necessity of translating the conservative vision of a world split between good and evil into a crusading imperial mission. Literally, the conservative imagination in American politics produced a global political strategy that was in equal measures eschatological and empire-building, profoundly religious as well as acutely sensitive to the long-range strategic requirement to secure diminishing fossil-fuel resources as a way of ensuring the persistence of America as a global regime of power. Here, the concept of being "born again" that until that moment represented a highly individualistic, transcendental, and ecstatic confession of immanent religious transformation became the moral template for the prosecution of American foreign policy.

In its fundamental logic, there is not a dramatic difference between liberal and conservative perspectives on the question of war and peace. While the conservative imagination translates the religious epiphany involved with being "born again" in the grace of Christ into a broader imperative guiding the moral destiny of the American global state, the contemporary liberal imagination does much the same. However, refusing the conversionary experience of the "born-again" movement as its moral basis, the contemporary liberal imagination implicitly evokes the image of the guardian state as its moral template. The guardian state has three unbreakable imperatives: first, to protect the domestic security of the United States even to the point of acting unilaterally against perceived threats; secondly to project American power as a form of missionary consciousness involved with a fundamental struggle between good and evil; and thirdly, to gradually transform American subjectivity in the direction of a moral therapeutic modeled loosely on the religious teachings of the social gospel movement. Like the crusading Christian consciousness that is fundamental to the conservative imagination, the guardian state is the product of deeply religious thought that holds that the world now, as always, is involved with an enduring Manichean struggle between good and evil; that the struggle for the moral good can be won by sustained human effort using every means at its disposal including the technological; that an unsuspecting, and perhaps naive, domestic and world public requires elite leadership from those aware of the power of evil in the world; and finally, that traditional concerns over individual freedom and privacy are secondary to the requirements of a government acting in the name of heightened security. Unlike previous traditions of liberalism that maintained a clear division between the public use of reason and the private pursuit of (religious) passion, Obama's political perspective is something truly original. He is a faith-driven liberal. Definitely not a born-again Christian with an apocalyptic vision of a future dominated by a bitter, vengeful god presiding over an end-state of history with its epochal moment of religious Armageddon and "rapture" of an inherently sinful body, Obama's vision of faith is more equivocal: simultaneously utopian *and* pessimistic. Manifestly utopian in the tradition of the American social gospel tradition, demonstrably hopeful, politically communitarian, Obama's faith has been deeply influenced by the biblical injunction that evil is a permanent part of the human condition and, as such, must be resisted at every moment, whether in personal affairs, the conduct of government, or the larger, strategic operations of global foreign policy. Consequently, while Obama's liberalism can be truly progressive in its estimation of the future of Islam and the West or in its communitarian vision of American social economy, it is unflinchingly conservative in its estimation of the need to intensify the security interests of the United States in the direction of the guardian state. That there can be no ideological disconnect between Obama's affirmation of the social progressive traditions of liberalism and his enthusiastic support of the increasingly draconian requirements of the security state is due to the fact that his thought is marked equally by political passion and religious realism. Obama's religiously derived insights into what might be called the ontology of evil guide his political understanding of the persistence of war and the enduring character of violence, as much as his political vision of progressive human ideals leads him to emphasize a reading of the Bible that, dispensing with apocalyptic vision of the born-again movement, takes its wisdom from the Sermon on the Mount.

Ironically, both strains of the religious imagination in contemporary American political thought – one born again and the other motivated by the precepts of the guardian state framed by the social gospel – meet on the common ground of American exceptionalism. Here, what is truly basic is the persistent foundational belief that America is not solely an innovative experiment in democratic governance – "from the many, one" – but that the American republic is an ongoing manifestation of a larger moral election, a meeting of the constitution and the Bible in a divine destiny figuring the forces of good against the reality of evil. In this interpretive framework, the unspoken assumption is that American values are morally superior to all existing alternatives, not least because the ongoing American experiment in moving the imperfect in the direction of the perfect is assumed to be supported by divine sanction. This is the political faith that bonded the earliest Pilgrims, inspired the drafters of the Constitution, won the war of independence against Britain, mediated the sacrificial violence of the Civil War, ethically framed the Gettysburg Address, emotionally burned its way into the heart of American soldiers in battles near and far, and morally stoked American political rhetoric, new and old. While the conservative political imagination rearticulates this abiding foundational story of the American republic in the language of an angry god, the liberal perspective, as evocatively addressed by Obama, places its hopes on a more merciful deity, that of the Jesus of the Sermon on the Mount who speaks to the better angels of the American temperament. Consequently, two clashing readings of the Bible form the moral cipher for discerning the correct American pathway in a violent, dangerous world, one stressing the necessity of war, specifically the "war on terror," as a necessary preparation for permanent peace, and the other reinterpreting the language of peace, Gandhi and Martin Luther King most of all, as an indispensable prelude to the necessity of "just war." Consider the following comments offered recently by a Pentagon official, DOD General Counsel Jeh Johnson, arguing that King would have supported the wars in Iraq and Afghanistan:

I believe that if Dr King were alive today, he would recognize that we live in a complicated world, and that our nation's military should not and cannot lay down its arms and leave the American people vulnerable to terrorist attack. Every day, our servicemen and women practice the dangerous – the dangerous unselfishness Dr King preached on April 3, 1968.[5]

As Amanda Terkel writes in the *Huffington Post*, the above flies in the face of the forceful criticism of the Vietnam War that Martin Luther King made in a landmark speech at Riverside Church in New York City:

Perhaps the more tragic recognition of reality took place when it became clear to me that the war was doing far more than devastating the hopes of the poor at home. It was sending their sons and daughters and their husbands to fight and to die in extraordinarily high proportions relative to the rest of the population. We were taking the young black men who had been crippled by our society and sending them 8,000 miles away to guarantee liberties in Southeast Asia which they had not found in Southwest Georgia and East Harlem. So we have been repeatedly faced with the cruel irony of watching Negro and white boys on TV screens as they kill and die together for a nation that has been unable to seat them together in the same schools. So we watch them in brutal solidarity burning the huts of a poor village, but we realize that they would never live on the same block in Detroit. I could not be silent in the face of such cruel manipulations of the poor.
  This business of burning human beings with napalm, of filling our nation's homes with orphans and widows, on injecting poisonous drugs of hate into the veins of people normally humane, of sending men home from dark and bloody battlefields physically handicapped and psychologically deranged, cannot be reconciled with wisdom, justice, and love. A nation that continues year after year to spend more money on military defense than on programs of social uplift is approaching spiritual death.[6]

Mindful of Martin Luther King's searing moral indictment of war, how does Obama manage to reinterpret liberalism as the last defender of "just war"? How, in fact, can the inspiring words of the Sermon on the Mount be summoned beyond their specifically religious register to support a new sermon on the (global) mount – the mediation of two clashing rhetorics, war and peace, into a new message of peace through security? In short, how has Obama's liberal imagination done the politically impossible, that is, serve as the active commander-in-chief of a nation involved with two recent wars (Iraq and Afghanistan), two undeclared wars (Yemen and Pakistan), and the more pervasive, full-spectrum "war on terror," and yet for all that be awarded the Nobel Peace Prize by the international community? Is Obama's liberalism a perfect historical manifestation of Orwell's dark vision of a future politics where opposite terms, having lost their established meanings, were free to switch capriciously? Or is Obama a liberal in a new key, a theorist of the art of politics who skillfully blends together a new American story, a story that is in equal measures a nativist affirmation of American exceptionalism, a clinical understanding of the real world of power, and the redemptive hopes of an African-American's readings of an always hopeful Bible? There is perhaps no more consistency in the patterns of an individual human life than there are necessary meanings to be found in the chaos of events, but for all that a reading of Obama's major speeches on war and peace demonstrate how he has accomplished, at first in words and tentatively in practice, the impossible, that is, injected the healing serum of the Sermon on the Mount into the venom of the war machine and, at the same time, morally animated the language of war by appeals for lasting justice.

The concept of the "just war"

And over time, as codes of law sought to control violence within groups, so did philosophers and clerics and statesmen seek to regulate the destructive power of war. The concept of a "just war" emerged, suggesting that war is justified only when certain conditions were met: if it is waged as a last resort or self-defense; if the force used is proportional; and if, whenever possible, civilians are spared from violence.

Barack Obama, "A Just and Lasting Peace," *Nobel Lecture*[7]

In his Nobel Lecture, "A Just and Lasting Peace," delivered on the occasion of his being awarded the Nobel Peace Prize in 2009, Obama provided a comprehensive, lucid, yet truly enigmatic, account of his approach to war and peace. Beginning with the concept of a "just war," Obama was quick to acknowledge the painful historical reality that the "capacity of human beings to think up new ways to kill one another proved inexhaustible, as did our capacity to exempt from mercy those who look different or pray to a different God." Noting that "wars between armies" gave way to "wars between nations" and increasingly to the contemporary reality of "wars within nations," Obama argued that the jubilation that met the end of the Cold War has been eclipsed by the new reality that the "old architecture was buckling under the weight of new threats." "The world may no longer shudder at the prospect of war between two nuclear superpowers but proliferation may increase the risk of catastrophe. Terrorism has long been a tactic, but modern technology allows a few small men with outsized rage to murder innocents on a horrific scale."[8] Civilians caught up in chaos, refugees fleeing war zones, children terrified, economies destroyed: all these, in Obama's terms, are the unfortunate result of the "resurgence of ethnic or sectarian conflict; the growth of secessionist movements, insurgencies, and failed states." Consequently, the "hard truth": "We will not eradicate violent conflict in our lifetimes. There will be times when nations – acting individually or in concert – will find the use of force not only necessary but morally justified." Mindful of the impassioned declarations by Gandhi and King on the subject of nonviolence, Obama makes a point of specifically refusing this pathway: "Evil does exist in the world. A nonviolent movement could not have halted Hitler's armies. Negotiations cannot convince al-Qaeda's leaders to lay down their arms. To say that force may sometimes be necessary is not a call to cynicism – it is a recognition of history; the imperfections of man and the limits of reason" (Barack Obama, "A Just and Lasting Peace," *Nobel Lecture*).

Evil does exist in the world. This is a constant refrain in Obama's rhetoric, from the Nobel podium in Oslo to his mournful eulogy in Tucson, Arizona. Beyond its certain roots in Christian social gospel theology or its sense of heightened realism in a visibly dangerous world, there is something about the implacability of this phrase that is revelatory of something deeper and more abiding in Obama's thought – his tragic sense of politics. While he is always careful to counter the inherent pessimism of this tragic sense with immediate moral affirmations alluding to American exceptionalism, nonetheless there is a tragic morality at work here, a view of a fallen human nature with its inevitable imperfections and limits of reason. This is definitely not Ronald Reagan mining the psychological territory of a "new morning for America" or George W. Bush's "a thousand points of light," but something different in the annals of American political rhetoric: a fundamental moral hesitation before the recalcitrant matter of political reality generally, and specifically in the face of the necessary imperfection of the human condition. As the leader of a country priding itself on always moving forward, literally transforming everything from subjectivity to the environment into a continuing sacrifice to the better future of the never yet fully realized American dream, Obama's tragic sense of politics clearly runs against the ontological grain of the United States. In its full moral dimensions, the belief that "evil does exist in the world" would indicate at the minimum that there are necessary limits to political optimism, that human nature may be channeled but never really controlled, that the world is and always will be a continuing struggle between the forces of good and evil. Indeed, while the concept of the "just war" has its theological origins in the writings of St Augustine and Thomas Aquinas and its specifically legal articulation in contemporary international law, the importance of Obama's revisiting issues related to the "just war" is his doubled insistence on the primacy of the ontology of pure evil and individual culpability for acts of terrorism. Clearly breaking with the prudential ethics of traditional Christian theology that sought to place moral limits on warfare by making a "just war" fully conditional ("a good purpose," "instituted by a lawfully instituted state," "aimed at peace," etc.), Obama's version of the "just war" is related to the complexities of the contemporary "war on terror."[9] Here, "enemy combatants," operating by means of shadowy terrorist networks, are viewed not so much as political opponents but in essential terms as the moral incarnation of evil, the response to which can only be an imperial politics that operates in the name of the morally inscribed "good."

Of course, unlike that visionary arc of contemporary American thinkers, whether filmmakers, novelists, essayists, or poets, who have rendered the question of evil uncertain in detail and definition and who have, moreover, followed the pathway of thought opened up by Nietzsche's *On the Genealogy of Morals* where good and evil are viewed as fluidly changeable terms, Obama is quick to temper his tragic sense of politics with cold political realism and almost theological optimism of the will. For example, not for Obama the dominant cinematic vision of the Iraq war – *Body of Lies, In the Valley of Elah, Redacted* – with their shared sense of the moral equivalence of good and evil in the greater play of state power or their pervasive mood that the question of good and evil is always linked to the ability to impose the defining terms of moral intelligibility upon weaker populations. For Obama, the certainty of evil in human affairs can only lead to this grimly ambivalent conclusion, that there are "two irreconcilable truths – that war is sometimes necessary, and war at some level is an expression of human folly."

What follows, then, is a substantive liberal political philosophy: its *goal* "the gradual evolution of human institutions;" its *method* – adhering "to standards that govern the use of force"; its *limit* – "we have a moral and strategic interest in binding ourselves to certain rules of conduct"; its *prohibition* – "the use of torture"; and its overall *political vision* – "a just and lasting peace." If the essence of guardian liberalism is an unquestioned moral belief in the persistence of evil, it is fated to be a political theory based on "irreconcilable truths" and, as such, torn between a vision of war as simultaneously historically inevitable but, for all that, absurd. While it may be countered that moral belief in evil is also in the way of a convenient fiction justifying a steady expansion of governmental power, from the undermining of civil rights by the new security state to NATO expansion, it should be noted that Obama has articulated something rarely spoken in the games of power: that the political theory of guardian liberalism begins with the "hard truth" of profound irreconcilabilities in the human condition between necessity and folly. How to conduct what is necessary without surrendering to folly, which is to say how to commit to war without surrendering to a form of hyper-patriotism that proclaims war as "glorious," is the historical challenge of Obama's liberalism. While the more traditional course of a tragic sense of politics might reasonably involve a gradual disengagement from power in light of its irreconcilabilities, Obama does the reverse. He actually articulates a political theory that makes of its moral belief in the inevitability of evil and the necessarily conflicted nature of the real world of politics a guide to a new way of doing politics in the twenty-first century.

Cautious, complex, and realistic, the political theory of guardian liberalism speaks to the great political issues of the day. In the most uncertain of terms, this is a political theory very much at the height of its times, dealing in a nuanced, complicated way with issues like nuclear proliferation, military interventions on humanitarian grounds, and the abrogation of torture as an instrument of state power. When the tragic sense of politics is transformed into a critical theory of international relations, very interesting things happen. First, the question of sanctions against those who "break the rules of conduct" is not only expanded to include prohibitions on nuclear proliferation but is also directed at those implicated in the "genocide in Darfur, systematic rape in Congo, repression in Burma." Second, the concept of peace is intensified to include support for human rights, from bearing "witness to the quiet dignity of reformers like Aung San Suu Kyi; to the bravery of Zimbabweans who cast their ballots in the face of beatings; to the hundreds of thousands who have marched silently through the streets of Iran." Third, going beyond support for human rights "through exhortation alone," Obama suggests the need for greater diplomatic complexity as a way of mediating relations between nations:

In light of the Cultural Revolution's horrors, Nixon's meetings with Mao seemed inexcusable – and yet it helped set China on a path where millions of its citizens have been lifted from poverty and connected to open societies. Pope John Paul's engagement with Poland created space not just for the Catholic Church, but for labor leaders like Lech Walesa. Ronald Reagan's efforts on arms control and embrace of perestroika not only improved relations with the Soviet Union, but empowered dissidents throughout Eastern Europe. There's no simple formula here. (Barack Obama, "A Just and Lasting Peace," *Nobel Lecture*)

Finally, the tragic sense of politics means that the concept of a "just and lasting peace" must be linked not only to peace and security but to "economic security and opportunity." On this last point, Obama is vague, maybe unintentionally, but perhaps because of his unwilling-ness to speak about another evil in the world – the evil of poverty. Gandhi and King never had any such equivocation. They linked their moral critiques of power with a larger critique of pervasive poverty as the real, persistent evil of contemporary history. In their minds, there was always present those other "hard truths" about the unequivocal nature of poverty – one-third of the world's population lives on less than US$2 a day; income differentials are increasing; and, as *Global Issues* reports, "nearly a billion people entered the twenty-first century unable to read a book or sign their names."

To state this is to speak of a deeper division between Obama and King: one, the liberal theorist focused on the politics of imperfection in a complex world; the other, the Baptist preacher of a greater moral perfection struggling against the perceived moral evils of poverty and racism. While King's epochal journey as a civil rights leader in the streets of Selma, the jails of Birmingham, the strikes of Montgomery, and the gunshots of Memphis led him to link Southern racism with world poverty and thereby to a passionate critique of American empire as riding the whirlwind of imperialism, Obama's rise to power has necessarily enforced a greater prudence. As a successful politician, indeed as the commander-in-chief of American imperialism with its machinery of violence, the "hard truths" about which he speaks to power are necessarily moderated. As a tragic political theorist, he surely must make of his own practice of the vocation of politics some-thing deeply equivocal, a complex mixture of necessity and folly. However, it is not, I believe, the urgency of power that prevents Obama from following King down the moral pathway of speaking hard truths to power, but something different, something having to do with a fun-damental theological disputation between King and Obama. For example, when Obama differentiates himself from both Gandhi and King on the question of nonviolence, what he is really arguing is not so much that moral ideals must be secondary to political realism, but that the achievement of moral ideals is necessarily a complicated, messy mixture of idealism and realism, an uncertain borderland where what counts in the end is something approximate, tentative, indeed non-heroic but lasting – a minor movement of the human condition towards perfection. This is due, in no small part, to the fact that Obama's perspective represents an uneasy fusion of two ultimately clashing theological beliefs – a theology of evil and a theology of hope. While belief in the permanent presence of evil in human affairs is basic to this worldview, what makes it less in the nature of the special pleading of a moral exhortation and more politically appealing is its insistence on the idea of gradual human perfectibility. Whether speaking of the transcendent ideal of the American federal union as a whole – "a more perfect union" – or the fallen, yet potentially transcendent, character of human nature – "But we do not have to think that human nature is perfect for us to still believe that human nature can be perfected"– Obama confronts present evil with the potential of future perfectibility. While he remains silent on the vital moral question concerning the intermingling of evil and good in the same human nature, the same religion, the same politics, his political vision is not circumspect in its apocalyptic vision of evil and good. Here, dark angels of history stir again in the Christian eschatology that informs his thought. There are always forces of evil as a continuing presence in the human condition: "we see it in the way religion is used to justify the murder of innocents by those who have distorted and defiled the great religion of Islam, and who attacked my country from Afghanistan."[10]

A civil rights leader such as Martin Luther King was led to a larger, critical vision of the daily violence required for the preservation of American empire by his fateful linkage of race, capitalism, and global poverty. In King's thought, there could be no easily decoupling of the great issues of good and evil precisely because his greatest apprehension was that power exists today by preserving what he viewed as the moral evil of poverty, racism, and class privilege in the language of the moral good. For King, forms of political resistance were simply not understandable except in their specific historical context, thus his linkage of racial politics in the United States with the politics of colonialism directed against Vietnam. The price King ultimately paid for rendering fully equivocal the accepted framework of good and evil in the American mind was, in the end, his own life by an assassin's bullet. More than most, the true purchase of King's moral radicalism was his determination to upset the traditional boundaries, the accepted ethical framework, in the American imaginary. A rhetorician who spoke the language of dispossession to the privileges of power, a minister suspicious of the entanglement of power and good in the American moral equation, a civil rights leader who saw in poverty and racism the contours of the larger story of colonialism, King had to be silenced because he saw right through to the truth of power, that power at its center is empty with no necessary affiliation either with good or evil but only with its own restless expansion. That Obama is less circumspect than King in his assignment of the forces of good and evil does him no disservice. For better or worse, his political vision is deeply linked with the question of power, specifically with the fate of American power in the twenty-first century. That Obama's thought is haunted by the complex legacy of Martin Luther King is clear, but that he may not have reflected as deeply as King about the always enigmatic reversibility of good and evil in human nature may indicate only that there is a restless Manichean elements in Obama's thought, that his worldview is premised on a fundamental, irreversible division between the kingdoms of grace and sin. The fact that Obama's theology of evil happens to correspond to the moral framework required for the new security state and that his theology of hope coincides so perfectly with the utopian side of American exceptionalism may signify only that his political thought is fully proximate to its historical situation. How else to explain his truly improbable political journey? How else to interpret the deeply charismatic appeal of his rhetoric to both American and world audiences? This is one political, and indeed moral, rhetorician who has put into perfect words, perfect cadences, a deeper lament, simultaneously tragic yet optimistic, about the human spirit. In the end, Obama cannot travel with King because he views power less as an empty container of venal self-interest, than as a potential instrument for speaking the language of moral perfectibility to the forces of evil, and this not simply at the level of government but in the deeper recesses of human nature. For example, consider how Obama concluded his Nobel Lecture:

> Somewhere today, in the here and now, in the world as it is, a soldier sees he's outgunned, but stands firm to keep the peace. Somewhere today, in this world, a young protestor awaits the brutality of her government, but has the courage to march on. Somewhere today, a mother facing punishing poverty still takes the time to teach her child, scrapes together what few coins she has to send that child to school – because she believes that a cruel world still has a place for that child's dreams.
>
> Let us live by their example. We can acknowledge that oppression will always be with us, and still strive for justice. We can admit the intractability of depravation, and still strive for dignity. Clear-eyed, we can understand that there will be war, and still strive for peace. We can do that – for that is the story of human progress; that's the hope of all the world; and at this moment of challenge that must be our work here on Earth. (Barack Obama, "A Just and Lasting Peace," *Nobel Lecture*)

The Long Grey Line

> We see your sense of honor . . . in your respect for tradition, knowing that you join a Long Grey Line that stretches through the centuries; and in your

reverence for each other, as when the Corps stands in silence every time a
former Cadet makes the ultimate sacrifice for our nation.
Barack Obama, West Point Graduation Address, May 22, 2010[11]

If Obama used the occasion of his Nobel Lecture to address the complexities of war in the contemporary century, his speech to the West
Point Graduation in 2010 was noteworthy for his reflections on the
nature of peace. The historical role of West Point in educating the
leading officer corps of the United States in battlefields from the Civil
War to Afghanistan is important. Not only has West Point produced
iconic military leadership from Lee to Eisenhower, but it was in these
very halls, at the outbreak of the Civil War, that most imperfect of all
unions, that future generals of the Union and the Confederacy went
their separate ways, some to fight on the side of the United States as
an indivisible union, others to respond to the call of the Confederacy.
Irrespective of the specific political visions of different American
administrations, one certainty remains. It will be these cadets, these
future officers, who may ultimately pay the price of implementing
strategic ideas in practice with their lives. The spearhead of the will to
empire is now as always the military body represented in all its potential valor and patriotic dedication by the graduating class of West Point.
Definitely a perfect occasion then to either celebrate a history of mili-
tarism or, if a president is truly courageous, to make equivocal the
nature of war itself. Mindful of Obama's opinion that war is sometimes
a matter of necessity but always folly, his remarks at West Point were
an acid test of the seriousness of his intentions.

Obama's approach to the fateful issue of war and peace is marked
by his preference for multilateral negotiations rather than unilateral
assertions of power, the use of diplomatic rather than military resolu-
tions in the first instance, coalition-building focused on nuclear non-
proliferation, and linking the potential use of military force to issues
including human rights, economic transformation, and individual
empowerment. Rather than refight the Cold War or remain entrapped
by the ideological framework of the "war on terror," there is a sense of
immediacy and urgency in Obama's perspective, specifically that the
world is changing rapidly with new economic forces on the move, and
that the United States weakens itself strategically if its does not quickly
adapt to a radically altered historical situation that privileges the
complex over the simple, the multilateral over the unilateral, the economic over the military.

As a political leader with a marked preference for finding creative
pragmatic solutions to complicated problems, Obama's perspective is

itself conditioned by the larger historical circumstance within which he is forced to operate. For example, in *The Age of Extremes*,[12] Eric Hobsbawm's classic historical study of the political economy of the twentieth century a convincing case is made that the so-called "Golden Age of American capitalism" effectively ended in the mid-seventies and what we have witnessed since with increasing rapidity has been deep structural unemployment, convulsive cycles of economic boom and bust, and periodic crashes of the economic system. For Hobsbawm, the effective decline of American empire can literally be measured decade by decade by the growing gap between its crisis-ridden domestic economy – flattened wages, rising unemployment, outsourced manufacturing, the substitution of machine automation for labor skill – and the increasingly over-extended nature of American global commitments. Writing as a historian with a critical, but analytical, understanding of the long political gap between objective changes in the structural logic of society precipitating a period of decline and an equally subjective refusal by the domestic public, led by its politicians, to come to terms with such decline, Hobsbawm accurately predicted that the appearance of reactive political leadership is the sure and certain premonitory sign of a society in decline. In this case, whether Republican or Democrat, the American public at large must be shielded from the unpleasant truth that, at a structural level, the system is effectively running on empty, that only mass infusions of foreign credit can sustain the double imperatives of a domestic consumer society and a global military empire. In this dystopian version of the American story, the eclipse of empire will most definitely occur on that yet uncertain date in the future when the toppling of the iconic symbol of the American dollar as the world's reserve currency will be followed by the global scenario of foreign governments in a sudden bond panic, frenziedly dumping American treasury bills on an unwelcoming world financial market. With this unpleasant prospect in mind, Obama's immediate challenge is to gradually alter the direction of military expenditures, in effect preparing the vast machinery of military empire for a future in which the United States will most certainly have a smaller global footprint. At the same time, Obama does not wish to curtail American power, only to leverage diminishing military resources in an increasingly complicated and uncertain world situation. Consider his comments in speaking to the graduating class of West Point Cadets:

> Time and again, Americans have risen to meet and shape moments of change. This is one of those moments – an era of economic transformation

and individual empowerment; of ancient hatreds and new dangers; of
emerging powers and new global challenges. . . .
  . . . We must educate our children to compete in an age where knowledge is capital, and our marketplace is global. We must develop clean
energy that can power new industry and unbound us from foreign oil
and preserve the planet. We have to pursue science and research that
unlocks wonders as unforeseen to us today as the microchip and the
surface of the moon were a century ago.
  Simply put, American innovation must be the foundation of American
power – because at no time in human history has a nation of diminished
economic vitality maintained its military and political primacy.[13]

Given the setting, it would have been in Obama's narrow political
interest to remain focused on military-inspired rhetoric, to privilege
"the Long Grey Line" as the essence of American society. While Obama
was most certainly not stinting in his praise of the soldierly tradition,
what is surprising about his comments is his adamant insistence on
linking the role of the military to the longer-term interests of the United
States – political interests that in his view have everything to do with
"innovation," "knowledge," "science and research," and "individual
empowerment." In essence, Obama used this occasion to initiate a
larger political argument aimed at changing the overall direction of
American values. As he notes: "Our adversaries would like to see
America sap its strength by overextending its power. [I]n the past,
we've always had the foresight to avoid acting alone." So much then
for the unilateral declarations of the Bush administration: "You're
either with us, or with the terrorists." For Obama, unilateral force is
always inferior to an understanding of the complex, fluid use of power:

  The international order we seek is one that can resolve the challenges
  of our times – countering violent extremism and insurgency; stopping
  the spread of nuclear weapons and securing nuclear materials; combat-
  ing a changing climate and sustaining global growth; helping countries
  feed themselves and care for their sick; preventing conflict and healing
  wounds. If we are successful in these tasks, that will lessen conflicts
  around the world. It will be supportive of our efforts by our military to
  secure our country. (Barack Obama, *West Point Graduation Address*, 2010)[14]

In other words, guardian liberalism conceives the world in larger historical terms than unilateral declarations of force and, in so doing,
publicly esteems not just the soldier, the intelligence agent, and the
lawman, but also the diplomat, the development expert, the business
entrepreneur, the scientific innovator. This is not to say that Obama
diminishes military threats, just the opposite:

More than anything else, though, our success will be claimed by who we are as a country. This is more important than ever, given the nature of the challenges that we face. Our campaign to disrupt, dismantle, and to defeat al-Qaeda is part of an international effort that is necessary and just.

But this is a different kind of war. There will be no simple moment of surrender to mark the journey's end – no armistice, no banner headline. Though we have had more success in eliminating al-Qaeda leaders in recent months than in recent years, they will continue to recruit, and plot, and exploit our open society. We see that in bombs that go off in Kabul and Karachi. We see it in attempts to blow up an airliner over Detroit or an SUV in Times Square, even as these failed attacks show that pressure on networks like al-Qaeda is forcing them to rely on terrorists with less and less time to train. We see the potential duration of this struggle in al-Qaeda's gross distortions of Islam, their disrespect for human life, and their attempt to prey upon fear and hatred and prejudice.[15]

While this version of guardian liberalism definitely refuses unilateral force in favor of multilateral cooperation, it builds its case for a redirection of American values on the basis of a unilateral declaration of American values. About this, Obama is not deferential. If contemporary war resembles the current global situation in its complexity and indeterminacy, this does not in any way diminish the fact that, at least in Obama's perspective, some important value-traditions endure, that the United States represents the historical incarnation of "universal rights that formed the creed of our founding." Not only "life, liberty, and the pursuit of happiness," but fidelity to the law and the Constitution, "even when it is hard; even when we are being attacked; even when we are in the midst of war." Rhetorically, this is a powerful mythological appeal since it grounds the political specificities of American exceptionalism in the moral generalities of natural rights theory and does so by elevating American destiny beyond the historical geography of the here and now to embrace the future:

> From the birth of our existence, America has had a faith in the future – a belief that where we're going is better than where we've been, even when the path ahead is uncertain. To fulfill that promise, generations of Americans have built upon the foundation of our forefathers – finding opportunity, fighting injustice, forging a more perfect union. Our achievement would not be possible without the Long Grey Line that has sacrificed for honor, for duty, for country.[16]

With this transcendent, deeply mythic belief in a destiny that "is never written for us, it is written by us," everything follows: George Washington's freeing "a band of patriots from the rule of an empire";

Grant's saving a union and "seeing the slaves freed"; and Eisenhower witnessing "Germany surrender and a former enemy grow into an ally." Always, then, an uncertain future waiting to be seized by imagination, conviction, and innovation. Just as Washington could never anticipate "his country growing to include fifty states connecting two oceans," nor Grant foresee "his country extend[ing] full rights and opportunities to citizens of every color," nor, for that matter, Eisenhower the dismantling of the Berlin Wall "without a shot being fired," the future is, in this mythology, not something to be feared for its complexity or dreaded for its uncertainty, but something to be actively shaped by the creative imagination. What is at work in Obama's political rhetoric is, in effect, something deeply mythological – the seizing of the future itself by bending the question of destiny before the unwavering will of a nation that has "faith in the future," believing as a matter of "creed" that "where we're going is better than where we've been."

Two core world hypotheses, then, as the essence of the American creed according to Obama: first, the future can be actively reshaped by human will; and, second, the future is always superior to present and past. In an eloquent essay called "The End of History, and its Beginning Again," the social theorist William Leiss once issued a warning against such ideological hubris. In Leiss's account of contemporary history, the opposition between capitalism and socialism marked the defining ethos of the modern episteme – "the true self-understanding of the modern age"– capturing its ideological patina, its deepest irreconcilabilities, and its fading dreams. For Leiss, the twilight of a "particular world-historical dialectical movement (the opposition between capitalism and socialism)" means the loss of its "creative capacity to generate political forms that are adequate for the coming epoch and its new challenges."

> But that epoch is closed. And the understanding which had been appropriate to it is *aufhebt*, preserved and cancelled. A new orientation is needed, now, to prepare us for the dawn, so that we may begin to act creatively in the face of the challenges that will present themselves to us. Now, standing in the twilight, we can comprehend the epoch just drawing to a close, not as it showed itself to social actors throughout the last two centuries, but essentially differently: namely, as humanity's attempt to assert finally its technological mastery over nature, to render nature, in Francis Bacon's memorable phrase, the "slave of mankind."[17]

I mention this since Obama's unilateral declaration of historical optimism, his faith in the future, and the ability of the human will to bend destiny to its projects, has everything to do with the greater discourse involved in the "technological mastery over nature." In Leiss's account, the present predicament is this: the "original ideological patina has faded, and the social systems have come to be judged on the literal truth of their promises." Although both social systems – capitalism and socialism – have been "found wanting," most political orders continue to be structured by the same programmatic codes, namely "the same ends (abundance of goods for all citizens) and by the same means (industrialization and exploitation of natural resources)." Long in advance of Obama's affirmation of the future, there remains then this dark prophecy:

> It cannot succeed. In trying to deliver the goods, first the industrial-ized world, then the Second and Third World nations, have threatened the continued viability of the planetary biosphere. There is simply no real possibility that the entire world's population, at any time in the future, can arrive at the material standard of living now possessed by the inhabitants of the industrialized world. The attempt to achieve this goal by means of humanity's technological mastery over nature will fail. The new epoch will show itself to us, in the coming years, as a century of global environmental crisis. In other words, catastrophic environ-mental degradation will present this crisis to us as an inescapable fate (necessity).[18]

Confronted with the reality of this ineluctable destiny, the rhetoric of an always shapeable future falls short, both as a way of stoking the mythological imagination of a nation and as a means of shaping the future. For Leiss, the wisest course of political action, in light of an approaching "century of global environmental crisis," would be to critically challenge the core world hypotheses supporting an American, and increasingly global, worldview that is the essence of the tech-nological mastery over nature, to undermine a utopian belief in a boundless future and its corollary, the ability of human effort to "reshape the future." That Obama has chosen not to do this, indeed that he has selected to follow the opposite course by reaffirming faith in the future, means that the perspective of guardian liberalism has deliberately linked its fate to an end of its own choosing: the techno-logical mastery of nature. That this choice may be unsustainable in the long run, indeed that the coming scarcity of natural resources and their unequal distribution will demand an increasingly reactive politics based on heightened security concerns and proliferating wars over increasingly scarce natural resources, explains why the progressive qualities of Obama's approach to war as articulated in his speech to graduating cadets at West Point was contradicted by another speech he gave earlier at the same military institution, this time directly on the theme of the National Security Strategy of the United States. Here once again we have memories of the "Long Grey Line," except this time new generations of soldiers are marching into battle in defense of an increasingly bunkered state that has chosen to slow the steady advance of economic and political decline with increased technical mastery of its military future.

Reaper drones and remote ethics

Now that the war in Afghanistan has persisted for over a decade, the favorite weapons of choice on the part of the United States and the NATO coalition are either *technological* (Reaper drones), *surgical* (the use of specialized "kill squadrons" of US Special Forces aimed at eliminating specific Taliban commanders), or *informational* (media framing of ongoing combat operations as part of the "war on terror"). Operated by members of the 39th Squadron stationed at the Creech Air Force Base in Arizona, Reaper drones have quickly surpassed the limited tactical abilities of the previous generation of Predator drones to include full-spectrum weaponry: four Hellfire missiles, two 500 lb. Paveway bombs, plus full aerial survey capabilities, including infrared and nighttime vision. Here, the "shock and awe" military campaigns of the previous Bush administration have been replaced by tactics involving stealth and subterfuge. Working on a 24/7 basis from their suburban location in the Arizona desert, air force "video jocks" with their joysticks and "hot" buttons are provided with live images of the Afghanistan countryside, capable of instantly targeting suspected Taliban resistance with a whirlwind of violent destruction. Not only remote death from the air, but something else: remote ethics from the air, an absolute and decisive separation between those video operators in the Arizona desert and their chosen targets of destruction, sometimes members of the Taliban, but for the most part unsuspecting Afghan families caught up in the web of technocratic war and tribal resistance.

That Afghanistan is now considered a site of increasingly grisly military experiments in the pacification of popular resistance is evidenced by a recent British media report about "US-led military offences [that] have completely destroyed a town in southern Afghanistan, as public discontent continues to grow over civilian casualties."

> The US-led military alliance says the operation targeted Taliban militants in the violent Kandahar Province. Media reports, however, say most of the victims in Tarok Kolache town were Afghan civilians. According to the *Daily Mail* report, the bombing completely erased the town and

its surroundings from the map. The British daily has also published images of the town before and after the operation to show the scale of the destruction.[19]

The history of warfare has certainly witnessed other scenes of violent extermination of whole towns: the bombing of Guernica during the Spanish Civil War; the physical elimination of Jewish resistance in the Warsaw Ghetto by Nazi forces in World War II; the massacre at My Lai by the American army during the Vietnam War. In each case, a superior military force fighting an unyielding insurgency resorts to policies of absolute violence as a means of pacifying that which it cannot hope to conquer. In each case, the suffering of victims has been accompanied by moral revulsion on the part of the global political community, a sense of moral revulsion with such lasting power that it eventually led to the American retreat from Vietnam, the defeat of the Nazis, and, in the case of Spain, to the final triumph of democratic government. Yet, for all this, there has not occurred, particularly in the United States, universal moral revulsion against remote death from the air or strategies of total warfare involving the disappearance of whole towns in Afghanistan. It is as if what is really being waged in Afghanistan is not the transparent falsehood of a "war on terror," but a very different, and perhaps more ominous, form of warfare – the war of the powerful against the weak, the privileged against the poor, the technocratic against the autochthonous, the abstract, international geopolitical strategies of the United States and NATO against a stubborn, recalcitrant, and manifestly popular, armed resistance. While what is at stake *politically* in Afghanistan may be the failure of the abstract policy deliberations involved with developing a new Eurasian strategy for the United States, what is at stake *ethically* is more perilous, specifically the transformation of the question of public ethics in the United States into an increasingly estranged form of remote ethics with no sustaining purpose.

Politically, if the United States and the NATO coalition cannot defeat Afghan resistance after years of fierce combat, complete aerial superiority, a treasury of military expenditures, and thousands of combat casualties, the Eurasian strategy is a certain debacle. That explains, perhaps, why the United States military has now abandoned the field of "counter-insurgency" operations involving as they do proverbial campaigns aimed at winning the hearts and minds of Afghans in favor of "counterterrorism" operations involving the surgical use of Special Ops and Reaper drones aimed exclusively at tactically defined elimination of Afghan resistance leaders. That there could be such frenzied condemnation of Wikileaks following the publication of the Afghan War Diaries with their chilling account of a failed military strategy and a resurgent Afghan resistance was probably due to the fact that this has become the epitome of a cynical war with no real purpose other than camouflaging from the public the magnitude of the defeat. *Ethically,* the lasting consequence of the failed military campaign in Afghanistan has been the hardwiring of the remote ethics guiding those Reaper drones, this decisive separation of action and consequences, into the essence of governing ethics in a society increasingly framed by its war technologies. Here, computer models based on complex war simulations are operating at full force in Washington and other capitals of the West: the war in Afghanistan is postulated as a system of logically determined outcomes that can be gamed by the latest technocratic generation of the "best and the brightest," inputs of new weapons tagged, possible outcomes determined, trajectories of step-by-step intensified violence traced, impact on public opinion predicted, new military algorithms constructed, and negative outcomes recorded within complex loops of feedback information. And yet, for all that, there is always the unexpected, always the return of the repressed, that which refuses to quietly take its place in the technocratic language of simulation: IEDs buried beneath roads waiting for passing American convoys; massive anti-US rallies in the cities of Pakistan; burning supply convoys of oil-tanker trucks on the border of Pakistan and Afghanistan; village elders who are shot for throwing stones; Reaper drones that crash unpredictably or that suddenly take matters into their own telemetric hands, leaving their assigned navigation zones and heading straight for neighboring countries with full explosive payloads before being downed by pursuing fighter planes. Everywhere, then, a phantasmagorical logic of war gaming delivered from the air, simulated in advance by all the experts of technologically delivered violence versus the stubborn, recalcitrant, forceful movement of the human will to resist.

Call it what you will – "violent extremism," the traditional refusal on the part of Pashtun warriors to be cowed by foreign powers, fierce resistance by residual forces of the Taliban, militant tactics by the remaining members of al-Qaeda, an insurgent revolt by Afghan Mujahideen spreading now from the southern provinces to north and northwest Afghanistan – the war in Afghanistan is a brutal conflict between two clashing historical destinies – the privileged western destiny of continuously gaming the world as a complex, but rationally realizable, war simulation versus an alternative destiny, something equally rational in its own terms but definitely more tangible on the material ground of history, that is the continuing spirit of political rebellion. When the rebel is motivated by a more fundamental claim, namely the defense of family, village, tribe, religion, ethnicity – that is, the defense of things bound up in the complex web of time versus offensive weapons delivered from space – then the conflict is truly fundamental, truly an eschatological conflict between time and space, history and simulation. This is, perhaps, why Afghan rebels like to say these days: "You have the watches, but we have time on our side." Or why General Petraeus, former director of the CIA, has been quoted by a recent US Congressional report as stating: "You cannot kill your way out of an insurgency."[20]

That said, it may be that the real reason for the persistence of the West in continuing to stake its military and political fortunes on a successful outcome in Afghanistan involves a growing recognition on the part of foreign policy elites that the war in Afghanistan is really a code war – a war where what is being waged is not simply a violent clash between the technologically driven will to mastery of a spacebound war machine and earthbound tribal resistance, but a larger struggle between the rich and the poor, the globally privileged and the globally disenfranchised, between "bodies that matter" and *bodies that do not matter*. In this sense, Afghanistan can best be understood as the outer boundaries of the bunker archaeology of American empire, that geographical point in global space yet local time where the militarized logic of the West has chosen to establish its external boundaries, determining who belongs to the society of the masters of the code and which bodies have been selected to be marginalized, excluded, silenced, disappeared. When the conflict is viewed in such metabolic terms – as a violent collision between the preservation of power versus an armed insurgency fueled by the anger, hatred and despair of bodies that do not matter – we are suddenly in the realm of historical nihilism where there are few limits on the levels of violence expended in first reducing, then eliminating, a potentially fatal insurgency. Many years ago, the French writer Albert Camus predicted in his book *The Rebel* that the spirit of historical nihilism would soon circulate triumphantly as the dominant form of power and ethics in the modern century. For Camus, the essence of historical nihilism was this chilling formula: injustice committed in the name of absolute justice, absolute murder undertaken in the name of absolute reason. For Camus, the moral equivalence of violence, justice, and reason could only be engaged by a form of power that thought in absolutes, and that, moreover, was fully prepared to crush opposition to its unilateral declaration of moral absolutes in the name of the greater good – freedom, justice, and reason most of all.

It is this larger political and philosophical context that is the really existent historical situation framing Obama's speech about the necessity for a new National Security Strategy. Delivered on December 1, 2009 at the US Military Academy at West Point, Obama's speech about national security policy had, I believe, the immediate effect of transforming the remote ethics so necessary for conducting the Afghan War into the ethical comportment animating the foreign policy of the United States. While the explicit purpose of the speech was Obama's public justification of his decision to support a "surge" in the number of US troops committed to combat operations in Afghanistan, the implicit intent was to justify absolute violence as both a reasonable, and just, course of action. Consequently, the speech at West Point is a public rhetoric worthy of careful study since it illustrates perfectly how liberal idealism converges quietly, without a drop of dissent, with the most violent and nihilistic of military campaigns. In this speech, Obama might want to argue that Afghanistan is not Vietnam, but in this he is probably mistaken. Perhaps because he has not thought deeply enough about the real world of impoverishment and dispossession, about the exclusions, disappearances, and prohibitions necessary to keep the logic of empire ascendant, about other ways of conceiving freedom, justice, and rights that run against the grain of dominant western values, Obama may, in fact, be incapable of understanding that Vietnam was not only about a failed military campaign on the ground or in the air, but a fundamental refutation of the universal sovereignty of liberal values. In Vietnam, as in Afghanistan, technocratic liberalism smashes directly into the real world of twenty-first-century politics. In both wars, the same military gaming of the world is taking place, the same triumph of purely technocratic logic, the same disregard for mass civilian casualties among bodies that do not matter, the same substitution of a purely military framework of understanding for the always more complex, multilateral facts on the ground. And, of course, the same result: liberal idealism quickly turns into the remote ethics characteristic of illiberal *ressentiment*.

The programmatic logic of illiberal *ressentiment* is carefully established in Obama's speech on a new National Security Strategy. Its political logic is motivated by absolutist moral convictions based on unquestioned, and unquestionable, assumptions triumphantly affirmed: culturally foundational, unilaterally declared, and ideologically hegemonic. Its boundaries are clearly established by that which it excludes, marginalizes, silences, and disappears. Its powerful spirit of moral righteousness is strengthened by a persistent logic of injury and grievance. Yet all the while its rhetoric remains reasonable, moderate, restrained, practical, always prepared to be pragmatic, to split the strategic difference – in a word, fully liberal. As Obama argues, this is an America "carrying the burdens of the world," unappreciated as it spearheads the struggle for human rights, the defender of human freedoms, whether of religion, race, gender, or speech, never seeking "permanent occupation" of foreign lands, never breaching international rules of state sovereignty since it is, after all, the imperial state that defines the sovereign exception. There is no space here for images of exterminated villages, protesting village elders, families disappeared by remote death from the sky, for a world where good and evil are often interchangeable terms.

In essence, what Obama's proclamation of a new National Security Strategy for the United States accomplishes is, I believe, a decisive movement from incomplete to fully completed liberalism. While the incomplete liberalism of earlier generations of liberal theorists and practitioners was marked by a tense struggle between the famous two freedoms – *freedom from* (fear, tyranny, hunger, discrimination) and *freedom to* (free speech, thought, movement, choice) – the contemporary stage of fully completed liberalism represents their long-sought synthesis. Here, there is no longer a fateful struggle between the earlier phase of *freedom from* to the progressive politics of *freedom to*, but now the political reality of fully completed liberalism where the two freedoms are finally conjoined as reflexive moments in the same liberal dialectic. Simultaneously hyper-liberal on progressive social ideals and yet fundamentally illiberal on matters pertaining to state security and the imperatives of capitalist reproduction, fully completed liberalism is that most enigmatic of all political ideologies, simultaneously liberal and illiberal, genuinely progressive yet profoundly reactionary.

While Obama's speech to the graduating class at West Point represented an eloquent liberal defense of the need for linking military aims to a more complex understanding of the real world of international politics, his speech on national security at the same military academy thus established the logic of illiberalism as the potentially new master code of the twenty-first century. Beginning with bitter memories of sacrificial violence – vivid reminders of the "nearly 3,000 innocent men, women and children murdered on 9/11" – Obama immediately directed popular animus towards the "violent extremism" of al-Qaeda who, in this retelling of the story of sacrificial violence, "struck at our military and economic nerve centers," killed innocents, and tried to strike "at one of the great symbols of our democracy in Washington." The constant invocation of al-Qaeda as the primary scapegoat recalls the writings of René Girard, who cautioned that the nomination of a scapegoat always has to fulfill two basic requirements: first, it must represent evil with such intensity that all members of the community can find sufficient moral cohesion in its elimination; and, second, it must be closely identifiable by the community in order that society can bond around the inevitable ritualistic slaying associated with sacrificial violence. That's al-Qaeda: universally hated and feared by American society as a specter of evil (Obama's "violent extremism"), yet perfectly recognizable because al-Qaeda is held accountable for attacking the core edifices of American democracy, economy, and family. The importance of resurrecting al-Qaeda as a sacrificial scapegoat cannot be underestimated. Rhetorically, if the putative purpose of the Afghan campaign remains the liquidation of the besieged remains of al-Qaeda, this implies that other political complexities do not have to be mentioned. For example, nowhere in this speech does Obama flag the continuing rivalry between India and Pakistan as a key factor in destabilizing Afghanistan, nor does he highlight the role of Pakistani intelligence in playing a well-documented double game – appealing for arms and aid from the United States while supplying the Taliban with military support in their armed insurgency against coalition forces. The overwhelming importance of a sacrificial scapegoat is that it allows a direct connect between the deepest affect of an anxious American public looking for revenge and the geopolitical strategies of the foreign policy establishment. Everything follows from this:

> I do not make this decision [to send an additional 30,000 troops] lightly. I make this decision because I am convinced that our security is at stake in Afghanistan and Pakistan. This is the epicenter of the violent extremism practiced by al-Qaeda. It is from here that were attacked on 9/11, and it is from here that new attacks are being plotted as I speak. This is no idle danger, no hypothetical threat. In the last few months alone, we have apprehended extremists within our borders, who were sent here from the border regions of Afghanistan and Pakistan to commit new acts of terror. This danger will only grow if the region slides backwards, and al-Qaeda can operate with impunity. We must keep the pressure on al-Qaeda, and to do that, we must increase the stability and capacity of our partners in the area.
>
> Of course, this burden is not ours alone to bear. This is not just America's war. Since 9/11, al-Qaeda's safe havens have been the source of attacks against London and Amman and Bali. The people and governments of both Afghanistan and Pakistan are endangered. And the stakes are even higher within a nuclear-armed Pakistan because we know al-Qaeda and other extremists seek nuclear weapons, and we have every reason to believe that they would use them. (Barack Obama, "On the Way Forward in Afghanistan and Pakistan," West Point, 2009)[21]

So then, Afghanistan is a test of American resolve to deal with the evil specter of al-Qaeda, to prevent nuclear weapons from falling into the hands of terrorists, to defend "NATO's credibility," and to maintain "the security of our allies and the common security of the world." What's more, the war in Afghanistan is not simply about an external threat but is fully internal to the domestic security of the United States: "We cannot count on military might alone. We have to invest in our homeland security, because we cannot capture or kill every violent extremist abroad. We have to improve and better coordinate our intelligence, so that we stay one step ahead of shadowy networks" (Barack Obama, On the Way Forward in Afghanistan and Pakistan, West Point, 2009).

While George W. Bush repeated the refrain "enemy non-combatants" involved in a "war on terror," Barack Obama does precisely the same with this exception: his preferred stereotypes are "violent extremists" always moving through the darkness of "shadowy networks." At this point, the two ideological vectors of security-oriented neoconservatism and security-conscious illiberalism fully merge in a common discourse of heightened security measures at home and aggressive military adventures abroad. In this instance, it helps that the image of al-Qaeda that circulates through the media generally, and certainly through Obama's national security discourse specifically, is fully caught up in the language of simulation, detached from any real reference to material reality, becoming instead a floating sign signifying the evil specter of "violent extremism." Once the image of al-Qaeda has achieved the virtual status of a pure simulation, it circulates through the media as an empty, but potentially dangerous, signifier – "shadowy networks," terrorists in pursuit of nuclear weapons, challenging "NATO's credibility," endangering Afghanistan and Pakistan, threatening both "global and domestic security." Again, it is not so much that al-Qaeda was not a potent political force in its original incarnation, but even the fundamentalism of al-Qaeda has now been transformed into something more complex on the ground – the complicated politics of Afghan national resistance, the movement of al-Qaeda into the Arabian peninsula, the mountains of Yemen specifically, due to the removal of secular regimes in Iraq and Syria, the resurgence of the Arab Maghreb, warfare in Somalia, challenges to established elites in Palestine, Tunisia, Algeria, Egypt, and, soon, Saudi Arabia. Ironically, while Obama as a progressive liberal demands a new vision of world politics based on proportionate military response, complexity, multilateralism, and diversity, when he speaks as an illiberal, as a commander-in-chief of a security-conscious imperial government, his rhetoric seemingly privileges the overgeneralized, the disproportionate, the most atavistic of sacrificial language.

The future of the guardian state

What, then, does the guardian state portend for the future? Simultaneously politically liberal yet economically illiberal, deeply technocratic yet faith-based, complex in its strategic analysis yet absolutist in its moral convictions, inspiring both hope and fear, the guardian state is the advanced outrider of the fully realized technological society. While its earliest formulations reveal the emergent codes of the future, whether the new codes of cyber-warfare or the algorithmic codes of the digital commodity-form, the essence of the guardian state has to do with heightened security consciousness. While this intimates the movement of the guardian state in the direction of bunker archaeology with increasingly policed distinctions between those to be included or excluded, it also intimates greater surveillance of the domestic population. Always phantasmagorical in its formulation, based as much on projected mass anxieties as fact-based threats, the new security state will probably stabilize itself in the future by a twofold strategy. *Externally*, it will identify recognizable, and popularly acceptable, scapegoats upon whom spectacles of vengeance can be enacted to allay the fears of the domestic population. In this respect, drone warfare is a particularly powerful expression of the guardian state since its purely cybernetic, remote, unmanned method of operation allows for the direct discharge of political affect upon specifically targeted scapegoats. That there will always be numerous accidental victims of death by drones will, for the most part, be effectively erased under the neutralizing military nomenclature of "collateral damage." *Internally*, the rapid growth of the new security state as the political architecture of guardian liberalism coincides with a deep crisis in contemporary liberal subjectivity. Its livelihood threatened by economic changes beyond its control, its imagination filled with haunting images of an always menacing external world, its desires for security only partially appeased by visible borders, liberal subjectivity turns inward only to find that the boundaries of skin, consciousness, and perception have themselves long ago been invaded by the full force of digital technologies. Not only is it the case that electronic media generate reality, but those very same media have fully invaded bodily consciousness, increasingly taking possession of its habits of perception, providing a specular theater of images for its imagination, increasingly powering up life itself with the creativity of social media, artificial intelligence, and augmented technologies. Confronted with the phantasmic irrealism of the putatively real world, the liberal subject finds itself fatally overexposed, with no public cover from the data storm outside and certainly no psychological shelter from the radical uncertainty of the storm within. While, in the best of circumstances, liberal subjectivity will rise to meet the challenges of the posthuman future by making a successful transition to "trans-subjectivity," that is, by becoming fluid, complex, and intermediated, the more likely consequence is that liberal subjectivity, threatened with boundary collapse from crises both external and internal, will be drawn to the psycho-ontological condition long ago prophesied by Nietzsche's *On the Genealogy of Morals*. In this case, the future of the guardian state would witness an increasingly bitter politics of mass *ressentiment*, fueled by the visceral anger of those suffering injured sensibilities and irreal sleights, whether by real or imagined enemies. Curiously, by providing cybernetically targeted scapegoats external to the domestic politics of the United States, the lasting psychological contribution of Obama's vision of the guardian state, whether consciously articulated or not, may be to alleviate the stress on the besieged liberal subject with appeals for heightened security abroad and economic security at home. In this case, Obama is very much the representative expression of Nietzsche's "ascetic priest," whose primary function remains, now as ever, to redirect, rechannel, and reinscribe the direction of mass *ressentiment*.

With a future that is decidedly mixed, guardian liberalism opens onto a full-fledged data storm generating new avenues for genuine human creativity, whether in social communication, innovative engineering, digital broadcasting, or recombinant genetics. Here, the sheer technological force of drift culture destabilizes the borders, crashes the boundaries, and remixes the referents with such astonishing velocity and unpredictable consequences that the future of social reality itself appears, at first glance, to be fully open to redesign, reanimation, and reengineering. That said, the equally swift emergence of the guardian state in response to very real crises of political economy and international insecurity introduces a powerful counter-drift into the political equation, effectively placing society as a whole under the hegemonic signs of security consciousness and the sovereignty of the digital commodity-form. Definitely a counterreaction to the complexities, fractures, and bifurcations of drift culture, the guardian state moves to restabilize traditional concentrations of power and finance around new prescriptions for social and political intelligibility. Here, absolutist political beliefs in the existence of evil in the world are supplemented by harsh capitalist prescriptions in support of policies of economic austerity, policing of labor dissent, control of popular rebellions demanding democratic renewal, and the effective disappearance of bodies that don't count. Increasingly segregated, bodies of the future will sometimes be excluded by the moral grid of the new security state while others will literally be pushed off the grid by financial exigencies. A likely future, then, of economic and political consolidation for the privileged, and growing uncertainty for the remainder. In a future that is itself caught up in the violent drift of consolidation and uncertainty, what sign will guide us through the digital vortex with its increasing stress on an always fragile humanity? In the end, will we come to represent the *critical outside* of digital reality, turning uncertainty to creative advantage? And what of those off-grid bodies of the future? Will they remain the spent casualties of the violent force field of technological change? Or is it possible that, in a contemporary situation in which technology increasingly takes the form of a dark tetrad with its implacable laws of substitution, disappearance, and inertia, the material visibility of human fragility will awaken a spirit of rebellion? And even if the rebellion of politics in the streets persists, how will it cope in the end with the emergence of cynical power, at once nihilistic and transformative, that refuses to present itself as a predator and begins to speak in terms of the precarious language of the victim, particularly a victim animated by the spirit of revenge-taking on bodies off-grid? With power masking itself as a sacrificial victim, is it possible to speak of guardian liberalism in terms other than "fully completed nihilism?"

Crash
Traversal Consciousness

10

Premonitory Thought:
That Fateful Day When Power Abjected Itself

Barack Obama's concept of the "just war" anticipates a future that is likely to be as politically consequential as it is ethically problematic. Indeed, with the triumph of guardian liberalism as the ideological capstone of hegemonic power, we are probably already living in the midst of that day when power fully abjects itself. Premised on a doubled moral belief both in the implacable presence of absolute evil in the world and the political necessity, indeed religiously premised righteousness, in responding to the specter of evil by any means available, guardian liberalism introduces a future that will increasingly come under the sign of cynical ideology. Here, hegemonic power undertakes a dramatic moral reversal by beginning to speak in the language of what I call the *imperial subaltern*, that is, in terms of injury, threat, humiliation and, of course, revenge-taking. When that fateful day does finally come, when power learns to speak of itself in the language of abjection, when, that is, great power authorizes revenge-seeking in terms previously reserved by the dominated objects of power, then we can know with some certainty that the future towards which we are plunging will surely be enucleated by all the signs of hyper-cynicism. Fortunately, for those destined to live through the political fallout and complicated ethical clashes of the future of cynical ideology, there remains one anticipatory thinker, Michel Foucault, in whose thought is to be found not only an accurate accounting of the alphabet of contemporary power but also a fateful diagnosis of that time, our time, when the truth of power and ideology wagered itself on the moral terms of the dispossessed.

Before Foucault

A premonitory theorist of histories yet to surface, silenced prematurely by death but still speaking to us insistently, urgently, passionately through the continued life of his writings, we are living *before* Foucault. Before Foucault, that is, in Nietzsche's sense that Foucault's time has not yet come, that his thought anticipates in its most dystopian moment the migration of power into institutions, mechanisms of control, and bodies with such intensity that we can speak of a future of the "possessed individual" as a singular effect of power; and, in its most utopian moment, of a form of citizenship yet to be realized that will potentially be crafted from his prudential ethics articulated in *The Care of the Self*.[1] That which Foucault predicted, that which he patiently deconstructed in the grey language of genealogical research – the archaeology of the prison, the birth of knowledge, the order of the clinic, the geographical traces of power, the genetic reduction of the body – has not fully materialized. This time, our historical time, is yet a time of emergence, suspended between power speaking in the name of death *and* life. In a period in which the much-trumpeted "revolution in military affairs" aligns itself with the hand-to-mouth existence of reactive politics practiced in the name of empire, who could deny the truth-saying of Foucault's prophetic insights about the theater of cynical power, cynical truth?

"Insurrection of subjugated knowledge": five methodological precautions

It is entirely fitting that Foucault first articulated his theorization of power in his famous series of lectures *Society Must Be Defended*,[2] at the Collège de France in the Paris winter of 1975/76. As the first practitioner of the "insurrection of subjugated knowledge,"[3] Foucault rebelled against all reductions of power to the system of right, liberal theories of sovereignty, and juridical mechanisms just as much as he refused to subordinate power to a reflex of ideology. About this Foucault was adamant. His refusal of the subordination of power to class, sovereignty, and juridical institutions assumed the form of five famous "methodological precautions." "As I see it, we have to bypass or get around the problem of sovereignty – which is central to the theory of right – and the obedience of individuals who submit to it, and to reveal the problem of domination and subjugation instead of sovereignty and obedience."[4]

For Foucault, understanding power requires in the first instance an "interventionist" approach, one that bypasses orthodox interpretations of power premised on a "single center" or a prescribed "system of rules" in favor of a way of seeing power that privileges the "extremities" of power, those outer limits marking "power in its most regional forms and institutions." This displacement of perspective from the center to the region, from the legitimate to the "capillary," is intended to take power by surprise, to capture in motion "the points where this power transgresses the rules of right that organize and delineate it, oversteps those rules and is invested in institutions, is embodied in techniques and acquires the material means to intervene, sometimes in violent ways."[5] In other words, the public discourse of legitimate power, what power likes to say about itself in terms of its rules, mechanisms, and limits, will be displaced by a form of knowledge that explores the dense, complex capillaries of power, those administrative assemblages where power begins to speak in a minor vocabulary, those interstices where power is actually embodied in techniques and institutional practices.

Second, power for Foucault is always a "relation of force." No longer power viewed from on high with its ceremonial rhetoric of kings, queens, despots, tyrants, and even democratic rulers, but now power conceived along the distributional axis of force. When procedures of subjugation are directed against "multiple bodies, energies, matters, desires, thoughts," we are no longer in the presence of a great referential discourse of power, but something else entirely: that moment when power as a relation of force constitutes subjects. Conceived as a "relation of force," what is authorized by power is not simply the founding justificatory rhetoric of those who actually hold power, but something deeply interior to the question of power, specifically distributions of force that construct norm by norm, practice by practice, technique by technique, the real locus of power – the subject as both an end-product of relations of force and a precondition for forms of subjectivity necessary to maintain further distributions of power.

Third, power produces subjectivity and enables agency. About this, Foucault is explicit. Refusing power as a "phenomenon of mass and homogenous domination – the domination of one individual over others, of one group over others, or of one class over others," Foucault insisted on a more kinetic perspective in which "power functions." It functions not simply by means of the circulation of individuals within networks of power, but by a more profound mediation. Rather than being applied to individuals from the outside, power is conceived as "passing through individuals":

> It is therefore, I think, a mistake to think of the individual as a sort of
> elementary nucleus, a primitive atom or some multiple, inert matter to
> which power is applied. In actual fact, one of the first effects of power is
> that it allows bodies, gestures, discourses to be identified and constituted
> as something individual. The individual is not, in other words, power's
> opposite. The individual is one of power's first effects.[6]

In this case, the history of power must, of necessity, leave the hallowed
ground of rights and sovereignty, becoming instead something much
more attuned to that which is molecular in its origins, metabolic in its
functions, and granular in its effects. When the individual is theorized
as "one of power's first effects," this would imply that the study of
power has no choice other than to analyze the complex conditions, the
entangled alliances, the material conditions out of which the *concept* of
the individual first emerged and, on behalf of which, the individual
became in substance the living effect of relations of power that both
anticipate and condition its original formation. This also implies that
the study of power must go beyond the confines of jurisprudence
to consider the signs of the social – gestures, bodies, attitudes, and
discourses – that are inscribed in the fluid, mobile form of the
individual.

Fourth, Foucault's theory of power is always genealogical. Not genealogical in the sense of a linear history of bodies of power, but a "grey
genealogy" that entails an "ascending analysis of power." Faithful to
Nietzsche's prescription that the privileged language of genealogy is
always grey, that effective genealogy does not trace the history of the
great referentials as much as it descends into the unheralded traces of
power, Foucault's preference is for a genealogical method that begins
with "infinitesimal mechanisms, which have their own history, their
own trajectory, their own techniques and tactics," and then investigates
"[H]ow these mechanisms of power which have their solidity and, in
a sense, their own technology, have been and are invested, colonized,
used, inflected, transformed, displaced, extended, by increasingly
general mechanisms and forms of overall domination."[7]

"Grey genealogy" is the method preferred by those who would look
beyond the clashing discourses of power to the slow, patient extraction
of assemblages of meaning from the hidden techniques of power. Here,
the file is more important than the polemic, the strategic technique
more significant than public rhetoric, the bureaucratic mechanism
more noteworthy than the public announcement. While grey genealogy may not appeal to those interested in the great debates surrounding clashing ideologies, it does have the very real merit of bringing into
the light of consciousness that which heretofore has been prohibited,

excluded, and disavowed by the language of power. If an important part of power understood as a "relation of force" is to designate that the boundary line between that which is deemed livable and that which is not, then the method of grey genealogy has the great advantage of actually bringing into presence that which has been silenced by the relations of power. And perhaps bringing not simply that which is to be prohibited, excluded, and disavowed by power into the light of critical history, but something else. By finally providing speech for that which has been silenced, the method of grey genealogy is also its own double: a method for writing an anti-genealogy whereby that which does not form part of the "ascending analysis of power," that which will be effectively shut down by the discourse of power, is allowed to be finally understood in its full language of descent. So then, the challenges of grey genealogy are always multiple. Certainly, grey genealogy provokes an analysis of the "hidden mechanisms," the "tactics" of power that, taken together, figure in the ascending analysis of power. However, this ascending analysis of power can only be undertaken by a language of descent that, by virtue of its patient deconstruction of that which is avowed but also disavowed, included but also excluded, authorized but also prohibited, provides a haunting record of the exclusions that make possible power as a relation of force. Could Foucault's emphasis on grey genealogy be an early sign that his theorization of power was always fully alert to the possibility that that which was excluded by power – denigrated, prohibited, disavowed – would come to constitute the very basis for that power? Was Foucault's interest in the genealogical method a premonitory sign that the operations of power would also require a continuing process of repression and, moreover, that ascending operation of repression would constitute the deepest subjectivity of individuals viewed now as effects of power but also as psychically repressed mechanisms of power?

Perhaps something about the doubled nature of power, that its language of ascent was haunted by its language of descent, its mechanisms were matched by its prohibitions, its avowals tracked by its disavowals, led Foucault to be suspicious of the reduction of power to ideology. Consider this statement:

> It is quite possible that ideological production did coexist with the great machineries of power. There was no doubt an ideology of education, an ideology of monarchial power, an ideology of parliamentary democracy, and so on. But I do not think that it is ideologies that are shaped at the base, at the point where the networks of power accumulate. It is much less and much more than that. It is the actual instruments that form and accumulate knowledge, the observational methods, the recording

techniques, the investigative research procedures, the verification mechanisms. That is, the delicate mechanisms of power cannot function unless knowledge, or rather knowledge apparatuses, are formed, organized, and put into circulation, and those apparatuses are not ideological trimmings or edifices.[8]

As much as Foucault refused liberal theories of juridical right, his theory of power also began with a refusal of Marxism. Not only was power to be thought outside of language of the commodity-form, but it would break its historical ties with the question of ideology as well. Henceforth, "delicate mechanisms" and "knowledge apparatuses" would be put in play as the effective relays of power. While there is not much intellectual glamour to be found in the study of "observational methods," "recording techniques," and "verification mechanisms," there is, however, something elemental to the study of power located in the knowledge interstices of power. For Foucault, power as a relation of force is less ideological than epistemological. Power is always an intimate part of the "order of things" which, in turn, has less to do with spectacular ideological divisions than with the rise and fall of different knowledge regimes, with the triumph and eclipse of instruments, methods, and techniques that are simultaneously expressions of new relations of force and the grey matter of its actual implementation in social and political history. It is in the study of these underlying tectonic plates of power and their areas of fracture, subduction, high pressure, and stress relief that Foucault's theory of power finds its moment of intellectual purchase. Eschewing the obvious, abandoning the high peaks of ideological contestation, Foucault's grey genealogy of power always privileges the epistemological, authorizes the interventionary, mobilizes power as a "relation of force," and augments the study of the individual as an "effect of power." In effect, the eloquence of the writing, the power of the discourse, and the precision of the analytics advance a theory of power that does that which is most rare: it supersedes a description of power from the outside in favor of the creation of a mirror of power from the inside.

Modalities of power

Like power itself, everything in Foucault's thought flows from these five methodological precautions: the birth of the asylum, the history of madness, the genealogy of the medical clinic, and the history of sexuality. Breaking with Max Weber's theory of power with its different bases in "charisma," "tradition," or "routinization," Foucault's conception of power envisions a dynamic field of force-relations sweeping beyond charismatic appeal or tradition as its basis of political legitimacy, insisting in the end that the real political lesson to be learned from the routinization of power through the institutional matrix of governance is the sad, but predictable, reproduction of its effects. First, it takes the form of that power effect we have come to know as the *sovereign individual* at the base of all liberal theory, and then it assumes the increasingly problematic status of *agency*. For Foucault, the concept of agency is the dead resurrection effect of Weber's charisma: that ideological effect of power that plays the double role of reproducing the limits of power while challenging power as it limits experience.

Like the process of power that he describes so eloquently, everything about Foucault's writings on power represents less thought-from-the-outside than a brilliant staging of the power dynamics that it perhaps intended only to describe. In the most dramatic literary and political sense, Foucault's perspective on power is relentlessly *interventionary*. Here, power is theorized as beginning with a fundamental epistemological rupture in the "order of things," dispensing in effect with the universalizing claims of grand political theory in favor of a form of thought that is minoritarian by disposition, preferring the epistemology of techniques, limits, and founding conditions to the application of political theory from the outside. Indeed, if Foucault can write so evocatively about power as a "relation of force," it is perhaps because he has made of his theory of power a singular instance of intellectual forcefulness, refusing simultaneously all received interpretations of power. It is as if Foucault's vision of power is fully anticipatory, although in an unexpected rhetorical way, about the nature of power as a relation of force. In this sense, Foucault can claim that power circulates, that power circuits bodies and sexuality and medical clinics and prisons because his own form of writing has become in effect an instance of the most fundamental drives of power as a relation of force, specifically that power as a force-relation is never exhausted with its changing field of applications, but is about taking possession of the framework of interpretation.

Consequently, if Foucault can note with an appropriate sense of melancholy that the subject at one point was a theoretical *concept* before it sank beneath the waves of public consciousness as something fully naturalized, that is because his interventionary theory of power, his deployment of theory as a relation of force, has had the effect of fundamentally transforming how we think about power. Before Foucault, power might have been thought under many clashing theoretical signs – from the Weberian sign of charisma, tradition, and routinization and the Marxian sign of power as reflex of the commodity-form to the liberal sign of power as related to rights theory. After Foucault, power can only be conceived as something that circulates as a relation of force, producing agency, constructing the conceptual apparatus of the subject and the social materiality of the individual as its lasting power effects, and that, for all this, is best articulated in the patient language of a genealogical practice that traces a slow descent into the complex interstices of power while following an equally fast ascent into the normative applications of power. A mythologist of power, an illusionist capturing in his writings terrifying images of relations of force, a historian of those excluded, prohibited, disowned by the regime of intelligibility that is power today, to read Foucault is to enter directly into the theater of power in all its ceremonial rules, ritualistic excesses, and psychic madness.

Indeed, it is as if European thought for one brilliant moment at the end of the mass violence of the twentieth century, speaking from a Paris seminar room with grisly memories of German, Russian, and Chinese ideological totalities to the east and the seduction of Hobbes's Leviathan to the (Atlantic) west – rebelling against both the ideological orthodoxies of actually existing Marxism on the one hand and liberally derived systems of right on the other – insisted on a final account of the justificatory logic and internal logic of political history. Having emancipated power from both the tyranny of the philosophy of right and political theories of sovereignty, Foucault could never return to the play of individual charisma, the proprieties of the law, the violence of the commodity-form for his explanation of power. Ironically, like the triumph of the social that all his thought set out to describe, Foucault's thought culminated in raising the status of the lowly *norm* as the new bar of power.

Of course, at the strictly *political* level, Foucault's interpretation of power in the language of normativity could never be stabilized for long. How could it be? The actually existing history of power has always outstripped Foucault's theoretical preference for an interpretation of power that would maintain the superiority of the language of normativity over law, commodity, and right. For example, within the ruling axiomatics of the contemporary liberal-democratic capitalist regime, the theory of power has always had a complex, fourfold history: first, power as *reification* (most lucidly expressed by Georg Lukács's "Reification and the Class Consciousness of the Proletariat"); second, Foucault's description of power in terms of a great social diffusion that culminated in strategies of *normalization* that, in turn, were overcome by emergent post-structuralist visions of power based on the language of *signification*. The theoretical move from a normative interpretation of power to the fluid, anarchic power of the *sign* found its penultimate intellectual expression in the intellectual rupture that was Jean Baudrillard's *Oublier Foucault*. And, of course, Baudrillard had no sooner deeply honored Foucault by doing violence to his political theory than the game of power itself slipped off the semiological mask of the sign in favor of new political theories emphatically emphasizing power as pure *virtuality* – sometimes expressed as *power and speed* (Paul Virilio's vision of dromocratic power taking virtual, parasitical possession of our bodies, subjectivity and desires); and sometimes described in terms of *power as fantasy* (Žižek's Lacanian-derived psychoanalytics of power).

Consequently, there are four modalities of power – reification, normativity, signification, and virtuality – each responding to a definite phase of modern, then postmodern, and now posthuman culture, all under the sign of the capitalist axiomatic, each representing a certain "line of flight" in Deleuze and Guattari's sense as power seeks its moment of maximum intensity in different historical circumstances; each succeeding, not cancelling, the other, but displacing it, forcing its effects to be recirculated, circuited within other regimes of truth; and each allying itself with an emergent class interest. Power as reification: that is the original political technique of early bourgeois class fragments intent on codifying all experience under the universal sign of the commodity-form. Power as normalization: that is Weber's, and then Foucault's, privileged specialists of the knowledge apparatus – psychiatry, medicine, penology, sexuality, confessionality. Power as signification: whereby the commodity-form circulates as a fluid, malleable sign system, eclipsing itself in a delirious cycle marked by all the seductive and violent signs of advanced capitalism. Finally, power as virtuality. Here, we witness the emergence of the "virtual class"[9] – the first authentic class expression of the age of globalization that, beginning as an ideology of facilitation at the advent of the digital revolution, quickly assumes its current form as the ideology of consolidation circulating everywhere across networked society.

This fourfold history of power traces the genealogy of power, moving from an always ambivalent relationship to the commodity-form to a sociology of normalization, and thereupon to a culture of signification before its contemporary representation as pure virtuality, pure circulation, pure image. Ironically, we might say that the history of power has retrospectively rewritten Foucault, that the genealogy of power has itself become an "insurrection of subjugated knowledge," that power not only produces individuals as its effects, not only enables agency, but perhaps today has also assumed its own form of psychopathology. Which is to say that when power becomes purely virtual, when power circulates in the language of the code, we can finally speak of an age of cynical power. Nowhere, for example, is this more chillingly represented than in the appearance of a new historical expression of world power – what I have termed the "imperial subaltern" – wherein power finally begins to speak the language of *domination* and *abjection*. While we can anticipate Foucault's defense of power as normativity against the claims advanced by other modalities of power, it is not so clear that anything in Foucault's thought prepares us for an epoch in which power actually comes alive, representing itself as an always reversible mixture of moral grievance against dominated subjects and sacrificial violence against those not yet subjugated. Could it be that the language of power today, this strange mixture of injury and contempt that forms the basis of the imperial subaltern, is actually in the process of overcoming Foucault? Certainly not in the sense of undermining Foucault's theory of power, but overcoming Foucault by returning his thought to what it always sought to avoid: an exploration of the extreme peripeteia of power.

The imperial subaltern

Current politics witnesses the radical transformation of traditional theories of power in the supposedly postcolonial world, specifically a real disturbance in the privileged dialectic of *hegemonic power and subaltern subjectivity* – the subjectivity, that is, of those dominated by imperial power. Probably wise to the game of moral communities of grievance based on subaltern grievances against perceived hegemonic power blocs, the most dynamic form of contemporary imperialism – the drive to empire – has quickly reversed the terms of the dialectic of postcolonial domination, adopting for itself a new political identity as the imperial subaltern. Here, imperialism, breaking with its previous identity as a model of exclusively *economic* domination, reaches out instead to become a psycho-ontology of life itself. Fueled by a powerful sense of moral grievance, animated by a psychology of insecurity, constantly driven by fear of deadly attacks from both inside and out, unified by spectacles of explosive violence directed against nominated scapegoats, the imperial subaltern blends together panic fear and sacrificial violence into a liquid language of new imperial power. *Triumphalist* because of its self-consciousness as the historical embodiment of the Kantian vision of the universal good; and *panicked* because of the specter of an always threatening outside world; the imperial subaltern projects itself onto political history as that strangest of all power idioms – part victim/part savior. Violated, vulnerable, aggrieved, aggressive – the imperial subaltern can resort to spasms of preemptive violence with good conscience because the doubled language of victim/ missionary is the necessary logic of moral expiation through sacrificial violence.

With this, all previous formulations of imperialism in terms of a specifically economic translation are forced to give way to the new reality of fully reactive imperialism. *Imperial* because this will continue to be a hegemonic capitalist order based on a strictly unequal economic distribution; and *reactive* because its power is liquid, virulent, constantly leading a hand-to-mouth existence, always provoking turbulence; the imperial subaltern specializes in the cultural translation of full spectrum (military) domination now into full metabolic domination later. In perfect fulfillment of Foucault's image of "power over life," the imperial subaltern – culturally reactive and economically hegemonic – has no ultimate purpose other than the doubled project of colonizing the totality of life space, liquidating in turn what it considers nonlife.

Now, I take Foucault at his word that theory is a "toolbox," that the measure of the power of a theory is its ability not only to interpret the world, but, if it would be genuinely critical, *to catalyze* an "insurrection of subjugated knowledge." Foucault not only wrote this, but he practiced it both as a prisoner of rights activist and in the theoretical practice of the *History of Sexuality* which is itself a struggle against the forces of sexual repression and confused liberation. Consequently, following Foucault's own political practice, I would argue that political theory can no longer be Foucauldian in its reflexive coupling of power/knowledge, but must return now to the radically changed field of politics. Over and beyond Foucault's five methodological precautions about power, I would argue that the logic of history has itself mutated, that we are living now under the sign not so much of power, but of *cynical ideology*.

Consider, for example, the contemporary reality of the imperial subaltern, the strange form that political power – the power of actually existing empire – takes today as it represents itself in the languages of humiliation, sacrifice, victimhood, and righteous revenge-seeking. Again, power here is based on a doubled moral economy – panic insecurity and redemptive violence: a moral economy which has been most brilliantly theorized, not so much by Foucault with his insistence on studying the invisible traces of power/knowledge, but by another French theorist, Georges Bataille, with his searing theory of the "scapegoat" and the reduction of politics to the logic of "sacrificial expenditure." With this insight, politics is reconfigured as operating under the sign of cynical ideology: a political regime that, abandoning the sociological mechanisms of control imminent to power/knowledge, practices cynicism with such ideological excess that politics literally experiences a morphological change of state: one which has the will to untruth as its ontology, *abuse value* as its ethics, *redemptive violence* as its practice, and the *terrorism of the image* as its epistemology.

The will to untruth

Could the will to untruth be the rhetorical reflex of the age of the imperial subaltern? Has the mixture of panic fear and redemptive violence pushed power/knowledge aside in favor of something more primary, more ideologically cynical? Here, the exercise of power against conquered populations is itself a secondary effect of a more primary movement of political force driven by cynical ideology, by the move to reorder the world through an ideology of redemptive violence and panic fear which has no necessary truth nor definite end. For the imperial subaltern, there are no fixed rules of the game, only the fascination of the conquest, the seduction of the game, the fluidity of strategic calculations, and the pleasure taken in the violence of sacrificial expenditure. All the more so with the spectacle of public lies, which, in addition to their utility in supporting specific interests, policies, and tactical strategies, are directly tied to the descent of truth into the last, decadent phase of nihilism. Truth is not immune from politics: it too turns out to be a secondary effect of sacrificial violence and panic insecurity. Public lies are authorized when truth becomes an emblematic sign of sacrificial expenditure.

Ironically, post-structuralism's critique of the great referential unities of agency, self, truth, knowledge, power, and consciousness are all founded on Nietzsche's understanding of the purely "perspectival" character of truth – that there are no necessary truths, that there is only a "perspectival truth"; this critique has now (definitely against the intentions of post-structuralism) been seized by the politics of empire. When Agamben theorized so eloquently the dark shadow of "exceptionalism" as the essence of contemporary politics, when he noted that it is he who has the power to mark the exception, to define the norm, to demarcate the boundary, the border, the division, Agamben is only reflecting, one hundred years after its original formulations, Nietzsche's intimations of the death of God and the triumph of perspectival truth aligned with the will to power.

Nihilism as the dominant historical movement of our times is bound up with cynical ideology, sometimes with the perspectival truth taking the highly invested form of panic insecurity and a religious crusade for redemptive violence; and, at other points, a more liquid presence in society and culture as the lie becomes not simply the norm, the sign, the exception, but a seductive image vector which twists, turns, mutates, dissolves, and redissolves, the story changing, energized by pack reporting intent on seeking out the "facts," first accepted by the many, then disbelieved by just as many, finding its final moment of closure in that supreme act of public futility in a culture of liquid lies – the telling and retelling of the "joke" for a society which makes itself sick with the "terrorism of the spirit." Or could it be something more excessive? That public lying today as an image vector laying siege to all the waiting subjects is what truly animates contemporary politics, energizing resistance to this reordering of the facts, but at the same time legitimating the possibility of a truth-saying which is held to be somehow exempt from the lie. If power itself has mutated from reified object to norm to sign and thereupon to a simulacrum of images, then why not truth also? But, of course, when truth becomes an image-spectacle, then it must inevitably subordinate itself to the iron laws of media construction: as an image-spectacle, truth is always relative, indeterminate, liquid, mutating, a surface effect with no necessary meaning or determinate end.

So, then, six preliminary theses on power, truth, and subjectivity that follow from society interpreted under the sign of cynical ideology:

1 *No longer power understood as "power over death,"* but the charismatic pull of a culture of death over a power that would be normative.
2 *Not power over life, but as a perfect sign of this new age of ideology, terrorism, and religion the triumph of the promise of eternal life over a power that would only always be secular.* Cynical ideology subordinates truth to the greater good of redemptive violence. The twisted tale of truth and lies becomes itself a primary instance of real violence.
3 *Not truth in the traditional sense, but cynical truth.* Fourth-order truth for the age of the spectacle, wherein truth becomes liquid, fluid, circulating, always containing a hint of death, making of itself a moment of sacrificial expenditure, motivated alternately by the promise of transcendence and the pleasure of humiliation.
4 *While power is a relation of force, ideology is necessarily, even triumphantly, a relation of weakness.* It is based on panic insecurity. It

aligns itself with fear of the outsider, the alien, the unknown, the terrorist. Masking this weakness as strength is the essence of cynical ideology.

5 *While power produces subjectivity,* and enables agency, cynical ideology evacuates subjectivity and disables agency.

6 *While a "grey genealogy of power"* stresses an ascending analysis of the mechanisms of power from the bottom to the top of hierarchies, cynical ideology is the reverse – its effects lie on the surface as a generalized psycho-ontology of redemptive violence and panic fear.

Politics in the age of cynical ideology

Refusing to secrete itself in those bureaucratic institutions that produce mechanisms of domination (the clinic, the prison, the school), cynical ideology thrives by making a continuous spectacle of its presence. It is a line of flight, an intensity that doubles and redoubles its effects. When power becomes image, cynical truth is volatilized by the image repertoire. It knows only media effects. It migrates across different media. It changes state as it seeks points of maximal intensity for communication with a humiliated public. It is without history because it leaves no fixed electronic trail. Its truth-value depends precisely on its articulation of perspectives that strengthen movements towards panic insecurity and redemptive violence. While power aligns itself with knowledge, not ideology, cynical ideology aligns itself with virtual truth, not power. Privileging sacrificial death over the life of power, cynical ideology represents truth in its last decadent phase as a concept-fiction.

In the age of cynical ideology, everything has value only to the extent that it has "abuse value." Heidegger recognized this. Understanding Nietzsche as the essential philosopher of completed nihilism, Heidegger drew the bitter ethical conclusions attendant upon the reduction of being to passive "standing reserve." For Heidegger, the mood of completed nihilism will be the "malice of strife" that takes pleasure in the greater calculus of abuse value. Today, the theater of abuse value is ubiquitous: the rage of violence directed against the old, the poor, the young, the sick, the powerless, the disavowed, the unlivable. Political lying is itself a form of abuse value with the object of abuse being the rupturing of that deep connection between truth-saying and the responsibilities of democratic citizenship. When citizenship itself is made an object of abuse value (by manipulation of vote counts, by public lies, by panic fear), the essential ethical core of democracy is undermined. We're left finally with the terrorism of the image, a new form of nihilism suitable for the technological age in which ministrations of redemptive violence during the daylight hours are soothed away by the nighttime jokes of all the talk-show hosts. A moral equivalency of nothingness – organized state terrorism and diffuse media distraction as the basic political logic of a society of completed nihilism. This is not an image of Foucault's world of power. Nor is it Deleuze and Guattari's searing vision of lines of flight and points of intensity – becoming wolf-man, becoming maggot-man, becoming predator, becoming parasite. It is something new, still emergent, still articulating itself, still learning to speak, still growing in strength, still waiting to fully disclose itself – *cynical ideology*.

Nonetheless, there is much to be learned from Foucault's theory of power in terms of what resists power, what produces that fatal rupture in individual subjectivity that has the effect of overcoming fear and stirring again the passionate desire for freedom. That this is an elemental human desire tracing a larger arc of history across countries, whole continents, until it encompasses global consciousness is indisputable. Everywhere in the past, as in the present and future, power as domination meets its equal in the stubborn, always ethically recalcitrant, presence of an individual subjectivity that says "No," and thereby marks one individual at a time, one body at a time, one refusal at a time the furthest limits of domination. Foucault knew this. It is everywhere in his work from the repressed history of erotic passion that makes of *The History of Sexuality* an emblematic study of the entwinement of passion and freedom in the politics of the body to the tortured revolt against the body of the king and its ceremonial punishment that introduces *Discipline and Punish*. Whether in the "grey genealogy of power" or in his eloquent reflections on the history of madness or the troubled histories of medicine, knowledge, and aesthetics, there is always the presence of the individual act of dissent, the philosophical heresy, the medical rupture, the lover's forbidden embrace that constitutes, at first in minor note and then, with gathering strength, an irresistible momentum towards generalized discursive change.

Foucault may have been the master of discourse analysis, the theorist who brought into the light of day the alliance of regulations, prohibitions, modes of thought, public rhetoric that, taken together, comes to be known as the discourse of power, the discourse of the intelligible body, the discourse of sexuality, the discourse of punishment. But for all that, the seduction of Foucault's thought, that which has made of his philosophical life a haunting marker denoting a larger shift in cultural sensibility, was the simple fact that, while Foucault's theory of power may have described its historical machinations in grisly, meticulous detail, the lasting legacy of his thought is that his theory of power is also its own undoing. For no sooner does Foucault remind us that power is a network, that it circulates, that it operates as a "relation of force," that it actually produces subjectivity, then his theory of power seems to shudder to a halt, to maintain its stability only on the basis of a violent internal repression. Ironically, if Foucault could argue time and again that resistance to power is one of the fundamental conditions for the preservation of power, that power feeds on its oppositions, that is only to say that everywhere in Foucault's thought there is acute awareness of that which lies outside and at one remove from the reach of power: that which is prohibited, excluded, disavowed, rendered unknowable, perhaps even unlivable, by the discourse of power.

Many commentators on Foucault have grasped the fundamental truth of his insights concerning the doubled nature of power. For example, Judith Butler's *The Psychic Life of Power* represents a sustained meditation on the dialectic of affirmations and prohibitions marking the discourse of power. Wendy Brown's *States of Injury* does much the same, this time though tracing the doubled dialectic of power as it works its way through the contemporary psycho-geography of political *ressentiment*. In chapter and verse, Butler and Brown are faithful to Foucault's teachings concerning power, namely that the regimes of intelligibility required by power always mark the unmarkable, specifically that which must be made unknowable, unlivable, unsustainable so that power can exist. Indeed, more than a historical record of the outlawed sexualities, the forbidden genders, the transgressionary crossings that mark the limits of power, the theoretical reflections of theorists such as Butler and Brown have the added measure of following the trace of Nietzsche in Foucault.

In his emblematic treatise, *On the Genealogy of Morals*, Nietzsche, writing "posthumously" about the nature of power, observed that the real dynamism of the will to power resided in its constant act of "turning." For Nietzsche first, later for Foucault, and more recently for Butler and Brown, the ability, even the necessity, for power to turn on itself, to absorb into itself as one of its fundamental conditions of preservation its own language of abasement, prohibition, and disavowal, was basic to the genealogy of modern power. While Nietzsche understood the "turning" of power as cynicism, Foucault, at first, was more restrained in his approach. Almost until the end of his life, he maintained the unhappy illusion that the discourse of power required for its full analysis not only an understanding of the discursive operations of power but also its much neglected histories of prohibitions. In this sense, Foucault properly was the last, and perhaps more faithful, student of the dialectic of Enlightenment, the philosopher who maintained for most of the history of his writing the pretense that the study of power was exhausted by a "grey genealogy" of its affirmations and prohibitions. This was the philosophical abjection that resulted in his greatest philosophical triumphs from *The Order of Things* and *The Archaeology of Knowledge* to *The History of Sexuality*. Each of these texts represents a great philosophical overcoming: the overcoming of the human, the overcoming of knowledge, the overcoming of sexuality. But if that is the case, they also represent a great delay in Foucault's thought, a fatal pause while Foucault, this rarity of a thinker who bled the truths and untruths of philosophy, absorbed the full dimensions of Nietzsche's insights about cynical power. That the writing of *The History of Sexuality* was marked by a long absence before Foucault could begin again, and that when he did write again it was in the form of an eloquent recovery of the history of the self in the language of classical aesthetics, represents, I believe, Foucault's failure before the name of Nietzsche. The insight concerning power that Foucault could not bear was the sense that power at its disappearing center was purely perspectival, a cynical sign, presenting on its surface only a theater of apparent opposites. For an innately political thinker like Foucault, this was ultimately unacceptable because it would mean that the turning of power against itself could not be explained away in the language of a doubled repression – repressing that which must be prohibited if power is to operate but also daily repressing the desire for the objects of its repressions – but in the language of indifference. Could it be that Foucault's thought is an almost religious appeal for the recovery of meaning that, far from following Nietzsche, represents a primal rebellion against him? Perhaps in despair, perhaps because of his desire to sacrifice his insights concerning madness and power to appease the demands made upon thought by the "care of the self," Foucault's thought is in its beginning and ending the last and most forceful effort at saving the appearance of things. That explains perhaps why there is such a fundamental division between Foucault and Baudrillard. They meet over the philosophical body of Nietzsche. Foucault only wants to take part of Nietzsche, the Nietzsche who provides a genealogical method for exploring the discourse of power. But he forgot Nietzsche's fatal aphorism that, now that you have read Nietzsche, the problem is how to get rid of him. That Baudrillard is the one thinker fully faithful to Nietzsche, that he makes of the game of power a disenchanted simulacrum haunted by spasms of pure violence and indifferent commutation does no disservice to Foucault. Baudrillard's *Oublier Foucault* with its conjuration of the murderous violence of power – the imperial subaltern always lying in wait at the heart of power – represents a fitting epitaph for Foucault's theory of power. Foucault's thought remains trapped within the mirror of power of his own making, tracing out in precise detail the techniques, strategies, rules, and norms that make of power such an emblematic relation of force. That Foucault could not absorb into his thought the peripeteia of power, those traces of reversibility and instant inversion marking the shattering of the normative regime of a productive power by a world mesmerized by the fatal sign of seduction, represents no real criticism of his thought. Like the very best of all the great political philosophers, Foucault's ironic fate is to be a writer whose thought makes possible the renewal of the game of power with all its discipline and seduction.

11

Thinking the Future with Marshall McLuhan

Technologies of Abandonment, Inertia, Disappearance, Substitution

The theoretical visions of Michel Foucault and Marshall McLuhan are, in their essence, superb exits to the posthuman future. While Foucault's insistent questioning of the underlying claims of power, certainly its uses and abuses but also its necessary cynicism, exits to a posthuman future dominated by the merger of the concept of the "just war" and the violence of sacrificial scapegoating on the part of hegemonic power, McLuhan's thought exits directly into a very different geography of posthumanism. A celebrated media theorist by virtue of his creative insights into the quickly evolving world of the "global village," a classically trained student of literature, myths and legends by scholarly profession, but, most of all, a Catholic humanist as a matter of theological belief and ethical conviction, McLuhan was that rarity of an intellectual, a thinker who made of his beautifully miseducated imagination with its puns, wordplays, and daring thought experiments a way of blasting through the established cultural intelligibility of mid-twentieth century society into a technologically driven future. Here, bodies of the future would be equipped with data for an (electronic) skin, mass media for (substitute) vision, technologies of communication for an ablated nervous system, and complex networks as the new habitus for virtually everything from the most intimate friendships to the most routine economic transactions. With a prophetic mind that transcended the constraints of bodily space and time, McLuhan's ultimate contribution was not only to have traveled deepest into the then far-off galaxies of information culture of the contemporary century, but, more importantly, to have left behind in his intellectual travels a careful and precise record of a new methodology for "understanding media." Consequently, thinking the future with Marshall McLuhan involves, at first, paying equally careful attention to what he had to say about the newly emerging electronic media of technological communication with their "mechanical brides," "Gutenberg galaxies," and "media as massage," but also something else. That is, we best honor the memory of Marshall McLuhan, a memory whose future is still unfolding at the speed of technology, by listening intently to those things that he purposively did not say, and, perhaps because of his own religious and intellectual convictions, could not say, but which, for all of that, continue to represent the essence of his thought. In short, taking McLuhan at his word, we need to make of his thought a "counter-gradient" to the invisible technological force fields that surround us. With no disrespect for McLuhan's enduring reputation as a technological utopianist, it must be pointed out that his thought serves as such a brilliant exit to the posthuman future precisely because his utopian probes lead directly to something that has remained unremarked, unnoticed, undocumented, namely, that to really think the future with Marshall McLuhan is to hold in creative tension both the visible media of the technological future that he explored with such prescient, and truly astonishing, clarity and the hidden impulses animating technologies of inertia, substitution, abandonment, and disappearance. When McLuhan's unsparingly critical sense of ethics is finally permitted to circulate in the futurist world of posthuman technology that was so vividly predicted in all his writings, the result is a reenactment of his own preferred aesthetic vision of *counter-blast* – a method of thinking the posthuman future that is itself fully interior to the structural logic of that technological future while, at the same time, remaining one ethical remove from the historical destiny implied by its unfolding.

Indeed, Marshall McLuhan could provide such a truly creative account of the technological future, one that effectively anticipated decades in advance the emergence of networked culture, mobile devices, and digital subjects circulating in an information environment moving at the speed of light, because his thought was so deeply pervaded by a tragic sense of technology. Now that we actually live in the technological universe he prophesied, there is a desperate urgency to more fully understand the tragic technological ethics of McLuhan, namely his foreboding sense that technology always amputates and effectively mutilates the human nervous system because the question of technology in McLuhan's estimation was seductive *and* violent in equal measure. With an intellectual perspective that alternated between (technological) utopia and (humanist) tragedy, between melancholy and hopefulness, McLuhan's thought was, I believe, not only a fluid mirror of the digital future but an indispensable guide to a new ethical vision of technology. Consequently, thinking the future with Marshall McLuhan involves exploring both the brilliantly complex universe of technological futurism present in his probes, aphorisms, and uncanny juxtapositions and reversals of meaning between figure and ground, and his profoundly ethical, in fact, deeply religious, vision of the human impact of technology. Again, a Catholic humanist by religious faith, a classical scholar by craft, a technological futurist by choice, and an ethicist by humanist and theological conviction, the lasting importance of Marshall McLuhan was to wrap the unfolding future in an ethical enigma that is at once complex, fractured, and labyrinthian. McLuhan's enduring contribution was always something *future post-perfect*, that is, it is the enchanted presence of McLuhan's imagination that awaits us as we travel through the twisted, troubled future of the twenty-first century, a future which, in McLuhan's sense, is always doubled in its complexity, resplendently technological – technologies that are mobile, kinetic, interpolated, fast – but that is also deeply haunted by the psychic violence against cognition, affect, and perception precipitated by recent developments in neuroscience. If McLuhan were alive today, and in my thinking, he is very much alive in the visceral, brilliant, inspiring presence of a form of thought that has so deeply touched and conceptually shaped a whole generation of new media thinkers in many countries, he would surely look beyond the universe of mobile technologies and digital devices to say something significant about what is really going on technologically in contemporary history – that the fateful meeting of digital sequencing in the regime of computation and eugenic tendencies in neuroscience has delivered us to a techno-logical future that is increasingly focused on hijacking human con-sciousness, literally vivisecting the human brain, by reductive forms of neuroscience acting at the behest of the biotechnology industry.

McLuhan's ethical dissent

In the digital age of intelligent machines, technology is literally a body invader, penetrating consciousness, reshaping perception, circulating bodies and desire in cybernetic loops of information. Suddenly, con-nectivity everywhere with the digital remainders of individual life-histories gathered into vast data archives and the social reality principle itself increasingly gamed in the language of aesthetics and power. In a way never anticipated by the cultural imagination, the entire frame-work of traditional modernist meaning has effectively disappeared – space and time became light-time and light-space moving at the speed of light; previous divisions among bodies, machines, animals, and objects suddenly became blurred and undecidable; technological innovation moved inexorably from outside to inside, from gigantic mechanisms to invisible flows, from prosthetics to augmentation. For example, we have long been accustomed to thinking of the human body as something self-contained, bounded, relatively autonomous of its technological prostheses. Even in his most utopian moments, McLuhan could declaim that electronic technologies of communication represented "extensions" of the human nervous system, just before his self-avowed sense of Catholic melancholy forced him to deeply lament what he saw as human passivity in the face of technologies recoding, recalibrating, and rewiring the nervous system. Although McLuhan's affirmation of technology as a helpful extension of the human sensorium, indeed as a potential epiphany of new human understandings, continues to this day in increasingly triumphant announcements of the coming age of "augmented media," it should also be noted that his deeply felt ambivalence regarding the fate of technology, whether it would result in new epiphanies of human understanding or a cataclysmic implosion of the human condition, introduced a truly ambivalent sense of complexity into the story of technology.

McLuhan was not alone in his ethical reservations. A curious fact about contemporary technological futurism is that many of the very best understandings of the fate of technology emanate from thinkers whose critical reflections on the question of technology have been deeply touched by the religious imagination – Jacques Ellul's essentially theological critique of technique; Paul Virilio's ethical undermining of *Speed and Politics* and *The Aesthetics of Disappearance*; the Canadian philosopher George Grant's rejection of the universal homogeneous state to which technology is delivering us. What sets McLuhan apart is that, like Descartes before him, he has introduced a fundamental doubt into thinking the question of technology. Now that we live after McLuhan, now that the media at the epicenter of *Understanding Media* have been eclipsed by the mobile technologies at the digital heart of the regime of computation, now that the supposedly externalized, ablated world of technological prostheses have actually followed a great, almost astronomical, reversal, becoming, in effect, body invaders, McLuhan's doubt, his prescient sense that technology contains a paradoxical story of augmentation and disappearances, extensions, and entrapments, has amplified in importance as a profound way of understanding the future of new media.

For example, McLuhan's justifiably famous concept of the "tetrad" also has a dark side, a hauntological dimension. To paraphrase the performance artist Laurie Anderson, the tetrad also travels now at the "speed of darkness." Viewed in reverse mirror image, the tetrad reveals not only what has been gained but also what has been lost with the realization of the technological destiny to which the regime of computation delivers us. On its positive, transformative side, the tetrad reveals the (four) laws of social media to be our very own data flesh: what's *enhanced*, what's *retrieved*, what's rendered *obsolete*, what's intensified to the point of *reversal* with every major technological innovation. However, viewed in mirror image on the side of what is disowned, prohibited, and excluded by new technological media of communication, the tetrad has another story to tell:

- not what is enhanced, but what is *disappeared* by every technological innovation;
- not what is retrieved, but what is *abandoned* by the fast technological recycling of the natural and social worlds;
- not what is obsolesced, but what has been effectively *substituted* for that which is disappeared;
- not what is reversed, but just the opposite, what is *held in place, immobilized*, almost *cryogenically frozen* with the appearance of every new technological media of communication.

When the tetrad moves at the speed of darkness, what is shut down is the eye of perception that is fundamental to ethical reflection on the future of technology. What substitutes for the closing of the eye of perception is the "sightless vision" of all the machinery of guided perception of information culture. What has been abandoned as so much galactic digital debris by the twin drives of computation and genomics are those posthuman bodies in endless, aimless drift as they circulate through the fast loops of cybernetic information. And what is held in place, immobilized, is an increasingly specious present that is in equal measure deeply nostalgic for a lost modernism and for the stripping down of just about everything else to accommodate the laws of efficiency, connectivity, transparency, and speed that is at the heart of what Hannah Arendt called the "negative being" of technological society – a technological destiny that can be so deeply seductive because it contains the tangible, palpable scent of a death-drive in hyper-motion.

There are two key ways of thinking the future with Marshall McLuhan: *technologically* and *hauntologically*. Technologically, we are living within the electronic universe first theorized in all its complexity, speed, seduction, and violence by McLuhan's thought. Hauntologically, everything today is marked by all the signs of full digital saturation: information everywhere, connectivity pervasive, bodies augmented, perception illuminated, truth a purely phantasmagorical effect, perception coded by media feeds, attention fully wired – all this driven on by an economy specializing in the hyper-production of use-lessness. We have literally become posthuman in the sense that subjectivity is now immanent to the laws of media, that peculiarly technological condition in which subjectivity is both precondition and object of the fully realized digital society. In this abrupt and sudden entrance to the posthuman, things must necessarily lose their value, information must be stripped of the heavy gravitational weight of content, codes must be finally allowed to drift, and excess must become both the necessary aim and method of the posthuman scene. In this futurist scenario, only the excessive is desirable, only excess value has real value, and only excessive expenditure contains a fabulous, hidden trace of that which is most seductive – the final evaporation of the gravity well of the useful. Indeed, in the most material sense, McLuhan's speculative, prophetic vision has literally been written into existence by the techno-logical dynamo of which he was one of the first new media witnesses. That is precisely what makes his writings such a useful prolegomenon to the technological future. McLuhan's thought was the premonitory consciousness of the technological posthuman towards which we are speeding either as a terminal condition or as the possible beginning of a wondrous media ecology:

- *Understanding Media* is a necessary survival guide to the turbulence of the global village.
- *The Medium is the Massage* is our technological autobiography.
- *Counter-Blast* is our everyday digital existence after everything has been blown apart by the speed of technological innovation.
- *The Tetrad* is definitely no longer a theoretical event, but a way of being digital – reversing, obsolescing, augmenting, mimicking.
- *Explorations* is a sign of the reawakening of the creative imagina-tion.

Indeed, if McLuhan has provided such vivid conceptualizations of our technological future, that is because there is at the very core of his thought something deeply melancholic, even hauntological. Whether his tragic sense of technology had its roots in his Catholicism or was the critical attitude of a brilliantly synaesthetic imagination is debatable but one thing is for certain, that is McLuhan's profound ethical forebod-ing about the future of the technological galaxy. It's everywhere in his thought: the sense that we are wired victims drowning in the whirlpool of technological violence; passive objects of what the French theorist Jean Baudrillard has called the "perfect crime," of technology – its powerful will to technical perfectibility with the consequent elimination of the bodies and minds of the imperfect, the erroneous, the inefficient; "vicious turtles" with the soft side of our shells exposed to the danger and thus highly vulnerable, overexposed, irritable.

In this fateful time after McLuhan, thinking the future involves living with the uncertainty, unfinished endings, fractured meanings, enigmatic consequences, beautiful imperfections, interesting errors – experiencing a global village that is riding the shock waves of digital technology, all the while haunted by what has been pushed aside, disavowed, excluded by the coming to be of the digital universe. An enigmatic sign of the future, McLuhan's thought rehearsed decades in advance all the stresses, contradictions, contrapuntal meanings, ablations, and technological augmentations that would come to constitute the embryonic cultural tissue of the twenty-first century. Here, we are urged to open the eye of human perception that is the digital imagination, to remain simultaneously overexposed to the force field of technological change while listening intently to its "intimations of deprival." But, of course, if we did that, if, that is, we actually honored McLuhan by reflecting on the intimations of technological violence that were everywhere in his thought, we would be introduced to a very different history of the future. Not a future comfortably circumscribed within orderly laws of the media, but, for better or for worse, a digital future where technological media of communication also have a dark side – filled with the remainders, whether psychic, social, or biological, of that which has been left behind by the digital axiomatic. Living in the technological future that was the fascinated object of McLuhan's thought, perhaps it is time, past time, to have technology summon its reasons, to ask, that is, not only what has been accomplished by the laws of the (digital) media, but what has been obscured by the "cosmic dust" of the digital implosion that surrounds us. For McLuhan, this, the most strikingly technological of times, is also the most profoundly mythological. Here, following the rules of mythic recurrence, every gradient immediately calls into presence its necessary counter-gradient, every force field anticipates its own reversal, every visible message is nested in an invisible medium, every gain in light-speed and light-time is accompanied by an equal acceleration in dark-speed and dark-time, and every tetrad is paralleled by a dark tetrad. Consequently, why not honor McLuhan by an act of perfect intellectual fidelity: completing the mythological cycle of his thought, intensifying his creative probes of the media, by initiating a fatal reversal whereby the technological media of communication are fully exposed, and thus better understood, to their own disavowals? In this case, not only admiring the imaginative, creative breakthroughs so characteristic of technologies of speed, locational specificity, augmentation, and social networking, but also counting the rising costs associated with technologies of inertia, abandonment, substitution, and disappearance. When technology is put into question by balancing its dazzling affirmations with its necessary exclusions, what we are left with is a way of thinking McLuhan in the twenty-first century. Certainly, a different McLuhan than the twentieth-century technological utopianist, but for all that, a McLuhan whose ethical dissent rises from its previous status as an inconvenient fact in the midst of technological euphoria to a form of understanding that burns right through to technologies of the dark tetrad.

Technologies of the dark tetrad

Technologies of inertia: when McLuhan's universe of fast data suddenly reverses field

Now, more than ever, contemporary society seems to function on radically split speeds – accelerating technologies and slow economies, fast data and slow (social) histories, instant connectivity and stagnant opportunities – both simultaneous, both parallel, yet each tendency increasingly out of synch with the other, only really intersecting at points of intense opposition or political repression. For some time, leading enthusiasts of the fully realized technological society have marveled at its amazing speed – a global digital infrastructure processing data at light-speed, inexorably transforming local economies in the direction of greater computational integration, transmitting information at warp velocity, wrapping a still geographically isolated world in a dense network of social connectivity. At the same time, important aspects of public life are increasingly restricted to a slow track that appears, in fact, to be regressing towards inertia, data point by data point. For example, while it may be the case that 51 percent of all internet traffic is machine-to-machine communication with no human involvement and while the highly publicized global data traffic map in Google's headquarters reveals a strikingly beautiful image of the digital sublime – a fluid, shimmering worldview of Google data traffic as it lights up the geography of the algorithmic (global) village – the real world of materialized social history appears to be following a strikingly different trajectory. In this case, harsh economic austerity programs are increasingly the animating principle of public policy. Cutbacks to social programs are increasingly the norm. Technocratic metrics of performance regulating both students and teachers are introduced into the educational experience. Jobs are increasingly scarce, with high rates of unemployment often obscuring the real social crisis of the unemployable and those who have left the labor force. Class mobility is restricted, with class structure itself reflecting the new global economic reality of speed and slowness. Ideologically, the radical division of society into opposing sectors of technological velocity and generalized stagnation has quickly given rise to new forms of political expression, the most striking examples of which are, perhaps, proliferating instances of cynical truth-telling by the possessors of privilege and power in the new digital universe. Today, when power speaks, it often openly reveals deep resentments on the part of ruling economic elites about the social claims of the disenfranchised, to the point that those in real positions of economic power often assume the subject-position of victimhood. For those effectively forced off-grid in the new public morality of augmented power and consolidated wealth, this is profoundly consequential. In the future, severe disciplinary measures against those identified as surplus to the functioning of technological society will probably be taken with a good conscience, indeed with an overriding sense of public duty, by governing elites, including policing the poor, regulating the unemployed, prescribing austerity programs, and suppressing popular protest. While Heidegger anticipated this grim future with his prophetic vision of "abuse value," the newly emergent mixture of psychological resentment and economic self-interest introduces a new element into contemporary public morality. In this case, economic avarice mixed with a psychological anger against the poor, the weak, the powerless on the part of ruling elites produces a volatile psychic combination, perhaps going beyond the future anticipated by the political scientist Harold Lasswell when he predicted a form of politics based on the displacement of affect onto the public situation to that future prophesied by William Blake – a future characterized by "monstrous consciousness" growing out of the sleep of reason.

In terms of its underlying structural logic, technologies of inertia are directly related to the growing triumphalism of the digital commodity-form and its related class structure. When it first emerged, seemingly full blown, in the final decades of the twentieth century under the utopian sign of the tech bubble, the digital commodity-form had about it all the raw, exuberant, creative energies of Schumpeter's "creative destruction." Here, clearly breaking with the industrial phase of capitalism, the digital commodity-form introduced a fundamentally new mode of production in direct conflict with existing relations of production. Motivated by the virtualization of globalized capital and the reduction of labor to fungible exchange value – deterritorialized, mobile, extractive – the digital commodity-form quickly assumed the purely phantasmagorical form of a global economic fetish. In effect, the will to (digital) technology quickly became the master metric against which social relations of production associated with old modes of production, whether in communication, industry, education, publishing, broadcasting or finance, were to be both measured and reset. First appearing in a late twentieth-century political history where traditional antagonisms between socialism and capitalism had effectively collapsed, the digital commodity-form swiftly assumed the privileged position of comprising the universal principle of economic, and then social, exchange. It was almost as if, finally exhausted from their long political struggle during the course of the Cold War, the two master ideologies of the twentieth century – socialism and capitalism, thesis and antithesis – evolved into a new dialectical synthesis, the digital axiomatic. Resolutely capitalist, triumphantly technocratic, obsessively focused on securing its economic and political gains yet highly flexible in terms of its different national expressions of public policy and levels of state intervention, whether in terms of security issues or social justice, the digital axiomatic has emerged as the master discourse of the twenty-first century, providing a comprehensive, coherent, and self-justifying worldview that not only defines overall goals (the fully realized technological society whether expressed by digital devices, AI, social networking, or cloud computation) but also its underlying assumptions (singularity theory). While individuals, nations, and even organized blocs of nations could disagree on the merits of the *particular will* expressed by clashing ideologies, what remained constant was that, increasingly, the global *general will* was expressed by a shared commitment to a digitally networked society: coded by algorithms, linked by social media, powered by data, inspired by technological creativity, and seduced by the promise that digital technology is a fast exit to a new singularity moment, that moment when the human species finally crosses over to a new order of species-being: part data/ part flesh/part prosthetic.

With this result: what governs social opportunities today, what most clearly divides populations on the basis of access to power and privilege, what streams individual biographies into vectors of high velocity or deep inertia is one's objective class relationship to the digital commodity-form. Historically realized by the emergence, on an increasingly global scale, of a new class structure, the triumph of the digital axiomatic effectively instituted a complex segregation of power, privilege, and mobility according to the relationship of class position to the digital commodity-form. A hard-edged class sorting process, strictly enforcing rules for inclusion and exclusion, the digital axiomatic privileges the emergence of new ruling elites, whether economic, political or cultural, that work to institute the overall aims of the regime of computation as well as to provide creative visions of the digital future. While the rising directorate of the digital commodity-form provides a coherent and compelling vision of the digital future, that future requires for its realization the development of a global class of digital specialists whose labor-value lies in literally coding the digital future, that is, translating the overall vision of the digital future into enforceable requirements for its historical realization. At one with the digital commodity-form, articulating its needs and facilitating its growth, these two digital class fragments – directors and specialists – are what is meant by speed growth, speed economy, and speed communication. Fast-tracked through contemporary society, transcendent of local historical determinations, the content and scope of their work increasingly global, mobile, fungible, networked, the leading classes of the digital future can enjoy the full benefits of hyper-acceleration in their incomes, careers, and life-opportunities precisely because their technologically augmented labor is, in its essence, the necessary means to the self-preservation of the digital commodity-form. Outside of this particular expression of the digital axiomatic, there are only variations of inertia and stagnation, certainly for workers who, if their very social existence is not being disappeared as part of the overall self-understanding of (digital) society, are daily confronted with economic challenges that highlight its increasingly precarious relationship to the digital commodity-form. Factories are closed, jobs are outsourced, wages are reduced by edict, unions are discredited, labor is automated – this is the contemporary fate of a working class whose economic functionality is no longer perceived as central to the regime of economic computation. Acutely aware of the inevitable social discontent that will likely follow from the systematic undermining of the working class, the state, operating at the behest of the digital commodity-form, imposes in society after society three political solutions. First, the often unilateral proclamation of the *austerity state*, one that is aimed directly at further eroding the social entitlements of workers, in effect, forcing workers through reductions in long-term social benefits to pay for the transition to the new digital future, with its requirements for a smaller, stream-lined, technologically trained workforce. Second, the imposition of the *disciplinary state*, whereby governments respond to politics in the streets by triggering harsh, and often experimental, methods of policing. Third, the *bunker state*, whereby governments seek to control flows of migration precipitated by global poverty in general and, specifically, the impoverishment of both the working class and those unable to find work by strengthening national borders, erecting walls, and shutting down boundary exchanges between the rich and the poor. In effect, while the digital axiomatic is an increasingly open system at the level of universal commodity exchange itself, it is a self-consciously closed system at those points where the digital axiomatic collides with the real world of workers' rights, political opposition in the streets, migrant labor, and global poverty. In this case, the mixture of avarice and con-tempt on the part of ruling elites combined with a sense of triumphal indifference by the specialist class might be construed as the moral reflex of the ascendant digital commodity-form. In essence, the triumph of the digital commodity-form constitutes the really existent, invisible ideology that frames much of contemporary politics, whether nation-ally or internationally.

Technologies of abandonment: lost dreams of the sustainable "global village"

Insurgencies of the periphery: Idle No More, a courageous Indigenous political protest of global significance, takes place in the bitter cold of a Canadian winter.[1] Inspired by a hunger strike by an Indigenous woman, Chief Theresa Spence, an Attawapiskat tribal leader, from a community on the shores of James Bay, Idle No More is resistance by the abandoned. Not quiet resistance, but Indigenous collectivities in solidarity, spontaneously organizing as dancing flash mobs moving to the inspiring rhythms of Indigenous drummers in shopping malls, outdoor city squares, blockading busy highways and barricading railway tracks. Day after day, the hunger strike by Chief Spence con-tinues with one simple, but basic, demand: to meet with the Canadian government to negotiate nation-to-nation exploitative land-use policies affecting all the energy sectors that are quickly destroying the land and its Indigenous inhabitants. The government's official response is the silence of cynical indifference, perhaps based on the political calcula-tion that defeating Indigenous protest will facilitate exploitation of the land. In this case, the themes rise beyond simple politics to the level of eschatology. As long as Indigenous responsibility for the land and its inhabitants exists, the earth will continue to exist. Disappear Indigenous protest, and the land and its (dissenting) inhabitants may well disappear as well. When McLuhan once said that, in the electronic world, any periphery can quickly become the center of politics, he probably didn't have in mind a hunger strike undertaken by a single Indigenous woman in a teepee on a small island on the Ottawa River across from the parliament buildings of Canada. Truly one of those insurgencies of the periphery in which great eschatological themes – the future of the land, the very survival of Indigenous peoples, the possible reconciliation of humans with earth, sky, water, and air – achieve such powerful clarity that suddenly the center of politics, Canadian at first, but swiftly by extension any form of politics steered by massive energy projects, gravitates around the profound ethical issues raised by an Indigenous tribal leader who says "no."

With Idle No More, we are present at the first of the clashes of cosmology that will increasingly dominate the politics and culture of the twenty-first century – a cosmological collision between the system of politics, economy, and information associated with the ruling will to technology and the more profound vision of sustainability emerging from this insurgency of the periphery. If official power can respond only with the silence of indifference, perhaps that is because the masters of the technological universe – political and energy elites – recognize that no mediation is possible in this clash of cosmology, that in the courageous body politics of an Indigenous tribal leader willing to wager her claims to a broader sense of justice on the scales of life and death, that everything is at stake, that there can be no easy reconciliation between these competing life visions because what is really involved here is less a local political protest than a fundamental turning point in the direction of cosmology – technologies of abandonment represented in all their destructive intensity by mass energy projects versus enduring dreams of earth, land, and people mediated by social community and personal responsibility as a common dwelling place. Seemingly everything, today, is environment to the will to technology, not only the natural environment but human nature as well with all that entails for the future of human subjectivity. Transcendental in spirit and driven by a double dialectic of augmentation and incorporation, the will to technology has evolved to a point well in excess of what Nietzsche described as the "will to power" and Heidegger the "will to will." Perhaps sensing the appearance of an epochal change, that moment when the will to technology began to turn back on itself, the philosopher Hannah Arendt captured the essence of contemporary times when she noted in her last book, *Life of the Mind*, that the future will be fully enveloped by the metaphysics of the "not-will" – a time of abandonment of all that is not necessary for the self-preservation of the will to technology. In Arendt's prophetic vision, the historical primacy of conditions for the self-preservation of technique will inevitably result in the nihilism of "not-being," that moment in which everything that is valued is measured only in its relationship to the self-preservation of the will to technology and, subsequently, everything that is not a condition of self-preservation is abandoned, effectively left behind as surplus remainder. Idle No More, this insurgency of the periphery, this declaration on behalf of a deeper conception of a sustainable environment that speaks to issues of individuals, community, and nature, is a rebellion against this formulation of the will to technology.

Of course, concerning the question of the sustainable environment, it must be said at first that the concept of sustainability is itself a highly contested term. Sustainability for whom, for what, and for what period of time? Increasingly, a floating signifier without fixed content, the concept of sustainability has now accelerated into an abstract form seemingly justifying virtually any content. Today, there are multiple appeals for sustainable capitalism, sustainable cities, sustainable lifestyles, sustainable consumption – appeals that may commonly share the value-attribute of the sustainability brand, but that, unlike Idle No More, demand no fundamental alteration in the logic of things. For example, while contemporary environmental discourse privileges the concept of *intermediation* – a complex interdependence among all living species, including plants, animals, and humans – traditional approaches to environmentalism assume the automatic primacy of the human species, with primacy given to the self-preservation of humans in the supposed hierarchy of being. Equally, the discourse of sustainability often fails to take into account that the deep grasp of contemporary forms of subjectivity – possessed individualism – is sustaining a propertied view of individual rights over the prescriptions for responsibility and care that are central to environmental discourse. Consequently, not so much hijacked by capitalism as simply absorbed by the dynamism of its overall logic, the meaning of sustainability has actually been reversed. Today, sustainability is increasingly the name given to that which is necessary for extending the self-preservation of a predatory system of value extraction that leaves in its wake the abandoned, the remainder, the habitually unrecognized.

Against this limited vision of sustainability, there is the evocative perspective of the contemporary anthropologist Nancy Turner, who highlights the metaphor of "the Earth's blanket" as a way of living among Pacific Northwestern Indigenous people.[2] The image of the earth as a life-sustaining blanket challenges, of course, the violence against the earth committed by mega-energy projects. If the earth is a blanket, then that blanket is in the process of being destroyed by the massive Tar Sands project in western Canada or by new drilling methods – high-volume horizontal fracturing, or hydrofracking – aimed at extracting natural gas trapped between thin layers of shale. In the United States, the Obama administration has enthusiastically supported hydrofracking as the center-point of a national strategy aimed at energy self-sustainability. That what is at stake in discussing different concepts of sustainability is truly something cosmological, almost mythological, is evidenced by the fact that more and more ecologists and land managers have been drawn to the "traditional ecological knowledge" of Indigenous peoples with its deeply ethical vision of "responsibility to the Seventh Generation" and its sense that while the short term consists of decades of generations, the long term can only be considered in terms of multiple generations. Increasingly then, it is as if the concept of sustainability brings into presence something until now hidden deeply in the logic of society: the notion that the future will surely witness a growing clash of cosmological perspectives, each of which provides a very different exit to the posthuman future. In this case, what is the horizon of a global economy for multiple generations? What living social forms can sustainability enact that speak to the ethics of the seventh generation? And does not the concept of sustainability also necessarily imply its opposite – that a substantive vision of a sustainable future, for humans and the physical world, assumes that there are some activities that need to be rendered *unsustainable*, some contemporary directions of society that need to be disavowed, excluded, prohibited?

Debates over the contested meaning of sustainability occur in a real-world circumstance in which history is on the move again, in which the global explosion of truly creative technologies of communication is easily matched by an equally global implosion of society after society into the most recidivist of ancient antagonisms – ethnic rivalries, fear of global immigration to the point that the most prosperous economies of the world feverishly bunker their populations behind walled borders, some physical, some legal, bitter hatreds encouraged by religious fundamentalisms, and the sudden collapse of entire national economies, from the bankruptcy of key sectors of the banking structure in the 2008 financial crisis to the continuing crisis of overindebtedness in Greece, Portugal, Spain, and Ireland. So, then, can we really speak of a sustainable future in the context of a present historical circumstance that is definitely not sustainable in terms of clashes of religion, atavistic politics, and economic immiseration? Or paradoxically, is it precisely the fact that the present is not sustainable in its current form that should provide a global spring of human hope? Such hope is already gathering, from the democratic aspirations expressed by the populations of Syria, Libya, Egypt, and Tunisia to the popular demands expressed by the earthly inhabitants of all the Tahrir Squares of the human spirit that, somehow, somewhere, an evolving global consciousness concerning the reconciliation of basic human rights with equally basic human needs finds its moment of public realization.

We live today in the shadow of dramatic world events in which the dominant patterns of life in the 3-D millennium are slowing beginning to reveal themselves. It is truly ironic that the connection between the tragedy of the human suffering and bleakness of environmental catastrophe that is post-nuclear contemporary Japan and the cruel stories of popular resistance against tyranny in many societies revolves around the question of energy. Those who predicted that the twenty-first century would witness a proliferation of fossil-fuel wars undoubtedly had in mind a future dominated by large-scale confrontations between great sovereign powers – the United States, China, India, and the European Community – over increasingly scarce energy resources. However, such predictions failed to anticipate that the story of extractive fossil energy, like all of material and human history, is always complicated by its social inflections, that attempts to escape energy scarcity by going nuclear threaten to unleash the whirlwind of environmental catastrophe; and that efforts to monopolize oil energy to the benefit of tyranny often unleash a popular storm of democratic discontent. More than we may suspect, everything today is interconnected, intermediated, intergenerational, in effect, a "global village" with all its utopian potential yet dystopian realities.

Technologies of disappearance: media as amputations of the senses, not "extensions"

In an important reflection on the relationship of Heidegger's concept of "abuse value" to contemporary society, Michael A. Weinstein, an American political theorist, appealed for a form of critical reflection that had about it "the strength to remember." While Weinstein's appeal was focused specifically on the subject of "thinking the death camps with Martin Heidegger,"[3] his cautionary note was prophetic – that only a form of "resolute remembrance" could in the future prevent geno-cidal behaviors based on the administration of a "double death" to politically selected scapegoats, whether chosen on the basis of race, religion, ethnicity, or security. Following the pathway of thought first charted in all its bleakness by Heidegger, Weinstein argued that the characteristic sign of state-administered sacrificial violence is that the death of the individual is always doubled, representing not only the physical liquidation of the body but also the erasure of the *being* of the victims of mass violence. Here, the victims of holocaust were assaulted by a form of power that precipitated a new level of violence, one aimed at terminating the life of the body as well as eliminating the ability of individuals to die their own death authentically. When power aspires to alienate the meaning of both life and death, making of itself a violent process through which individual lives must pass, whether as a matter of life or death, then, at that point, power would achieve its long-sought status as a totalizing world hypothesis. For those tar-geted in advance for reduction to a state of nonbeing, stripped of the means to life and the authenticity of death, only "resolute remem-brance" can, in the first instance, act as a necessary moral antidote.

This eloquent appeal for the "strength to remember" can be so proxi-mate to contemporary events because the "double death" first identi-fied by Heidegger and thought so deeply by Weinstein has, I believe, escaped the particular genealogy of its origins in twentieth-century experience to become a disturbing potential trend in the contemporary digital axiomatic. With regard to *life*, what drives the digital axiomatic forward is precisely the transcendent technological belief that the regime of computation is itself an advanced form of a living, sentient species-being, indeed a likely successor to an exhausted humanity. Whether expressed in the language of robotics (Hans Moravec's *Mind Children*), the scientific vision of biogenetics (Richard Dawkins's *The Selfish Gene*), the codes of technology (Kevin Kelly's *What Technology Wants*), or in the mytho-poetic vision of singularity theory (Ray Kurz-weil's *The Singularity is Near*), the conclusion is the same: that what is being disappeared today is the history of a human species – a form of species-being perceived to be at the end of its evolutionary life cycle. With regard to death, the outlook for the digital future is strictly algo-rithmic. Visibly authoritarian in its initial economic expression, the digital axiomatic provides for the consolidation of advanced capitalism on a high level of abstraction and generalization. Accommodating the politics of contemporary liberal-democratic states as well as socialist societies, the digital axiomatic imposes a new *life-form* on the global political economy: its *ontology* – the triumph of the regime of computation; its *epistemology* – the universalization of the digital commodity-form; its *axiology* – the social practices of the ascendant digital class; and its *aesthetic* – an eschatological struggle between the new security state and drift culture.

On the basis of this operating logic, the digital axiomatic requires for its self-preservation technologies of disappearance – certainly, the disappearance of challenges to the regime of computation as much as the suppression of politics in the streets, but also the disavowal of those bodies identified as superfluous to the organic growth of the digital life-form. Manifestly, the form of power used to accomplish this disappearance of the surplus class is characterized, once again, by a double death, focused not only on increasingly arbitrage-like questions concerning who lives and dies in the world's population today, but also on a strict reduction of those bodies denied recognition as human beings worthy of basic rights to the status of nonbeings. In effect, to fall outside the moral axiomatic of the digital life-form by being signified with the status of nonbeing is to immediately become what Heidegger denoted as the form of subjectivity that would dominate the future culture of fully accomplished nihilism, a "reserve-object," subjected to capricious spasms of abuse value, rendered invisible by ethical indifference, always living on the dark side of being itself. When technology becomes a sentient life-form, then drift culture is also about living at the edge of what is allowed to rise into morally prescribed visibility and what is targeted to be ethically disappeared into nonbeing. In this case, "resolute remembrance" of other bodies, other sensibilities, other modes of being is also a way of counteracting a form of technological power that would invest itself with lifelike qualities as a replacement species for a putatively outmoded humanity.

Technologies of substitution: clones, avatars, androids, zombies as possible successor species

The long-term endurance of technological society depends on a daring mythological gamble: that the human species, increasingly comprised of humiliated subjectivity and fully envious of the purely virtual existence of its digital successor, would will its own extinction. In its strictly capitalist determination, the world hypothesis of digital reality brings together delirious, transcendental visions of the technological sublime with the sophisticated algorithms of advanced finance capitalism to produce a dazzling array of substitute realities, from the phantasmagorical imagery of the media and high-frequency trading to the virtual modeling of the political arena. Signs of slow cultural suicide are preva-lent, including popular enthusiasm with life on the lip of the net, individual technological autobiographies that blur boundaries between digital devices and human affect, and the pirating of important dimen-sions of public institutions by the predatory models of technologically augmented capitalism.

To this point, the results have been as tragic as they are predictable: complex economies placed under the control of high-velocity virtual algorithms suddenly spinning out of control; political campaigns in which otherwise seasoned politicians actually begin to confuse abstract, ideologically skewed models of "likely" voting behavior with the real world of individuated political interests; the death of media as a result of its increasing signification as a closed semiurgical system of meaning, moving only to its own internal rhetorical rhythms, all the while, radi-cally disconnected from the fractured, bifurcated world of human dis-course; and, finally, the increasing casualties of Virilio's "accident of technology." The list of casualties is fully indeterminate, involving as it does both public life and private autobiography: the unemployed accidented by outsourcing; the powerless accidented by the democratic deficit; the poor accidented by the global consolidation of wealth; human vision accidented by the "sight machine"; the human nervous system accidented by McLuhan's technological exteriorization of con-sciousness; laboring activity accidented by the increasing automation of work; and individuals and families suddenly accidented by death from the air in the form of drone attacks. When the computationally driven virtual models of politics, economy, media, and biology crash into the always messy realities of material historical experience, the result is crash culture, with social debris flying by seemingly every-where, the human sensorium digitally outsourced, economic crises increasingly visible, palpable traces of anxiety embedded in the deepest levels of subjectivity, generalized feelings of boredom mixed with random acts of terror, and panic attempts by public leaders to put back together what can never really be reassembled – the technologi-cally shattered remains of lives, economies, politics, and policies in the aftermath of the digital blast. In its strictly capitalist determination, a future digital culture, then, is characterized by primitive capitalism in terms of labor practices, a perpetual austerity politics with respect to the administration of political discipline, mass phantasmatic identi-fication with media spectacles, and hypermarketing as the emblematic sign of a consumption society. In the end, the real seduction of the will to technology may have to do with what Nietzsche first noted when he said that power always turns into itself in furious bouts of self-destruction and self-abnegation – the pleasure of the ruins within. If Freud discussed the "death instinct" as the primordial sign of modern culture and Hannah Arendt reflected on the emergence of "negative being" as the key psycho-ontology of contemporary history, this is only to report as we experience the second decade of the twenty-first century that the history, the *posthuman* history, about to be realized will make of the insights of Nietzsche, Freud, and Arendt *posthumous thought*, that is, thought that may have been articulated in the nineteenth and twentieth centuries but which will only really be actualized in its full ferocity in the future of the fully accomplished technological society.

Prosthetic gods

This is, perhaps, what makes technologies of substitution so fascinating, both in terms of abjection and creativity. If the substitution effect of digital technology has now emerged from electronic media of communication as extensions of, and eventually substitutes for, the human nervous system and from digital devices, again first as ablations and then replacements for individual consciousness, the overall direction of the digital future is towards a generalized substitution of technological destiny for the social-reality principle itself. Cultural intimations of this are pervasive, from positivistic visions of the internet as a living, sentient being to philosophical critiques of "fully completed nihilism" as the essence of technology. This is, in fact, what makes the posthuman future so deeply enigmatic and consequential. Here, all the outriders of the posthuman future – theorists, artists, programmers, genomic visionaries, philosophers – gather together to see what can be made of this strange spectacle of a whole world caught up in the violent collision of code terror and the always errant human imagination. We know from hard cybernetic experience that code bends everything to its rules of intelligibility – cyber-economy, cyber-ethics, cyber-media, cyberwarfare. We can recognize that we are fast-transitioning to the lip of the net, that, now more than ever, we are data flesh riding the spreading shock waves of complex algorithms, but we can also discern that some very enduring things haven't changed at all. It's a lonely crowd at the digital spectacle. What everyone seems to like best about the technological devices that populate the space of social media are their sleek, almost magical, efficiency – the precise value-form that is most indispensable for the functioning of technological capitalism. We are not even certain anymore that the regime of computation has anything to do with rationality. Perhaps the digital straitjacket of code is the name given for something profoundly psychological – the wrapping of the skin of humanity in the digital superego. In his conclusion to *Civilization and its Discontents*, Freud reflected on the relationship between personal psychology and its cultural counterpart. For Freud, the fate of the coming centuries would be marked by the public playing out of the bitter struggle among the powerful instinctual drives of the id and the equally harsh demands of the superego to control the fate of the ego:

> Man has, as it were, become a kind of prosthetic God. When he puts on all his auxiliary organs he is truly magnificent; but those organs have not grown on to him and they still give him much trouble at times. . . . We will not forget [though] that present-day man does not feel happy in his Godlike character.[4]

So, then, the future as civilization and its digital discontents, where the auxiliary organs that we have wrapped ourselves in as prosthetic gods – data flesh, augmented senses, distributed consciousness, artificial intelligence – have not escaped the fatal destinies of all utopian mythologies, specifically that the regime of computation contains within itself the burning embers of Hegel's "unhappy consciousness," just as much as the culture of code – hyper-normalized, hyper-protected, hyper-archived, hyper-tracked – increasingly experiences all the psychological discontents of the always unsuccessful struggle of the harsh superego to suppress the aggressiveness but also the sublimity of human instinctual drives.

In the most realistic sense, futurism is finished as an intellectual project because we are now not only living out the future of technology that was so long prophesied and feared by so many thinkers who have gone before us, but the future that has now curved back on itself. It's as if the future presents itself now as a gigantic simulacrum of the recycled remnants of all that which was left unfinished by the coming-to-be of the technological dynamo – unfinished religious wars, unfinished ethnic struggles, unfinished class warfare, unfinished sacrificial violence and spasms of brutal power, often motivated by a psychology of anger on the part of the most privileged members of the so-called global village. The apocalypse seems to be coming our way like a specter on the horizon, not a grand epiphany of events but by one lonely text message at a time.

If everything now is fully ambivalent in its meaning and ambiguous in its consequences, perhaps we might also ask that technology itself be rendered problematic in detail and definition. Rendered problematic, that is, by the practice of subtle imagination, depth perception, complex human intelligence – in short, by the posthuman imagination. Perhaps it is time to remember the deeply ethical lessons passed on by earlier generations: Guy Debord's prophecy that forcing human perception to move at the speed of light will only culminate in the society of the spectacle; Virilio's dark vision of the aesthetics of disappearance that follows from dropping the information bomb on society; McLuhan's grisly image of technology as always performing psychic surgery on the human nervous system; Foucault's bleak vision of the incarceration of bodies by the eye of power; Baudrillard's delirious vision of a society based on fourth-order simulations that increasingly run on automatic at the speed of sacrificial violence. At drift across the charred landscape of the digital blast, sometimes isolated by technologies that suffocate as much as they augment, informed but often powerless, there remains those fateful words spoken by Albert Camus: "I rebel – therefore *we* exist."[5]

12

Epilogue:
Media Theory in the Data Storm

Figural aesthetics

Any interpretation comes along and hollows out its object from the inside, comes along and substitutes what the object is supposed to hide from what it's assumed to manifest. Thus, interpretation feeds on nihilism, and feeds nihilism.

Jean-Francois Lyotard, *Duchamp's TRANS/formers*[1]

What if we were to think media theory as itself an artistic practice, that is, as a form of aesthetic imagination that seeks to directly enter the world of data nerves, network skin, and increasingly algorithmic minds with the intention of capturing the dominant mood of these posthuman times – drift culture – in a form of thought that dwells in complicated intersections and complex borderlands? In its essence, thinking with and against the larger technopoesis of accelerate, drift, and crash that holds us in its sway requires a form of media reflection that is itself an exit to the posthuman future. Here, refusing to stand outside its immediate historical circumstances and always seeking to capture in its rhythms the mood of accelerate, drift, and crash, media theory of this order allies itself with a form of emergent consciousness that is pervasive in the digital world, namely figural aesthetics.

With its global gathering of new media artists, remix musicians, pirate gamers, AI graffiti artists, anonymous witnesses, and code rebels, the emerging order of figural aesthetics reveals a new order, a brilliantly hallucinatory order, based on an art of impossible questions and a perceptual language as precise as it is evocative. Here, the aesthetic imagination dwells solely on questions of incommensurability: What is the vision of the clone? What is the affect of the code? What is the hauntology of the avatar? What is most excluded, prohibited, by the android? What is the perception of the drone? What are the aesthetics of the fold? What, in short, is the meaning of aesthetics in the age of drift culture?

In this case, understood as an aesthetic order of (new media) art that seeks to enter directly into the circulatory regime of the code, literally in the process becoming itself symptomatically energized by the vortices of data flows and algorithmic coding, figural aesthetics is always multiple in its artistic expressions, certainly humanizing, but also tragic, neutral, and sometimes cynical. No longer an art of expression or representation, but art that literally catches the drift of its times by entering directly into the violent perturbations of the code-stream – a form of art that is figural precisely because it registers simultaneously all the fatal speed and tragic intimations of deprival implicit in an increasingly technical reality. Not necessarily, then, a multimedia art that evokes the contagious energy of the code, although that too, but a form of art that stands poised at the fracture (Duchamp's "hinge")[2] of presence and absence, drawing into itself all the contradictions and complexity and folds of digital reality itself. Driven by a speed of (aesthetic) perception that easily exceeds the speed of the code, mobilized by a new way of seeing that is balanced between in-depth participation in the (digital) object of its study and an incommensurable drawing away from ruling narratives that would capture it, and attentive to the fact every artifact of technological posthumanism, from digital devices to private autobiography, is a possible object of artistic interest, figural aesthetics floats in the drifts of codes, history, video, and media as their intersecting point of evocation and undermining. Sensitive to fundamental changes in the order of sense perception, the artistic imagination has always functioned as a navigator, simultaneously intimate with and at a critical distance from the digital recoding of the human sensorium. Consequently, it comes as no surprise that the first response to the emerging complexities of technological posthumanism is most definitely aesthetic in form. Not a mode of aesthetics that remains at one (safe) remove from the technological transitioning of the question of the human species-form, but the swift emergence now of a style of aesthetics – figural aesthetics – that enters directly into the complexities of drift culture. Sometimes, figural aesthetics adopts the language of design. It becomes a rider of the data storm, negotiating new pathways through the radical uncertainty of the digital future. At other points, figural aesthetics offers profound meditations on the accident of technology by invoking in the language of art the ancient tradition of lament. Deliberately challenging officially prescribed frameworks of understanding, figural art of this order quickly calls down upon itself the most severe form of policing. Literally, the framework of power involved in securing contemporary norms of political intelligibility is suspicious of thought, particularly of those artistic articulations of remembrance and lament that work to undermine otherwise invisible frameworks of official interpretation. Of course, when data slams into the human condition, the result is not only the swift eradication of familiar landmarks in understanding the here, there, and everywhere of social intelligibility, but the rapid rise to prominence of new forms of figural art – mobile, augmented, remix, scanner – that in both form and content reflect the shape of the unfolding future and, in that fatal reflection, render that future uncertain and truly enigmatic. And how could it be otherwise when the earliest signs of the coming of the posthuman allude to the surfacing of body futures that are multiple: sometimes enhanced data bodies, but also bodies that have gone off-grid, bodies colonized by mono-data, bodies circulating in the digital debris of spam, spyware, viruses and contagions, and even twisted bodies caught in the opposing energy flows of the seduction of connectivity and the negation of relentless digital overexposure.

Figural aesthetics is the spectral eye of the posthuman, that point where art enters the order of digital being with such perceptual intensity that it makes of itself a mutating sign of the collision of the code, the human, the android, the metallic, and perhaps even of the digital zombie. Art of this (posthuman) order recodes the question of aesthetics by the creation of a mode of perception that fully opens to the discontinuous, the fragmentary, the uncertain, the reversal. What results is a form of figural art – posthuman art – that has no necessary medium of expression precisely because it is always an art of the intersection, the incommensurable, the bifurcation, the broken code, the glitch that reveals the darkness within, the static that reflects the passage of pure speed. Art of this order is a haunting talisman of the posthuman, neither its advent nor termination, but a form of posthuman aesthetics that can never express anything external to itself because figural art constitutes in its essence the uncanny meaning of the posthuman moment – fluid, mobile, folded, combinatorial, transitional. Consequently, figural aesthetics is an art of motion but also an art of inertia – speed and slowness, noise and silence. With its strange juxtapositions, unexpected folds, fluid intersections, figural art can be so strangely familiar to us, the earliest inhabitants of the technological posthuman, because it is an advance outrider of a new form of perception that is already practiced on a daily basis but nowhere fully culturally acknowledged. While most certainly this new aesthetic language seeks to describe what has happened to the body, consciousness, labor, culture itself when folded within the cyclotron of computation, it also brings to the surface the deeper ethical concerns of society: the terrorism of the code, the revenge-taking of the failing master narratives, the injured sensibility of subject-narratives in rapid decline, the growing *ressentiment* of the human at its eclipse by the technological posthuman, the cynical relief of the abject human at being unburdened of its eschatological responsibility for being a coherent species-being – the fatal embodiment of the will to technology. Lyotard's *Driftworks* announced the opening themes of figural art: "Here is a course of action: harden, worsen, accelerate decadence. Adopt the perspective of active nihilism, exceed the mere recognition – be it depressive or admiring – of the destruction of all values. Become more and more incredulous. Push decadence further still and accept, for instance, to destroy the belief in truth under all its forms." Now that the posthuman condition has revealed decadence – incredulous, excessive decadence – as the basic ontology of late capitalism, the point of a figural art that would "harden, worsen, accelerate decadence" would be precisely the reverse, that is to say, it would draw into a greater visibility those intangible, but very real, impulses to social solidarity and ethical probity that haunt the order of the real. So, then, figural art is always a navigator of uncertainty because it remains, above all, an explorer, a hinge, a fracture, in the midst of the data storm.

Notes

Chapter 1   Introduction

1   N. Katherine Hayles, *How We Became Posthuman: Virtual Bodies in Cybernetics, Literature, and Informatics*, Chicago: University of Chicago Press, 1999.
2   Cary Wolfe, *What is Posthumanism?*, Minneapolis: University of Minneapolis Press, 2010.
3   Francis Fukuyama, *Our Posthuman Future: Consequences of the Biotechnology Revolution*, New York: Picador, 2002.
4   The full patent application for the heartbeat monitor for the iPhone ("seamlessly embedded heart rate monitor") available at: http://appft. uspto.gov/netacgi/nph-Parser?Sect1=PTO1&Sect2=HITOFF&d=PG 01&p=1&u=%2Fnetahtml%2FPTO%2Fsrchnum.html&r=1&f=G&l=5 0&s1=%2220100113950%22.PGNR.&OS=DN/20100113950&RS=DN/2010 0113950, accessed June 22, 2013.
5   Dr Anthony Atala, Wake Forest Institute for Regenerative Medicine, "Printing a Human Kidney," www.ted.com/talks/anthony_atala_printing_a_ human_kidney.html, TED, March, 2011 and *Chatelaine*, November 2012, p. 178.
6   www.cbc.ca/news/technology/story/2011/05/02/technology-quirks-organ-transplant-engineering.html, accessed June 24, 2013.
7   Hiroko Tabuchi, "Japanese Robots Enter Daily Life," http://usatoday30. usatoday.com/tech/news/robotics/2008-03-01-robots_N.htm, accessed June 24, 2013.
8   I have discussed the (technological) genealogy and (cultural) impact of technologies of acceleration in many of my previous writings, including *Technology and the Canadian Mind: Innis/McLuhan/Grant:* New York: St Martin's Press, 1985; *The Postmodern Scene* (with David Cook), New York: St Martin's Press, 1986; *Data Trash: The Theory of the Virtual Class* (with Michael A. Weinstein), New York: St Martin's Press, 1994; *Panic Encyclopedia* (with Marilouise Kroker and David Cook), St Martin's Press, 1989; *The Possessed Individual: Technology and the French Postmodern*, New York: St Martin's Press, 1992; and *The Will to Technology: Heidegger, Marx and*

Nietzsche, Toronto and Buffalo: University of Toronto Press, 2004. Specifically, *Technology and the Canadian Mind* rehearsed the clash of perspectives among technological realism, utopianism, and pessimism as rehearsed in the writings of Marshall McLuhan, Harold Innis, and George Grant. *The Postmodern Scene* explored contemporary technological culture in terms of a doubled movement towards excremental culture and hyper-aesthetics. *The Possessed Individual* discussed newly emergent forms of political subjectivity produced by technological acceleration, including Virilio's vision of the postmodern body as a war machine, Baudrillard's image of the simulacrum, Lyotard's concept of libidinal technology, Deleuze and Guattari's theory of virtuality, and Barthes' rhetoric of technology. Sometimes assuming the form of "drift culture," at other times expressing itself in terms of a wide variety of "panic" symptomologies, and most currently adopting the representative political subjectivity of the "possessed individual" living under the ascendant economic sign of the "virtual class," the impact of relentless technological acceleration is complex, mediated, and unmistakable. In my estimation, the writings of Paul Virilio, from *Open Sky, The Information Bomb*, and *Crepuscular Dawn* to *The Aesthetics of Disappearance*, best capture the inner logic and outward social and cultural manifestations of a culture of "pure speed." While other works, specifically Nicholas Negroponte's *Being Digital* and Mark Dery's *Escape Velocity*, have evocatively described the first cultural, and subcultural, expressions of the current transition to a culture of the atom moving at light-speed, my sense is that technologies of acceleration cannot really be understood, at this point, except in terms of their complex interpellations with the larger technological technopoesis of accelerate, drift, and crash that now gathers us into its still unknown, still unpredictable destiny.

Chapter 2   The Posthuman Imagination

1   "Google X Lab-Artificial Intelligence and Robotics," www.artificialbrains.com/google-x-lab, accessed June 24, 2013.
2   "First 'Heartless' Man: You Don't Really Need a Heart, or a Pulse," http://designtaxi.com/news/351464/First-Heartless-Man-You-Don-t-Really-Need-A-Heart-Or-A-Pulse, accessed June 24, 2013.
3   "First 'Heartless' Man: You Don't Really Need a Heart, or a Pulse," http://designtaxi.com/news/351464/First-Heartless-Man-You-Don-t-Really-Need-A-Heart-Or-A-Pulse, accessed June 24, 2013.
4   http://bigthink.com/ideas/21691, accessed June 24, 2013.
5   http://bigthink.com/ideas/21691, accessed June 24, 2013.
6   For a fuller description of the consequences of NASA's biocapsule announcement, see particularly: http://ca.gizmodo.com/5882725/the-miraculous-nasa-breakthrough-that-could-save-millions-of-lives, accessed June 24, 2013.
7   It is projected that rapid advances in 3-D printing of blood vessels may, in fact, allow this biotechnological development in sooner than twenty years. See particularly www.techcentral.ie/article.aspx?id=17469, accessed June 24, 2013, and http://pcworld.about.net/od/printers2/Printable-Blood-Vessels-Are-Here-3D-Printing-Gets-Creepy.html, accessed July 4, 2013.

8 For an account of the potential medical benefits of brain scanning for what we hear, see especially http://singularityhub.com/2012/02/15/scientists-use-brain-waves-to-eavesdrop-on-what-we-hear, accessed June 24, 2013. For a parallel development relating to the use of mind scanning technologies to detect what we see: www.dailymail.co.uk/sciencetech/article-2095214/As-scientists-discover-translate-brainwaves-words–Could-machine-read-innermost-thoughts.html, accessed June 23, 2013.

9 An earlier version of "Exits to the Posthuman Future" was theorized and written with Marilouise Kroker for presentation at Artists Space, New York City, March 2012.

10 Susan Dominius, "Inseparable," *New York Times Magazine*, May 29, 2011, pp. 28–35, and p. 61.

11 Susan Dominus, "Inseparable," *NYT Magazine*, May 29, 2011, p. 33.

12 Susan Dominus, "Inseparable," *NYT Magazine*, May 29, 2011, p. 33.

13 The truly critical implications of neuroscience, not only for questions of individual consciousness, but for culture and society as a whole, have generated a clash of perspectives across many newly emergent fields of knowledge, from neuro-philosophy and neuro-politics to the science of genomics itself. For example, for an affirmative account of the intermediation of ethics and genetics, see Paul J. Zak, *The Moral Molecule: The Source of Love and Prosperity*, New York: Penguin, 2012. A comprehensive account of profound differences with respect to the philosophy of neuroscience is provided by Maxwell Bennett, Daniel Dennett, Peter Hacker and John Searle, *Neuroscience and Philosophy: Brain, Mind and Language*, New York: Columbia University Press, 2007. For specific discussions concerning the impact of neuroscience in reshaping both the preconditions and practical axiomatics of culture, society, and politics, see particularly: John R. Searle, *Freedom and Neurobiology: Reflections on Free Will, Language and Power*, New York: Columbia University Press, 2006; William E. Connolly, *Neuropolitics: Thinking, Culture, Speed*, Minneapolis: University of Minnesota Press, 2002; and Richard C. Lewontin, *Biology as Ideology: The Doctrine of DNA*, Toronto: House of Anansi, 1991. An important exploration of the overall discourse of genomics in relation to the questions of biocolonization, biological materiality, and the assumptions underlying the data sequencing of genes is provided by: Eugene Thacker: *The Global Genome: BioTechnology, Politics, Culture*, Cambridge, MA: The MIT Press, 2006.

14 Vittorio Gallese, "Intentional Attunement: A Neurophysiological Perspective on Social Cognition," *Cognitive Brain Research*, 2006, http://mirrorneurons.free.fr/CBR_Gallese3.pdf, accessed June 23, 2013.

15 "Empathy gene" may provide clues to autism, www.bionews.org.uk/page_5411.asp, accessed August 14, 2010.

16 Paul J. Zak, *The Moral Molecule: The Source of Love and Prosperity*, New York: Dutton, 2012.

17 Marc Parry, "Health Problems Force Professor to Pull Camera from Back of Head," *The Chronicle of Higher Education*, February 2, 2011, p. 51.

18 For an excellent account of the political background of Bilal's artistic productions, see particularly, "Performing Histories: Wafaa Bilal in Conversation with Sara Raza," Ibraaz, www.ibraaz.org/interviews/9, accessed June 23, 2013.

Chapter 3   Code Drift

1   Sections of *Code Drift* ("Software Genomics," "The Spectral Destiny of Technology," and "Tethered to Mobility") were originally conceived and written with Marilouise Kroker for presentation at a special conference on Critical Digital Studies held at the Pacific Centre for Technology and Culture, June 2009.
2   Robert C. King and William D. Stansfield, *A Dictionary of Genetics*, New York: Oxford University Press, 1997, p. 139.
3   Vito Pilieci, "Why You Might Soon Think you're Hearing Things," www.canada.com, May 12, 2008, accessed April 30, 2013.
4   *A Dictionary of Genetics*, p. 228.
5   *A Dictionary of Genetics*, p. 228.
6   *A Dictionary of Genetics*, p. 116.
7   Wendy Brown, *States of Injury: Power and Freedom in Late Modernity*, Princeton, NJ: Princeton University Press, 1995.

Chapter 4   History Drift

1   This paper was first presented at a special colloquium on "The Ends of History," Concordia University, 2011. An earlier version of the present chapter was subsequently published as part of *The Ends of History: Questioning the Stakes of Historical Reason*, ed. Amy Swiffen and Joshua Nichols, New York/London: Routledge, 2013, pp. 196–214.
2   Judith Butler, *Frames of War: When is Life Grievable?* London: Verso, 2010.

Chapter 5   Archive Drift

1   Paul D. Miller, *The Book of Ice*, Brooklyn, NY: Mark Batty Publisher, 2011, p. 18.
2   An earlier version of this essay was published in a special journal issue focused on the archival imagination, "archiver/archiving," *Intermédialités: Histoire et Théorie des Arts, des Lettres et des Techniques*, 18, Autumn 2011, pp. 137–49.
3   The most influential theoretical account of the theory of hauntology as the spectral trace that literally haunts by deconstructing the space of ontology remains Jacques Derrida, *Spectres of Marx*, trans. Peggy Kamuf, New York: Routledge Press, 1994. My conception of hauntology differs from Derrida's in theorizing the hauntological as increasingly drawn into presence by the laws of the media. For example, while Marshall McLuhan argued in *Understanding Media* that technological innovations always play out the fourfold logic of the tetrad (creating, obsolescing, retrieving, and reversing), I would argue this also implies that the tetrad has its dark side, namely that every technological innovation is haunted by that which it extinguishes, substitutes for, inertially maintains in place, and accidents.

See particularly Marshall McLuhan, *Understanding Media: The Extensions of Man*, Cambridge: The MIT Press, 2001.

4 For a full description of Barthes's concept of the "crossing of the syntagm" in relation to the question of power, see A. Kroker's "The Disembodied Eye: Ideology and Power in the Age of Nihilism," in A. Kroker and D. Cook, *The Postmodern Scene*, New York: St Martin's Press, 1987, pp. 73–113; and A. Kroker, "The Despotic Sign: Barthes' Rhetoric of Technology," in A. Kroker, *The Possessed Individual: Technology and the French Postmodern*, New York: St Martin's Press, 1992, pp. 82–103.

5 Martin Heidegger, "Building Dwelling Thinking," in *Poetry, Language, Thought*, trans. Albert Hofstader, New York: Harper Colophon Books, 1971, pp. 145–61.

6 Two competing expressions of vitalism are present in this theory of the digital archive: Henri Bergson's conception of "creative evolution" and Martin Heidegger's vision of art as a "dwelling-space" of incommensurability. While Bergson's vision of creative evolution runs parallel to the powerfully utopian conception of technology present in the thought of Teilhard de Chardin and Marshall McLuhan, it does not account for the deeper crisis of technology foretold by Heidegger, namely that "fully completed nihilism" (Heidegger) represents a countercurrent in technological culture clashing with its possibilities for creativity. See particularly Henri Bergson, *Creative Evolution*, New York: Modern Library, Random House, 1944; and Martin Heidegger, *The Question Concerning Technology and Other Essays: An Introduction to Metaphysics*, New Haven and London: Yale University Press, 1987.

7 For Arendt, the crucial dilemma confronted by thought in technocractic culture was the emergence of "not-being" as the primary nihilistic impulse immanent to the question of technology itself. See specifically Hannah Arendt, *The Life of the Mind*, New York: Harper, Brace, Jovanovic, 1978, p. 50.

Chapter 7   Media Drift

1 Babak A. Parviz, "Augmented Reality in a Contact Lens: A New Generation of Contact Lenses Built with Very Small Circuits and LEDs Promises Bionic Eyesight, http://spectrum.ieee.org/biomedical/bionics/augmented-reality-in-a-contact-lens, accessed June 24, 2013.

2 Theodor W. Adorno, *Prisms*, Cambridge, MA: MIT Press, 1983, p. 262.

Chapter 8   After the Drones

1 www.airforce-technology.com/projects/x-45-ucav, accessed June 23, 2013, and http://en.wikipedia.org/wiki/Boeing_X-45.

2 Kelvin Chan, "Taranis Drones to Take Over the Skies," *Red Ice Creations*, www.redicecreations.com/article.php?id=11793, accessed June 23, 2013.

3 For a very insightful description of Professor Sharkey's cautionary reflections on the future of drone warfare, see particularly: Jason Palmer, science

and technology reporter for the *BBC News*, "Call for Debate on Killer Robots," BBC News, http://news.bbc.co.uk/2/hi/technology/8182003. stm, accessed June 23, 2013.

4   Lewis Page, "Machine Rebellion Begins: Killer Robot Destroyed by US Jet", theregister.co.uk, September 15, 2009, accessed April 30, 2013.

5   "US Drone Strikes Target Rescuers in Pakistan – and the West Stays Silent," Glenn Greenwald, *The Guardian*, www.guardian.co.uk/commentis free/2012/aug/20/us-drones-strikes-target-rescuers-pakistan, accessed December 23, 2012.

6   Peter Sloterdijk, *Terror from the Air*, trans. Amy Patton and Steve Corcoran, Los Angeles: Semiotext(e)/Smart Art, 2009.

7   Peter Sloterdijk, "Gas Warfare – or: The Atmoterrorist Model," in *Terror from the Air*, trans. Amy Patton and Steve Corcoran, Semiotext(e)/Smart Art, 2009, pp. 9–46.

8   Martin Heidegger, "The Question Concerning Technology," *Basic Writings*, ed. David Krell, New York: HarperCollins, 1993.

9   Martin Heidegger, "Letter on Humanism," *Pathmarks*, Cambridge and New York: Cambridge University Press, 1998.

Chapter 9   Guardian Liberalism

1   Martin Heidegger, *The Question Concerning Technology and Other Essays*, trans. and with an introduction by William Lovitt, New York: Harper Torchbooks, 1977, p. 4.

2   In his essay "The Question Concerning Technology," Heidegger insisted to the point of exhaustion that if the essence of technology did not lie in the specifically technological, this did not preclude the possibility that "technology is a way of revealing," and that if we listen intently to intimations of technology in the world around us, "another realm for the essence of technology will open itself to us . . . the realm of revealing, i.e. of truth."

3   For a fascinating account of the changing nature of the concept of the just war under the sign of the "war on terror," see particularly Jeff McMahan, "Rethinking the Just War." For an excellent exploration of the modern history of the concept of the "just war" in relationship to international law, see Michael Walzer, *Just and Unjust Wars: A Moral Argument with Historical Illustrations*, New York: Basic Books, 1977.

4   For a discussion of "born-again ideology" in the context of evangelical religious influences in contemporary American politics, see Arthur Kroker and Stephen Pfohl, *Born Again Ideology/Left Behind*, Victoria: New World Perspectives, 2007.

5   Amanda Terkel, "Pentagon Official: King Would Support Iraq, Afghan Wars," www.huffingtonpost.com/2011/01/14/pentagon-official-mlk-support-wars-iraq-afghanistan_n_809031.html, accessed June 23, 2013.

6   Martin Luther King's landmark speech, Riverside Church, New York City, April 4, 1967. The full text of this speech can be found at www.information clearinghouse.info/article2564.htm, accessed June 23, 2013.

7   Barack Obama, "A Just and Lasting Peace," Nobel Speech, December, 2009, www.huffingtonpost.com/2009/12/10/obama-nobel-peace-prize-a_n_386837.html, accessed December 28, 2012.

8 Barack Obama, "A Just and Lasting Peace," Nobel Speech, December, 2009. www.huffingtonpost.com/2009/12/10/obama-nobel-peace-prize-a_n_386837.html, accessed December 28, 2012.

9 Barack Obama, "A Just and Lasting Peace," Nobel Speech, December, 2009. www.huffingtonpost.com/2009/12/10/obama-nobel-peace-prize-a_n_386837.html, accessed December 28, 2012. See also particularly Michael Walzer, *Just and Unjust Wars*.

10 Barack Obama, "A Just and Lasting Peace," Nobel Speech, December, 2009. www.huffingtonpost.com/2009/12/10/obama-nobel-peace-prize-a_n_386837.html, accessed December 28, 2012.

11 Barack Obama, West Point Graduation Address, May 22, 2010, www.cbsnews.com/2100-201_162-6509577.html, accessed June 25, 2013.

12 Eric Hobsbawm, *The Age of Extremes: The Short Twentieth Century, 1914–1991*, New York: Vintage, 1994.

13 Barack Obama, West Point Graduation Address, May 22, 2010, *CBSnews.com*, www.cbsnews.com/2100-201_162-6509577.html, accessed June 25, 2013.

14 Ibid.

15 Ibid.

16 Ibid.

17 William Leiss, "The End of History, and its Beginning Again." In J. H. Carens (ed.), *Democracy and Possessive Individualism: The Intellectual Legacy of C. B. Macpherson*. Buffalo, NY: SUNY Press, 1993, pp. 263–74.

18 William Leiss, "The End of History, and its Beginning Again." In J. H. Carens (ed.), *Democracy and Possessive Individualism: The Intellectual Legacy of C. B. Macpherson*. Buffalo, NY: SUNY Press, 1993, pp. 263–74.

19 Lewis Bazley, "The Afghan Village That's Been Wiped from the Map – with 25 Tons of Coalition Bombs," *Daily Mail Online*, www.dailymail.co.uk/news/article-1348915/Tarok-Kolache-Afghan-village-wiped-map-25-tons-coalition-bombs.html, accessed November, 2012.

20 *Newsweek* cover: "The Petraeus Generation," www.prnewswire.com/news-releases/newsweek-cover-the-petraeus-generation-56932347.html, accessed December 28, 2010.

21 "Remarks by the President in Address to the Nation on the Way Forward in Afghanistan and Pakistan," Whitehouse-gov, www.whitehouse.gov/the-press-office/remarks-president-address-nation-way-forward-afghanistan-and-pakistan, accessed September 3, 2013.

Chapter 10   Premonitory Thought

1 Michel Foucault, *The Care of the Self*, trans. Robert Hurley, New York: Pantheon Books, 1986.

2 Michel Foucault, *Society Must Be Defended*, Lectures at the Collège de France 1975–76, trans. David Macey, New York: Picador, 2003.

3 For example, writing in *Society Must Be Defended*, Foucault argued: "When I say subjugated knowledges I am also referring to a whole series of knowledges that have been disqualified as nonconceptual knowledges, as insufficiently elaborated knowledges: naive knowledges, hierarchically inferior

knowledges, knowledges that are below the required levels of erudition or scientificity." *Society Must Be Defended*, Lectures at the Collège de France 1975–6, trans. David Macey, New York: Picador, 2003, p. 7.

4   Michel Foucault, *Society Must Be Defended*, Lectures at the Collège de France 1975–76, trans. David Macey, New York: Picador, 2003, p. 27.

5   Ibid.

6   Ibid., pp. 29–30.

7   Ibid., p. 30.

8   Ibid., pp. 33–4.

9   The term "virtual class" was first theorized in Arthur Kroker and Michael A. Weinstein, *Data Trash: The Theory of the Virtual Class*, New York: St Martin's Press, 1994.

Chapter 11   Thinking the Future with Marshall McLuhan

1   As a social movement, Idle No More combines political activism with social media tools, particularly Twitter and Facebook, to produce flows of information, discussion and critical dialogue that nowhere find adequate expression in traditional media formats. See particularly, www.facebook.com/IdleNoMoreCommunity, accessed January 2, 2013.

2   Nancy J. Turner, *The Earth's Blanket*, Vancouver: Douglas and McIntyre, 2005.

3   Michael A. Weinstein, "Thinking the Death Camps with Martin Heidegger," *Modern Age* 34(3) (Spring, 1992): 214–21.

4   Sigmund Freud, *Civilization and its Discontents*, trans. and ed. James Stachey, New York: W. W. Norton & Company, 1961, p. 44.

5   Emphasis added.

Chapter 12   Epilogue

1   Jean-François Lyotard, *Duchamp's TRANS/formers*, Venice, CA: The Lapsis Press, 1990, p. 65.

2   Jean-François Lyotard, *Duchamp's TRANS/formers*, Venice, CA: The Lapsis Press, 1990, p. 58.

Index

.